Latin American
SPANISH
A COMPLETE COURSE FOR BEGINNERS

Juan Kattán-Ibarra

TEACH YOURSELF BOOKS

For UK orders queries: please contact Bookpoint Ltd, 39 Milton Park, Abingdon, Oxon OX14 4TD. Telephone: (44) 01235 400414, Fax: (44) 01235 400454. Lines are open from 9.00-6.00, Monday to Saturday, with a 24 hour message answering service. Email address: orders@bookpoint.co.uk

For U.S.A. & Canada order queries: please contact NTC/Contemporary Publishing, 4255 West Touhy Avenue, Lincolnwood, Illinois 60646-1975, U.S.A. Telephone: (847) 679 5500, Fax: (847) 679 2494.

Long-renowned as the authoritative source for self-guided learning – with more than 30 million copies sold worldwide – the *Teach Yourself* series includes over 200 titles in the fields of languages, crafts, hobbies, sports, and other leisure activities.

British Library Cataloguing in Publication Data
Kattán-Ibarra, Juan
  Latin-American Spanish
  I. Title
  467.98

Library of Congress Catalog Card Number: 93-85935

First published in UK 1994 by Hodder Headline Plc, 338 Euston Road, London NW1 3BH

First published in US 1994 by NTC Publishing Group
An imprint of NTC/Contemporary Publishing company 4255 West Touhy Avenue, Lincolnwood (Chicago), Illinois 60646 – 1975 U.S.A.

The 'Teach Yourself' name and logo are registered trade marks of Hodder & Stoughton Ltd.

Typeset by Transet Ltd, Coventry.
Printed in Great Britain for Hodder and Stoughton Educational, a division of Hodder Headline Plc, 338 Euston Road, London NW1 3BH by Cox & Wyman Ltd, Reading, Berkshire.

Impression number   16 15 14 13 12 11 10
Year   2002 2001 2000 1999

ABOUT THE AUTHOR

Juan Kattán-Ibarra was born in Chile, and has travelled extensively in Latin America and Spain. He has degrees from the University of Chile, Michigan State University, Manchester University and the Institute of Education, London University. He has taught Spanish at Ealing College and Shell International and has been an examiner in Spanish for the London Chamber of Commerce and Industry and the University of London School Examinations Board.

He is the sole author of *Teach Yourself Spanish*, *Teach Yourself Further Spanish*, *Teach Yourself Basic Spanish*, *Teach Yourself Business Spanish*, *Teach Yourself Spanish Grammar*, *Essential Business Spanish*, *Basic Spanish Conversation*, *Conversando*, *Panorama de la Prensa*, *Perspectivas Culturales de Hispanoamérica*, *Perspectivas Culturales de España*, and co-author of *Spain after Franco*, *Working with Spanish*, *Spanish at Work*, *Talking Business Spanish* and *Se Escribe Así*.

— ACKNOWLEDGEMENTS —

The author wishes to thank the following people for their help with recordings: Carlos García (Argentina), Ana María Rojas (Colombia), Marilú Jarufe, Guillermo Palma (Chile), Valeria Román (Ecuador), Jorge Vera, Clotilde Montalvo, Initia Muñoz (Mexico), Elizabeth Baldeolivar-Levy (Panama), Karina Tomas (Peru), Carmen Puig (Venezuela). Thanks are also due to Juan Luzzi for his revision of the manuscript and his many useful comments.

The author and publishers would like to thank the following for permission to use material in this volume: Camb16, Madrid (pages 78 and 192); La Epoca, Santiago de Chile (page 136); Executive Limousine Service, Santiago de Chile (page 55); El Mercurio SAP, Santiago de Chile (pages 96, 129, 150, 152, 167, 172 and 229); Parrillada Casa Brava (pages 92 and 94); Tiempo Libre (unomex, s.a. de c.v.), México (page 56).

Every effort has been made to obtain permission for all material used. In the absence of any response to inquiries, the author and publisher would like to acknowledge the following for use of their material:

Diario El Heraldo, México (page 43); Diario El Espectador, Bogotá, Colombia (page 117); Diario La Segunda, Santiago de Chile (page 153); Diario Los Tiempos, Bolivia (page 191); Lys Rent a Car, Santiago de Chile (pages 206–7); Asesoría de Comunicación del Programa Nacional de Solidaridad, Mexico (page 212); diario Novedades, México (page 228); El Diario de Caracas, Venezuela (page 244); Fondo de Cultura Económico, México (page 249).

Furthermore, the author and publisher would like to thank Radio Mar FM for use of material on the cassette that accompanies this book.

CONTENTS

INTRODUCTION

This is a complete communicative course in Latin American Spanish, which assumes no previous knowledge of the language. It is designed for beginners as well as those who, having done a general Spanish course, now wish to learn the language forms spoken in Latin America. Although the course has been written especially for people studying on their own, the material and exercises will also lend themselves to classroom use. The 13 units which make up this book provide ample opportunity to learn and practise the language used in practical, everyday situations, such as introducing yourself and others, giving personal information, making travel arrangements, ordering food, and shopping, etc. Those travelling in Latin America, for business or pleasure, and students engaged in Latin American studies will find the material in this course particularly useful.

How to use this course

Each unit is clearly divided into different sections, and the following procedure is suggested for working through each of them.

Communicative contents: At the start of each unit you will find a statement of its communicative contents, expressed in terms of how you will use the language, for example *Asking and saying what time places open and close*. Read this section before you start and try to identify within each unit how these objectives are achieved in different language forms and expressions. Make a note of these as you work through each unit, and try to learn and use them in other contexts.

Diálogos (*Dialogues*): All units contain two or more introductory dialogues centred around a main theme and highlighting the objectives of the unit. Each dialogue has a brief introduction which sets the scene and the country. Units 1 to 4 are set in Mexico, and most of the characters in the dialogues are Mexican; Units 5 and 6 are set in Colombia; 7, 8 and 9 in Chile, but including a speaker from Venezuela; 10 and 11 are set in Argentina; and 12 and 13 in Peru. Notes on the main pronunciation features in these countries are included in some units.

Read the dialogue, noting the new language forms and vocabulary, then look through the vocabulary list for new words and expressions. The **Notas explicativas** (*Explanatory notes*) give further explanations. For a more detailed explanation of important language points, read the relevant section under **Notas gramaticales** (*Grammar notes*). Once you have grasped the meaning of the dialogue, read it again two or three times, and if you have the cassette listen to it at least twice until you are satisfied that it is clear. Then turn to the comprehension exercise to test your understanding of the dialogue. To check your answers, refer to the **Key to the exercises** beginning on page 257.

If you have the cassette, listen to it while reading the text, paying special attention to the pronunciation and intonation of the native speakers. When you are familiar with the dialogue, listen to the recording a few times without looking at the text. Once you have learned a little Spanish, you can listen to the new dialogue before you read it, trying to get the gist of what is said. Listening will help you improve your capacity to understand spoken Latin American Spanish and to compare pronunciation and intonation of native speakers in different parts of Latin America.

Frases y expresiones importantes (*Important phrases and expressions*): This section brings together examples of the different language functions outlined at the start of the unit and also includes other related words and phrases. Read it carefully, as it contains the key language of the lesson, which you will practise in the exercises.

Notas gramaticales (*Grammar notes*): Here the grammatical content of the unit is explained in English and demonstrated in sentences. You will learn all major grammatical points, including all main tenses, from the frequently used present tense to the future and past tenses. You will also become familiar with the grammatical differences between Peninsular and Latin American Spanish. Study the language points in this section and note how they are used in the introductory dialogues and in the exercises which follow. You may want to study some of the points in more depth, in which case a reference grammar book such as *Teach Yourself Spanish Grammar* may be helpful.

Actividades (*Activities*): This section contains a series of exercises which practise using the language for communication. Most are communicative in nature, centring on the aims outlined at the start of the unit. Follow the instructions for each exercise, then check your answers in the **Key to the exercises**.

Some of the activities in this section involve listening practice, but the material can be used for reading comprehension if you do not have the cassette. The aim of these exercises is to understand the gist of what is said, so whether you are using the book with or without a cassette, you should read or listen to the text as many times as you think necessary before you start the exercise.

The recordings are authentic and offer the opportunity to hear speakers from several Latin American countries, including Argentina, Chile, Colombia, Ecuador, Mexico, Panama, Peru and Venezuela. Some have also been taken from Latin American radio. A transcript of the recordings is given on page 265.

Imágenes de Hispanoamérica (*Images of Latin America*): This section includes useful information about Latin America on topics such as travel, accommodation, food and telecommunications. It also gives general background information on themes such as indigenous languages, population, emigration, politics and economics. Some information is given in English but there are also passages in Spanish, a few of which are taken from Latin American newspapers. This will help increase your vocabulary as well as your capacity to understand the written language. A list of key words is given to help comprehension, and follow-up questions allow you to check comprehension. Answers to these are given in the **Key to the exercises**.

—— Latin American Spanish ——

Spanish is the main means of communication for more than two hundred million people, most of them living in Latin America. Latin American Spanish differs from Peninsular Spanish, just as British English differs from American English or from that spoken in other parts of the world. Yet, despite these differences, educated speakers from all over the Spanish-speaking world understand each other.

The main differences between Latin American and Peninsular Spanish are in vocabulary, pronunciation and intonation. Differences in grammar also exist but are less marked. Naturally, there are language variations within Latin America itself, just as there are differences within Spain.

Latin American Spanish has borrowed a number of words from indigenous languages in the region. Some of these terms have found their way into Peninsular Spanish and even other European languages. Words like **tomate**, **chocolate** and **maíz**, among others, have their origin in the Americas. Apart from Spanish words which have acquired a different meaning in Latin America, the region as a whole sometimes shows preference for one Spanish word instead of another. By and large, however, most of the Latin American lexicon is Spanish in origin, and most standard words used in Spain will be understood in Latin America.

Some variations in Spanish within Latin America have their roots in the Spanish colonisation of the region; others stem from the influence of Indian languages and from that of non-Spanish settlers, mainly African and European. This has given rise to distinctive linguistic areas within the region. The Spanish spoken in Mexico, for instance, sounds quite different from that spoken in the River Plate region, in countries like Argentina and Uruguay. This in turn differs from that of the Andean countries or that spoken around the Caribbean. In addition to using forms which will be understood in most Latin American countries, *Teach Yourself Latin American Spanish* also explains some of the main differences between various forms of Spanish. Differences in pronunciation and intonation between major regions are demonstrated by means of the cassette which accompanies the course.

Radio broadcasts
The BBC Spanish Latin American Service can be heard on the
following short wave frequencies:

*00.00 – 01.30	6.11	9.825	11.765	15.39MHz
*03.00 – 04.00	6.11	9.515	9.825	11.965	15.39MHz
11.00 – 11.30	5.975	9.67	9.69	15.19	21.49MHz
13.00 – 13.30	6.13	11.775			15.315MHz

*Saturdays and Sundays: 00.00–01.15; 0300–03.45

—— Symbols and abbreviations ——

This indicates material included on the cassette.

This indicates dialogue.

This indicates exercises – places where you can practise using
the language.

This indicates key words or phrases.

This indicates grammar explanations – the nuts and bolts of
the language.

m – masculine;
f – feminine;
sing – singular;
pl – plural;
fam – familiar;
pol – polite;
Mex – Mexico;
Arg – Argentina;
Ven – Venezuela;
Col – Colombia.

1

_ ¿CUÁL ES SU NOMBRE? _

What is your name?

In this unit you will learn how to

- use simple greetings
- introduce yourself and exchange greetings with people you meet
- ask and give personal information: name, place of origin and nationality

Diálogos (*Dialogues*)

1 En el hotel

A tourist arrives in a hotel in Guadalajara, Mexico.

Turista	Buenas noches.
Recepcionista	Buenas noches, señora. ¿Qué desea?
Turista	Tengo una reservación.
Recepcionista	¿Cuál es su nombre, por favor?

Turista   Ana González.
Recepcionista   Ah sí, es la habitación número quince.

en *in*	**por favor** *please*
el (m) *the*	**sí** *yes*
buenas noches *good evening*	**es** *it is*
¿Qué desea? *Can I help you?*	**la** (f) *the*
tengo *I have*	**número** (m) *number*
una reservación (f) *a reservation*	**quince** *fifteen*
¿Cuál es su nombre? *What is your name?*	

Notas explicativas
(*Explanatory notes*)

Mexican pronunciation

Units 1 to 4 of this book are set in Mexico, and most of the speakers in the dialogues are Mexican. The Mexican accent is very distinctive within Latin America. In general, there is a weakening of vowel sounds, for example in **buen(a)s noch(e)s**, unlike what happens in many other Latin American countries, where it is consonants which are reduced or even omitted altogether in certain positions. The pronunciation of final -s, or s- before a consonant is a clear example of the difference between Mexican accent and that of some other Latin American countries. The -s in **buenas noches**, for example, is fully pronounced in Mexico, whereas in places like Cuba, Venezuela, Chile and Argentina, it tends to be substituted by an aspirated **h**, rendering a pronunciation more like **buena(h) noche(h)**. This pronunciation is also heard in southern Spain.

As in the rest of Latin America and southern Spain, Mexicans use the **seseo**. **C** before **e** or **i**, as in the word **quince** (dialogue 1) and the letter **z**, as in **González** (dialogue 1) are pronounced like **s**, and not like the **th** in **think**, which is what you will hear in most parts of Spain.

Another feature of Mexican pronunciation, which is common to other Latin American countries, is the pronunciation of the letter **ll**, as in the word **llamo** (dialogue 4), which is pronounced like the **y** of **yo** (dialogue 2). The distinction between **ll** and **y,** which is made in certain parts of Spain, where **ll** is pronounced more like the **lli** of *million* and **y** more like the **y** in *yes*, is a rare phenomenon in Latin America.

Forms of address: señora, señorita, señor

Look at this sentence from dialogue 1:

Buenas noches, señora.   *Good evening, madam.*

Before a name, the word **señora**, used for married and older women, translates as *Mrs*, for example **señora González** (*Mrs González*). In forms and letter headings it is normally found in abbreviated form as **Sra**. An unmarried woman will be addressed as **señorita** (*Miss*), normally used also when you are not certain whether the person is married or not. For a man you use **señor** (*sir* or *mister*). In abbreviated form, **señorita** becomes **Srta**. and **señor Sr**.

Generally speaking in Latin America, strangers and people providing services tend to use these words more often than in Spain, for example **sí / no señor** (*yes / no sir*).

Una reservación (*a reservation or booking*)

This term is heard in Mexico and some other Latin American countries, such as Colombia. The standard term is **la reserva**, which is used in Spain and also in parts of Latin America, for example Argentina and Chile.

Una habitación (*a room*)

This word is standard and will be understood in all Spanish-speaking countries. In some Latin American countries, however, you may hear other words for *room* and you need to understand these when you hear local people use them. In South America, for example, people may ask for **una habitación** in a hotel, but normally use **el cuarto** or **la pieza** when referring to rooms in a house. The latter word is very common in Argentina and Chile. A standard word for bedroom is **el dormitorio**, which is called **la recámara** in Mexico.

¿Cuál es su nombre? (*What is your name?*)

You will hear this phrase very frequently in Latin America, sometimes shortened to **¿Su nombre?** (*Your name?*), in official situations. See dialogue 4 for an alternative form of asking someone's name.

The double question mark

Notice that in writing, interrogative sentences carry two questions marks, one at the beginning and one at the end of the sentence.

2 En el bar

In the hotel bar, a man is looking for someone he has not met before.

Señor	Buenos días, señorita.
Señorita	Buenos días.
Señor	¿Es usted la señorita Carmen Robles?
Señorita	No, yo no soy Carmen Robles. Soy Gloria Santos.
Señor	Disculpe.
Señorita	No se preocupe.

bar (m) *bar*		**soy** *I am*	
buenos días *good morning*		**Disculpe.** *I am sorry.*	
¿Es usted . . .? *Are you . . .?*		**No se preocupe.** *That's all right.*	
yo no soy *I am not*		(Lit. *Don't worry.*)	

Nota explicativa
(*Explanatory note*)

La señorita, la señora, el señor

¿Es usted la señorita Carmen Robles?	*Are you Miss Carmen Robles?*

In indirect address, **señorita**, **señora** and **señor** are preceded by the Spanish equivalent of *the*: **la** for feminine, **el** for masculine. Compare the above sentence with **Buenos días, señorita**, where **la** is not used.

3 Mucho gusto

Señor Peña, a Chilean businessman, has come to meet señor Palma, a Mexican businessman. Pay special attention to the Spanish equivalent of *Pleased to meet you*.

Señor Peña	Buenas tardes. ¿Usted es el señor Gonzalo Palma?
Señor Palma	Sí, so yo.
Señor Peña	Yo soy Luis Peña, de Chile.
Señor Palma	Encantado, señor Peña.
Señor Peña	Mucho gusto.
Señor Palma	Siéntese, por favor.
Señor Peña	Gracias.

Mucho gusto.	*Pleased to meet you.*	**de Chile**	*from Chile*
buenas tardes	*good afternoon*	**Encantado.**	*Pleased to meet you.*
¿Usted es . . .?	*Are you . . .?*	**siéntese**	*sit down*
soy yo	*it's me*	**gracias**	*thank you*

Notas explicativas
(*Explanatory notes*)

Encantado/a, mucho gusto (*Pleased to meet you*)

A woman will say **encantada**. **Mucho gusto** does not change.

Hand-shaking

In a situation like that of the dialogue, people will normally shake hands. Hand-shaking is much more frequent in Latin America than in English-speaking countries. Even old friends and relatives will sometimes shake hands when meeting or leaving.

4 ¿Cómo se llama usted?

Mónica Lagos and Raúl Molina, both from Mexico, meet at a conference and introduce themselves. Observe the way in which they ask each other where they come from.

Señor Molina	Disculpe, ¿cómo se llama usted?
Señora Lagos	Me llamo Mónica Lagos. ¿Y usted?
Señor Molina	Mi nombre es Raúl Molina.
Señora Lagos	Encantada.
Señor Molina	Mucho gusto, señora.
Señora Lagos	¿De dónde es usted?
Señor Molina	Soy de Monterrey. ¿Y usted, de dónde es?
Señora Lagos	Yo soy de Puebla.

¿Cómo se llama usted? *What is your name?*		**¿y usted?** *and you?*
Me llamo Mónica *My name is Mónica.*		**¿dónde?** *where?*
Mi nombre es Raúl. *My name is Raúl.*		**¿De dónde es usted?** *Where are you from?*
		(Yo) soy de . . . *I am from . . .*

Responda en inglés (*Answer in English*)

(a) Where is señor Molina from?
(b) Where is señora Lagos from?

Notas explicativas (*Explanatory notes*)

Asking someone's name

¿Cómo se llama usted? Compare this way of asking someone's name with the one you learned in dialogue 1: **¿Cuál es su nombre?** The first sentence means literally *What are you called?*, while **me llamo ...** would translate literally as *I'm called ...* Both ways of asking someone's name are used in formal situations in Latin America, but **¿Cuál es su nombre?** seems to be more common. In Spain you are much more likely to hear **¿Cómo se llama usted?**, except in official situations in which you might hear **¿Su nombre?** (*Your name?*).

Giving your name

Me llamo ..., and **mi nombre es ...** (*My name is ...*) are both used by Latin Americans, whereas in Spain the second form is not used. Remember that you can also use **soy** (*I am*), as in **Soy Gloria Santos** (see dialogue 2).

Accent on question words

Words such as **donde** (*where*) and **cual** (*what, which*) carry an accent when used in interrogative sentences, e.g. **¿Y usted, de dónde es?** For an explanation of the use of accents see **Pronunciation** on page 252.

5 ¿Cómo te llamas?

All the people in the previous dialogues have used formal forms of address. **Usted** (*you*) is used to address a person formally. But in Spanish you can also address a person in a familiar way, using the **tú** (*you*) form. When you address a person in a familiar way you need to change the form of other grammatical words, verbs for instance. Observe the way in which Mark and Nora, two young people, address each other.

Nora	¿Cómo te llamas?
Mark	Me llamo Mark, ¿y tú?
Nora	Me llamo Nora. ¿De dónde eres?
Mark	Soy inglés, soy de Londres. Tú eres mexicana, ¿verdad?
Nora	Sí, soy mexicana, soy de Jalapa.

¿Cómo te llamas? *What's your name?* (fam)	**soy inglés** *I'm English*
¿y tú? *and you?* (fam)	**soy de Londres** *I'm from London*
¿De dónde eres? *Where are you from?* (fam)	**Tú eres mexicana, ¿verdad?** *You're Mexican, aren't you?* (fam)

Responda en inglés (Answer in English)

(a) What nationality is Mark?
(b) Where is he from?
(c) What nationality is Nora?
(d) Where is she from?

Notas explicativas
(*Explanatory notes*)

Familiar or formal address?

Latin Americans on the whole are more formal than Spaniards and they use the polite forms of address much more frequently than in Spain. Unless you are speaking to children or friends, it is best to use the **usted** rather than the **tú** form when you first meet somebody, then wait and see what the other person is using and do likewise. You'll find more on this under **Notas gramaticales**.

¿Cómo te llamas? (*What is your name?* (fam))

This is the familiar equivalent of **¿Cómo se llama usted?** The familiar equivalent of **¿Cuál es su nombre?** is **¿Cuál es tu nombre?**

6 Somos mexicanos

A Mexican couple meet a couple from Colombia.

Colombiano   Ustedes son mexicanos, ¿no?
Mexicano   Sí, somos mexicanos. ¿Y ustedes?
Colombiano   Somos colombianos.
Mexicano   ¿Y de qué parte de Colombia son?
Colombiano   Somos de Bogotá.

ustedes son . . . *you are . . .* (pl)	**¿Y de qué parte de Colombia son?**
somos *we are*	*And what part of Colombia are you*
¿y ustedes? *and you?* (pl)	*from?*

Nota explicativa
(*Explanatory note*)

Using ustedes

Ustedes son mexicanos, ¿no? *You are Mexican, aren't you?*

Ustedes (*you*) is the plural form of **usted**, used to address more than one person in a polite or familiar way.

Frases y expresiones importantes
(*Key words and phrases*)

- Using simple greetings
Buenos días.	*Good morning.*
Buenas tardes.	*Good afternoon.*
Buenas noches.	*Good evening / night.*

- Other ways of greeting people
¡Hola!	*Hello!* (fam)
¿Qué tal?	*Hi! How are you?* (fam)

- Introducing yourself and exchanging greetings with people you meet
(Yo) soy Luis Peña.	*I am Luis Peña.*
Mucho gusto.	*Pleased to meet you.*
Encantado/a.	*Pleased to meet you.*

- Asking someone's name and giving your name
¿Cuál es su / tu nombre? (pol/fam)	*What is your name?*
¿Cómo se llama usted? (pol)	
¿Cómo te llamas? (fam)	
Me llamo Mónica.	*My name is Mónica.*

- Asking people who they are and saying who you are
¿Es usted la Srta. Robles?	*Are you Miss Robles?* (pol)
¿Tú eres Carmen?	*Are you Carmen?* (fam)
(Yo) soy Gloria Santos.	*I am Gloria Santos.*

- Asking people where they are from and saying where you are from

¿**De dónde es usted?** (pol)	
¿**De dónde eres?** (fam)	*Where are you from?*
Soy de Londres.	*I am from London.*
¿**De qué parte de Colombia son ustedes?**	*What part of Colombia are you from?* (pl)
Somos de Bogotá.	*We are from Bogota.*

- Asking people what nationality they are and giving similar information about yourself

Usted es mexicana, ¿verdad? (pol)	
Tú eres mexicana, ¿verdad? (fam)	*You are Mexican, aren't you?*
Soy mexicana.	*I am Mexican.* (f)
Ustedes son mexicanos, ¿no?	*You are Mexican. aren't you?* (pl)
Somos mexicanos.	*We are Mexican.*

Notas gramaticales
(*Grammar notes*)

1   El, la (*the* (*sing*))

All nouns (words that name things or people) in Spanish are either masculine or feminine and the word for *the* is **el** for masculine nouns and **la** for feminine nouns.

el hotel   *the hotel*   **la** habitación   *the room*

2   *Masculine or feminine?*

Nouns ending in **-o** are usually masculine while nouns ending in **-a** are normally feminine:

el número   *the number*   **la** visita   *the vistor*

But there are many exceptions to the above rule, e.g. **el día** (*the day*), **la mano** (*the hand*), and there are many nouns which do not end in -**o** or -**a**, so it is advisable to learn each word with its corresponding article, **el** or **la** (*the*), for example:

el nombre	*the name*	la tarde	*the afternoon*
el bar	*the bar*	la noche	*the evening / night*

Nouns which refer to people will normally agree in gender (masculine or feminine) with the person referred to, and to form the feminine of such nouns you may find it useful to remember these simple rules:

(i) Change the -**o** to -**a**.

el mexicano (m)   *the Mexican*   la mexican**a** (f)   *the Mexican*

(ii) Add -**a** to the consonant.

el señor (m)   *the gentleman*   la señor**a** (f)   *the lady*

(iii) But if the noun ends in -**ista**, the ending remains the same for masculine or feminine.

el recepcionista (m) / la recepcionista (f)   *receptionist*

3   Un, una (*a/an*)

The word for *a* is **un** for masculine nouns and **una** for feminine nouns.

un hotel   *a hotel*   una habitación   *a room*

4   *Adjectives indicating nationality*

Adjectives are words which serve to qualify a person or a thing, for example a *Mexican* man, a *good* hotel. Adjectives of nationality, like many adjectives in Spanish, have masculine and feminine forms. To form the feminine from a masculine adjective of nationality or origin change the -**o** to -**a** or add -**a** to the consonant.

Masculine	**Feminine**
un señor mexicano	una señor**a** mexican**a**
a Mexican gentleman	*a Mexican lady*
un turista inglés	una turista ingles**a**
an English tourist	*an English tourist*

Other nationalities (masc and fem forms)

argentino/a	*Argentinian*
británico/a	*British*
colombiano/a	*Colombian*
cubano/a	*Cuban*
chileno/a	*Chilean*
escocés/escocesa	*Scottish*
galés/galesa	*Welsh*
inglés/inglesa	*English*
norteamericano/a	*American*
(*also* americano/a)	
peruano/a	*Peruvian*
venezolano/a	*Venezuelan*

Note that adjectives of nationality in Spanish are written with small letters.

5   Yo, tú, él . . . (*I, you, he* . . .)

To say *I, you, he*, etc. use the following set of words:

Singular		Plural	
yo	*I*	nosotros/as	*we* (m/f)
tú	*you* (fam)	ustedes	*you* (pl)
usted	*you* (pol)	ellos	*they* (m)
él	*he*	ellas	*they* (f)
ella	*she*		

The only difference with Peninsular Spanish is that Latin American Spanish does not use the familiar plural **vosotros** (*you*). In writing, **usted** and **ustedes** are normally found in abbreviated form as **Ud.** and **Uds.**, instead of **Vd.** and **Vds.** as is customary in Spain.

The form **nosotras** (f) (*we*), is used when all the people involved are women. If there are people of both sexes, use the masculine form **nosotros**.

Generally, words like **yo**, **tú**, **nosotros**, and so on are omitted in Spanish, except at the start of a conversation, to emphasise or to avoid ambiguity, as with **él**, **ella**, **usted** (and their plural equivalents) which always share the same verb forms.

Soy inglés.	*I am English.*
Somos mexicanos.	*We are Mexican.*
Él es mexicano.	*He is Mexican.*

In the first two sentences, **yo** and **nosotros** have been omitted, but in the last sentence **él** (*he*) has been used in order to avoid ambiguity. Without this, the sentence may also translate as *you are Mexican*. In context, however, this kind of ambiguity does not often occur. **Usted** is often used for politeness, but if there is no ambiguity it may also be omitted.

6 Giving personal information with ser

Basic personal information, such as name, place of origin, nationality, can be given with the verb **ser** (*to be*).

Soy Gonzalo Palma.	*I am Gonzalo Palma.*
Soy de Monterrey.	*I am from Monterrey.*
Soy mexicano.	*I am Mexican.*

The present tense forms of **ser** are as follows:

Singular		**Plural**	
yo soy	*I am*	nosotros somos	*we are*
tú eres	*you are* (fam)	ustedes son	*you are* (pl)
usted es	*you are* (pol)	ellos, ellas son	*they are* (m/f)
él, ella es	*he, she is*		

The plural familiar form **vosotros sois** (*you are*), is used in Spain but not in Latin America. To say *it is*, as in *It is a hotel*, use the word **es** on its own: **Es un hotel**.

7 Negative and interrogative sentences

Negative sentences are formed by placing **no** before the verb:

| Soy británico. | *I am British.* |
| No soy irlandés. | *I am not Irish.* |

Interrogative sentences can be formed in three ways:

(i) By reversing the word order in the sentence.

| Usted es boliviano. | *You are Bolivian.* |
| ¿Es usted boliviano? | *Are you Bolivian?* |

(ii) By using the same word order as for a statement, but with a rising intonation.

¿Usted es ecuatoriana?   *Are you Ecuadorean?*

(iii) By using the word **¿verdad?** (Lit. *true*) or the word **¿no?** at the end of the statement.

Tú eres uruguayo, ¿verdad?   *You are Uruguayan, aren't you?*
Ella es cubana, ¿no?   *She is Cuban, isn't she?*

8 Numbers

0	cero	21	veintiuno
1	uno	22	veintidós
2	dos	23	veintitrés
3	tres	24	venticuatro
4	cuatro	25	veinticinco
5	cinco	26	veintiséis
6	seis	27	veintisiete
7	siete	28	veintiocho
8	ocho	29	veintinueve
9	nueve	30	treinta
10	diez	31	treinta y uno
11	once	32	treinta y dos
12	doce	40	cuarenta
13	trece	45	cuarenta y cinco
14	catorce	50	cincuenta
15	quince		
16	dieciséis		
17	diecisiete		
18	dieciocho		
19	diecinueve		
20	veinte		

Before a masculine noun **uno** becomes **un** and before a feminine noun **una**:

un señor   *one man*
una señora   *one woman*

Note that only numbers from 21 to 29 are written as a single word in Spanish.

✔ ── Actividades (*Activities*) ──

1 It is early morning and you arrive in a hotel in Mexico where there is a room booked in your name. Use the guidelines in English to complete this conversation with the hotel receptionist.

Usted	*Say good morning.*
Recepcionista	Buenos días. A sus órdenes.
Usted	*Say you have a reservation.*
Recepcionista	¿Cuál es su nombre, por favor?
Usted	*Give your name.*
Recepcionista	Sí, es la habitación número veinte.
Usted	*Say thank you.*

2 You are in the bar waiting to meet señora Vargas, whom you have not met before, when a gentleman approaches you. He has obviously mistaken you for someone else. Use the guidelines to complete your part of the conversation.

Señor	Buenas tardes.
Usted	*Say good afternoon.*
Señor	¿Es usted Emilio/a Zapata?
Usted	*No, say you are not Emilio / a Zapata. Say who you are.*
Señor	Disculpe.
Usted	*Say that is all right.*

3 Here comes the person you think you are expecting.

Señora Vargas	Disculpe, ¿cuál es su nombre?
Usted	*Say your name and where you are from.*
Señora Vargas	Yo soy Isabel Vargas, de Veracruz.
Usted	*Say pleased to meet you.*
Señora Vargas	Encantada.
Usted	*Ask señora Vargas to sit down.*
Señora Vargas	Gracias.

4 Here is an informal situation. You are at a party when a stranger approaches you and starts a conversation. Reply accordingly.

Desconocido/a	Disculpa, ¿eres americano/a?
Usted	. . .
Desconocido/a	¡Ah! ¿Y de qué ciudad eres?
Usted	. . .

Desconocido/a	¿Cómo te llamas?
Usted	. . .
Desconocido/a	Me llamo Mario.
Usted	. . .
Desconocido/a	El gusto es mío.

desconocido/a *stranger (m/f)*	**el gusto es mío** *the pleasure is mine*

5 You are on your first visit to Latin America and you want to meet people, so be prepared to use greetings and ask some simple questions to make the first contacts.

How would you say the following in Spanish? (Use the polite form.)

(*a*) Good afternoon.
(*b*) What is your name?
(*c*) Where are you from?
(*d*) Are you Mexican?
(*e*) What part of Mexico are you from?

6 Read the sentence here written by Roberto Vera about himself, and then write a similar line about yourself.

> mi nombre es
> Roberto Vera, soy
> colombiano, de Bogotá.

7 Read this form with information about Ana González, and the line which follows.

Nombre:	Ana María
Apellidos:	González Ríos
Nacionalidad:	mexicana
Dirección:	calle Juárez 34, Monterrey

Ana María González Ríos es mexicana. Ana María es de Monterrey.

Use the information in this box to write a similar statement about Pablo Miranda Frías.

Nombre:	Pablo
Apellidos:	Miranda Frías
Nacionalidad:	venezolano
Dirección:	calle Bolívar 65, Caracas

apellido (m) *surname*		**dirección** (f) *address*	
nacionalidad (f) *nationality*			

Notas explicativas
(*Explanatory notes*)

Surnames

In Spain and in the Spanish-speaking countries of Latin America, people have two surnames. The first surname is that of their father, the second is their mother's. In Ana María's case above, for example, **González** is her father's first surname and **Ríos** is her mother's first surname. The second surname is used in more formal and official situations. Married women add their husband's first surname, preceded by the word **de** (*of*), to their own name or first surname. For example, if Ana María marries a señor Barros, she will be called **Ana María de Barros** or **Ana María González de Barros**.

Nacionalidad

Notice that the adjective of nationality must agree in gender with the word **nacionalidad**, which is feminine: **(nacionalidad) venezolana.**

8 Here are two recorded interviews with Mexican women and a brief introduction by someone from Panama. If you are using the cassette, listen to each piece as many times as you want until you

are confident that you understand what is being said. Then listen again, and as you do so, try to answer the questions below. If you are not using the cassette, read the transcripts on page 265, then answer the questions. First study these new words:

país (m) *country*	**para servirle** *at your service*

(a) What part of Mexico is Initia Muñoz García from?
(b) What sentence has been used to express the following: *What country are you from?*
(c) What part of Mexico is Clotilde Montalvo Rodríguez from?
(d) What sentence has been used to express the following: *Where are you from?*
(e) What city is Elizabeth from?
(f) How does she express the following: *My name is Elizabeth?*

Imágenes de Hispanoamérica (*Images of Latin America*)

As stated in the Introduction to this book, this section will give you general information about Latin America as well as some useful hints for people travelling on the sub-continent. Some of the information will be in English and some in Spanish, so that from the start you may become familiar with the written language and thus increase your capacity to understand. Remember, try to get the gist of what is said in the passages rather than attempt to understand or memorise every single word. The questions which follow will help you to check comprehension.

Spanish America

The land that extends from Mexico to Tierra del Fuego is generally known as Latin America (**Latinoamérica** in Spanish) and is sometimes incorrectly called South America, (**Sudamérica**). The first of the two words includes non-Spanish speaking countries such as

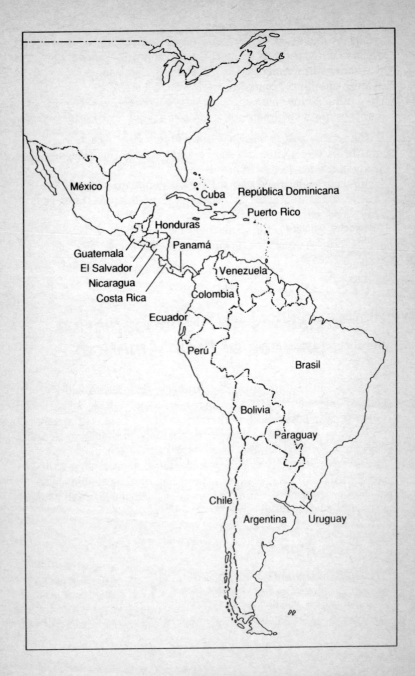

Brazil (Portuguese-speaking) and Haiti (French-speaking), while the second leaves out all of Central America, the Caribbean and Mexico, which is in North America. In this book, you will see the more inclusive term Latin America, but in Spanish you should refer to the Spanish-speaking countries of the American continent as **Hispanoamérica**, meaning *Spanish America*. The people of these countries are called **hispanoamericanos**.

In the passage which follows you will read about **Hispanoamérica** and the Spanish language, known as **el español** or **el castellano**. Study the key words before you read the text, then check your comprehension by answering the questions below.

hay *there are*	**los países** *the countries*
dieciocho *eighteen*	**también** *also*
está / están *is / are* (for location)	**estado asociado** *associated state*
el castellano *Castilian*	**a los Estados Unidos** *to the*
la lengua *the language*	*United States*

Hispanoamérica y los hispanoamericanos

En Hispanoamérica hay dieciocho repúblicas independientes. En Norteamérica está México; en Centroamérica están Costa Rica, El Salvador, Guatemala, Honduras, Nicaragua y Panamá; en el Caribe, Cuba y la República Dominicana; en Sudamérica, Argentina, Bolivia, Chile, Colombia, Ecuador, Paraguay, Perú, Uruguay y Venezuela.

El español o castellano es la lengua oficial en los países hispanoamericanos. El español es también lengua oficial en Puerto Rico, estado asociado a los Estados Unidos de América.

Responda en inglés (*Answer in English*)

(*a*) How many Spanish-speaking countries are there in Latin America?
(*b*) Where are Cuba and the Dominican Republic?
(*c*) What language is spoken in Puerto Rico?

Indigenous languages

The America's original inhabitants spoke a variety of languages, many of which are still spoken today. Thousands of Mexican Indians speak **Náhuatl**, the old language of the Aztecs, while **Maya** can be heard from southern Mexico to the highlands of Guatemala. **Quechua**, the ancient language of the Incas is spoken by more than eight million Indians, mainly in Peru, where it is an official language alongside Spanish. Another language in the Andean region is **Aymará**, spoken in the border between Peru and Bolivia, around lake Titicaca. In Paraguay, the old Indian language is **Guaraní**, still spoken by many Paraguayans alongside Spanish.

If you are travelling in Latin America, particularly in Mexico, Central America or the Andean countries of South America you will hear these languages spoken among Indians. However, most of them speak Spanish as well, so you should have no problems in communicating with them. Naturally, Spanish shows the influence of these indigenous languages, but this often proves to be an advantage rather than a disadvantage, as people tend to speak more slowly and clearly in these regions. You will notice this especially in Peru, Bolivia and Ecuador, all of which have a large Indian population.

2

¿DÓNDE ESTÁ?

Where is it?

In this unit you will learn how to

- ask and say where people and places are
- ask people how they are and say how you are
- ask and answer questions about location

Diálogos

1 En la recepción

Carmen, a Mexican, has come to see her friend Gloria Martín at her hotel in Mexico City. Gloria is from Colombia.

Carmen   Buenos días. ¿Cuál es la habitación de la señorita Gloria Martín, por favor?

| **Recepcionista** | Un momentito. (*Looking at the register.*) La señorita Martín está en la habitación número cincuenta, en el quinto piso. Allí está el elevador. |
| **Carmen** | Gracias. Muy amable. |

¿cuál . . .?	*which . . .?*	**allí**	*there, over there*
un momentito	*just a moment*	**elevador** (m)	*lift*
piso (m)	*floor*	**muy amable**	*that's very kind*
quinto	*fifth*		

Responda en inglés

(*a*) What is señorita Martín's room number?
(*b*) On which floor is it?

——— Notas explicativas ———

¿Cuál es . . .? (*Which is . . .?*)

¿Cuál es la habitación de la señorita Gloria Martín?

Which is señorita Gloria Martín's room?

Notice the use of **ser** (*to be*), in **¿Cuál es . . .?** (*Which is . . .?*) (for **ser** see Unit 1), and the use of **de** in **de la señorita Gloria Martín** (Lit. *of señorita Gloria Martín*).

Saying where someone is

La señorita Martín está en la habitación número 50.

Señorita Martín is in room 50.

Observe here the use of **estar** instead of **ser**, both translating into English as *to be*, to indicate location. More on this under **Notas gramaticales**.

Un momentito (*just a moment*)

Momentito is a diminutive of **momento** (*moment*). See **Notas gramaticales**.

El elevador (*lift*)

Probably due to the influence of American English (*elevator*), in Mexico and some other Latin American countries people use this word instead of the standard **el ascensor**.

Numbers

For numbers from 50 onwards and ordinal numbers from *first* to *sixth* see pages 36–37.

2   En la habitación número cincuenta

Gloria greets her friend Carmen.

Gloria	Hola, Carmen. ¿Cómo estás?
Carmen	Estoy bien, gracias. ¿Y tú, cómo estás?
Gloria	Muy bien. Siéntate. Me alegro mucho de verte otra vez.
Carmen	Yo también.
Gloria	¿Cómo están tus papás?
Carmen	Están muy bien.

estoy bien *I am fine*	**otra vez** *again*
muy bien *very well*	**yo también** *me too*
siéntate *sit down* (fam)	**¿Cómo están tus papás?** *How are*
Me alegro mucho de verte. *I am*	*your parents?*
very glad to see you. (fam)	

———— Notas explicativas ————

Asking someone how he or she is

¿Cómo estás? How are you? (fam)

To ask someone how he or she is, Spanish uses the verb **estar** (*to be*). For an explanation of this see **Notas gramaticales**. See also **Nota explicativa** under dialogue 4.

Los papás (*parents*)

This is more colloquial in Latin America than **los padres**, which is used in Spain.

3 ¿Dónde está la oficina?

Señor Alonso, a Colombian, has come to see señor Martínez, a Mexican businessman, at his office in Mexico City.

Señor Alonso	Buenas tardes. ¿Dónde está la oficina del señor Martínez, por favor?
Recepcionista	La oficina del señor Martínez está al final del pasillo, a la izquierda.
Señor Alonso	Gracias.

¿Dónde está . . .?	*Where is . . .?*	**pasillo** (m)	*corridor*
oficina (f)	*office*	**a la izquierda**	*on the left*
al final de	*at the end of*	**de nada**	*don't mention it*

Notas explicativas

Asking where places are

¿Dónde está la oficina?   *Where is the office?*

Notice here the use of **¿Dónde está?** to inquire about location. More on this under **Notas gramaticales**.

Del (*of the*), al (*at the*)

Notice the use of **del** and **al**, contractions of **de + el** and **a + el** respectively, in **La oficina del señor Matínez está al final del pasillo** (*Señor Martínez's office is at the end of the corridor*).

4 En la oficina del señor Martínez

Señor Martínez greets señor Alonso.

Señor Martínez   ¡Señor Alonso, buenas tardes!

Señor Alonso	Buenas tardes, señor Martínez.
Señor Martínez	Siéntese, por favor. Me alegro mucho de verlo. ¿Cómo le va?
Señor Alonso	Bien, gracias. ¿Y usted, cómo está?
Señor Martínez	Muy bien, gracias.

Me alegro mucho de verlo. *I am very glad to see you.* (pol)	**¿Cómo le va?** *How are you?* (pol)
	¿Cómo está? *How are you?* (pol)

Nota explicativa

Asking people how they are: alternative forms

Notice the two alternative forms: **¿Cómo está usted?** and **¿Cómo le va?** (*How are you?*). In familiar address, the latter form becomes **¿Cómo te va?** This, and the polite equivalent, are very frequent in Latin America.

5 Está a dos cuadras de aquí

At the Hotel Las Américas (no. 2 on the map overleaf) a Mexican visitor asks the receptionist if there is an underground station nearby.

Señorita	Buenas tardes.
Recepcionista	Buenas tardes, señorita. A sus órdenes.
Señorita	¿Hay una estación de metro por aquí?
Recepcionista	Sí, hay una, la estación de Cuauhtemoc. Está a dos cuadras de aquí, a la derecha, cerca del monumento a Cuauhtemoc.
Señorita	Muchas gracias. Muy amable.
Recepcionista	Para servirle. ¡Qué le vaya bien!

A sus órdenes. *May I help you?* (Mex)	**cuadra** (f) *block*
¿hay?, hay *is there?, there is*	**a la derecha** *on the right*
una estación de metro (f) *an underground station*	**cerca de** *near*
por aquí *nearby, around here*	**Para servirle.** *Don't mention it.*
	¡Que le vaya bien! *Have a nice day!*

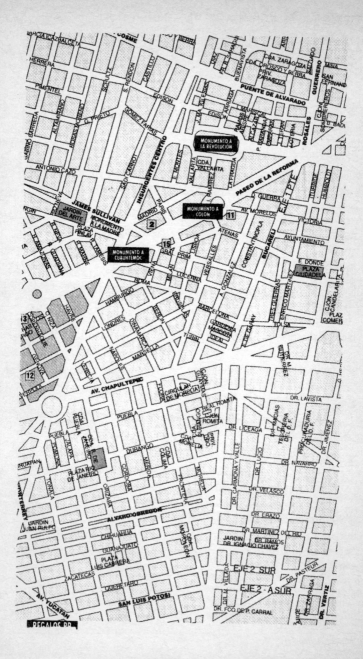

Responda en inglés

(*a*) Where is Cuauhtemoc station?
(*b*) Is it on the right or the left?

———— Notas explicativas ————

Formality

Notice the use of phrases such as **a sus órdenes** (*at your service*), **para servirle** (Lit. *at your service*), and **¡Que le vaya bien!** (*Have a nice day!*). Latin Americans, on the whole, and Mexicans in particular, are very polite, and you will encounter many such phrases when meeting Latin American people. Some of these phrases, like those above, are not used in Spain, where speech tends to be rather informal.

Una cuadra (*a block*)

a dos cuadras de aquí   *two blocks from here*

Notice the use of the word **a** to indicate distance. **Cuadra** (*block*), is used only in Latin America. Spaniards use **manzana** or **calle** instead: **A dos manzanas / calles de aquí.**

— Frases y expresiones importantes —

- Asking and saying where places and people are
  ¿Cuál es la habitación de la   *Which is señorita Gloria Martín's*
  señorita Gloria Martín?   *room?*
  La señorita Martín está en la   *Señorita Martín is in room*
  habitación número cincuenta.   *number fifty.*
  ¿Dónde está la oficina?   *Where is the office?*
  Está al final del pasillo,   *It is at the end of the corridor,*
  a la izquierda.   *on the left.*

- Other ways of expressing location
  Está arriba / abajo.   *It is upstairs / downstairs.*
  Está cerca / lejos.   *It is near / far.*

Está aquí / allí.	*It is here / there.*
Está acá / allá.	*It is here / there.*
Está a cinco minutos de aquí.	*It is five minutes from here.*
Está a cincuenta kilómetros.	*It is 50 km away.*
Está al lado del banco.	*It is next to the bank.*
Están detrás del bar.	*They are behind the bar.*
Están frente a la plaza.	*They are opposite the square.*

- Asking people how they are and saying how you are

¿Cómo estás?	*How are you?* (fam)
¿Cómo está Ud.?	*How are you?* (pol)
¿Cómo le va?	*How are you?* (pol)
¿Cómo te va?	*How are you?* (fam)
Estoy (muy) bien.	*I am (very) well.*
¿Cómo están tus papás?	*How are your parents?*
Están (muy) bien.	*They are (very) well.*
¿Qué húbole?	*How are you?* (fam, Mex)

- Asking questions about location and replying

¿Hay una estación de metro por aquí?	*Is there an underground station nearby?*
Sí, hay una, la estación de Balderas.	*Yes, there is one, Balderas station.*

Notas gramaticales

1 Los, las (*the (pl)*)

Most words form the plural by adding -**s**.

el piso	*floor*	**los** pisos	*floors*
la cuadra	*block*	**las** cuadras	*blocks*

Nouns ending in a consonant add -**es**.

el hotel	*hotel*	**los** hoteles	*hotels*
el señor	*gentleman*	**los** señores	*gentlemen*
la habitación	*room*	**las** habitaciones	*rooms*

(See page 254 for notes on stress and accentuation.)

Masculine nouns which refer to people may refer to both sexes in the plural.

el padre	*father*	los padres	*parents*
el hermano	*brother*	los hermanos	*brothers and sisters*

2 Ser *or* estar? (*to be*)

In Unit 1 you learned the use of **ser** (*to be*), to give personal information such as name (e.g. **soy Carlos**), place of origin (e.g. **soy de México**) and nationality (e.g. **soy mexicano**). Spanish has another verb, **estar**, which also translates into English as *to be* (e.g. **la señorita Martín está en la habitación número 50.**), and the uses of each are clearly differentiated by the native speaker and are identified in the following paragraphs.

3 Using estar *to express location*

General rules about when to use **ser** or **estar** are usually misleading, so it is better to learn each use separately. For example, if you want to refer to location or distance, use **estar**.

Allí **está** el elevador.	*There is the lift.*
Está a dos cuadras de aquí.	*It is two blocks from here.*

4 Using estar *to refer to a state or condition*

To refer to a state or condition which may be transitory, such as that of someone's health, use **estar**.

¿Cómo **estás**?	*How are you?*
Estoy bien, gracias.	*I am fine, thank you.*

5 The present tense of estar

Here is **estar** fully conjugated in the present tense.

yo estoy	*I am*	nosotros/as estamos	*we are* (m/f)
tú estás	*you are* (fam, sing)	ustedes están	*you are* (pl)
usted está	*you are* (pol, sing)	ellos/as están	*they are* (m/f)
él, ella está	*he, she, it is*		

Consider again the uses of **estar** in the dialogues and the examples listed under **Frases y expresiones importantes**.

6 Hay (*there is, there are*)

To say *there is* or *there are* and to ask questions regarding existence in general, Spanish uses the single word **hay**.

¿**Hay** una estación de metro por aquí?	*Is there an underground station nearby?*
Sí, **hay** una.	*Yes, there is one.*
¿**Hay** habitaciones?	*Are there any rooms?*
No **hay**.	*There aren't any.*

7 Diminutives

Diminutives are very frequently used in Latin America, and you will need to recognise them when you hear them. Their main function is to give a more friendly tone to words or statements. Diminutives are usually formed with **-ito** (m) or **-ita** (f) added to the word, for example:

un rato – un rat**ito**	*a while*
ahora – ahor**ita**	*now, straight away*
(very frequent in Mexico and other countries)	

Some words undergo other changes, for example:

un café – un cafe**cito**	*a coffee*
un poco – un po**quito**	*a little*

8 More numbers

50	cincuenta		300	trescientos
60	sesenta		400	cuatrocientos
70	setenta		500	quinientos
80	ochenta		600	seiscientos
90	noventa		700	setecientos
100	cien		800	ochocientos
101	ciento uno		900	novecientos
200	doscientos		1000	mil
210	doscientos diez		1501	mil quinientos uno
			2000	dos mil
1.000.000	un millón			
2.000.000	dos millones			

Numbers which finish in **-cientos**, e.g. **doscientos**, **trescientos**, must change according to the gender of the noun which follows.

el peso (Latin Am. currency)   doscient**os** pesos
la libra (pound)   doscient**as** libras
el dólar (dollar)   doscient**os** dólares

Cien (*one hundred*) does not change, e.g. cien pesos.

Note the way in which years are read in Spanish:

1850   mil ochocientos cincuenta
1994   mil novecientos noventa y cuatro

Ordinal numbers (1st to 6th)			
primero/a	**1st**	cuarto/a	**4th**
segundo/a	**2nd**	quinto/a	**5th**
tercero/a	**3rd**	sexto/a	**6th**

Ordinal numbers function as adjectives, therefore they must agree in gender (masc/fem) and number (sing/pl) with the word they refer to, for example **el segundo piso** (*the second floor*), **la segunda cuadra** (*the second block*), **las primeras cuadras** (*the first few blocks*). Before a masculine noun, **primero** changes to **primer**, and **tercero** to **tercer**, for example **el primer / tercer piso** (*the first / third floor*).

Actividades

1   A visitor has come to see a hotel guest.

Visita   ¿Cuál es la habitación del señor Valdés, por favor?
Recepcionista   El señor Valdés está en la habitación trescientos diez, en el tercer piso.
Visita   Gracias.

Make up similar dialogues using the information overleaf. You will find numbers on pages 19 and 36.

NOMBRE	HABITACIÓN	PISO
Sra. Marta Molina	220	2º
Sr. Cristóbal Salas	430	4º
Srta. Rosa Chandía	550	5º

Nota: The ground floor is **la planta baja**, which in some countries, for example Chile, is called **el primer piso**.

2 On a visit to Mexico, you meet Carmen, a Mexican friend you have not seen for some time. Complete your part of the conversation with her, using the familiar form.

Ud.	*Say hello to your friend and ask her how she is.*
Carmen	Estoy bien, gracias. ¿Y tú, cómo estás?
Ud.	*Say you are very well. Ask her to sit down and say you are very glad to see her again.*
Carmen	Yo también.
Ud.	*You have met her parents, so ask her how they are.*
Carmen	Están muy bien, gracias.

3 Señora Ramírez, a Latin American businesswoman, is visiting your company. She has come to see you in your office. Complete your part of this conversation with her, using the polite form.

Ud.	*Say good morning to her and ask her how she is.*
Sra. Ramírez	Yo estoy muy bien, gracias. ¿Y usted, cómo está?
Ud.	*Say you are fine and thank her. Ask her to sit down and say you are very glad to see her.*

4 Look at this dialogue between a receptionist and a hotel guest in Mexico.

Señor	Disculpe, ¿dónde están los teléfonos, por favor?
Recepcionista	Están al final del pasillo, a la izquierda, al lado del bar.
Señor	Gracias.
Recepcionista	Para servirle.

Now look at the plan of a hotel and make up similar dialogues.

Choose appropriate words and phrases from the dialogue and from those listed below.

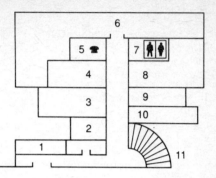

a lado de . . . *next to . . .*	**frente a . . .** *opposite . . .*
a la derecha *on the right*	**pasado el / la . . .** *past the . . .*
entre . . . y . . . *between . . . and . . .*	**antes de . . .** *before . . .*

KEY:
1 La recepción (*reception*)
2 El elevador (*lift*)
3 La agencia de viajes (*travel agency*)
4 El bar (*bar*)
5 Los teléfonos (*telephones*)
6 El comedor (*dining-room*)
7 Los baños (*toilets*)
8 El café (*cafe*)
9 La peluquería (*hairdresser's*)
10 La tienda de regalos (*gift shop*)
11 Las escaleras (*stairs*)

5 You will need to understand what people say to you when you inquire about a place or ask for directions. Listen to these conversations, then check your understanding by answering the questions. If you do not have the cassette, use the transcripts on pages 265–75 for reading comprehension.

In the first exchange, a man is seeking help from a young lady. Learn this new phrase and then listen to the conversation.

una casa de cambio (f)   *bureau de change*

Responda en inglés

(a) What is the man looking for?
(b) Where can he find one?
(c) How far is it?

In the second exchange, señor Ramos, a Colombian businessman, has come to see señor Silva at his office in Mexico City.

Responda en inglés

(d) Where is señor Silva?
(e) What number is his office?
(f) On which floor is it?
(g) Where exactly is it?

6   You are visiting a Latin American city for the first time and you need to find your way around. What questions would you need to ask to get these replies?

(a) Sí, hay una. La estación de Insurgentes.
(b) Está a cuatro cuadras de aquí.
(c) Sí, hay uno. El Hotel Reforma.
(d) No, está cerca. A cinco minutos de aquí.
(e) El Banco Nacional está en la plaza.
(f) La calle Panuco está a cinco cuadras de aquí.

minuto (m) *minute*		**calle** (f) *street*
banco (m) *bank*		

7   Now you are going to hear a conversation between a Colombian and a Chilean tourist who is visiting Bogotá, the capital of Colombia. The tourist is looking for the station (**la estación**). Most streets in the centre of Bogotá carry numbers instead of names: streets going in one direction are called **carreras**, those running across are called **calles**. If you do not have the cassette, use the transcript on page 266 for reading practice. The questions below will help you to check comprehension.

a pie *on foot*	**más o menos** *more or less*

¿Verdadero o falso? (*True or false?*)

(*a*) La estación está en la calle dieciséis.

(*b*) Está al final de la carrera diecisiete.

(*c*) Está a quince minutos a pie, aproximadamente.

8 You are going to hear part of a conversation with Jorge Vera, a Mexican from Veracruz. Jorge introduces himself as the director of a modern languages centre. Listen to the conversation or, if you are not using the cassette, read the transcript on page 266, then answer the questions below. First, familiarise yourself with these key words:

centro de lenguas modernas (m) *modern languages centre*	**una y media cuadra** *one and a half blocks*
localizado *situated*	**es decir** *that is to say*
media cuadra *half a block*	**parque** (m) *park*

Responda en inglés

(*a*) How far is the modern languages centre from the main street?

(*b*) How far is it from the main park?

—— Imágenes de Hispanoamérica ——

México

With a population of 88,598,000 inhabitants, Mexico is the largest Spanish-speaking country in the world, more than double the size of Spain. Its capital, Mexico City, known as **México** or **D.F.** (**Distrito Federal**, *Federal District*), is the largest city in the world, and has a population of 21,000,000 people, almost a quarter of the total population.

Like other Latin American countries, Mexico is a highly centralised country. The seat of the central government is in Mexico City, which is also the main centre for industry and commerce. Constant migration from rural areas into the capital forces the government to spend vast resources in providing services such as housing, health, education and transport. These are far from adequate, and cannot keep pace with the constant flow of people coming to look for better living conditions in the city. However, further industrialisation in other parts of the country, together with a decrease in birth rate, have led to a decline in population growth in the capital.

A friendly city

In spite of its size and its record as one of the most polluted cities in the world, Mexico City is a fascinating place to visit. Its people are friendly, perhaps more so than in other large Latin American capitals such as Buenos Aires, Santiago de Chile or Caracas. And Mexico City has a rich cultural life. There are excellent art galleries and museums, **el Museo de Antropología** being the best known. And those who can understand the language will be able to enjoy the best of Mexican theatre. On a lighter side, Mexico City, like the rest of the country, offers a variety of entertainment, especially music, and good food.

Travelling in Mexico City

Good transport facilities can quickly take the visitor around or outside the city. The underground transport system, **el metro**, is the most extensive and one of the most modern in Latin America, attractive, quiet and very clean, but usually overcrowded, as it is the main means of transport for over four million Mexicans. The alternatives are the buses, called **camiones** in Mexico and

buses in most other Latin American countries, or the minibuses, known as **peseros**. The **metro** has a fixed fare, no matter how far you travel, but on the **peseros** fares vary according to the distance you travel. The word for *ticket* in Mexico, as in the other Spanish-speaking countries of Latin America, is **el boleto** (not **el billete**, as in Spain), so from the start of your visit to Mexico City you may need phrases such as **un boleto** or **dos boletos, por favor**. On a **pesero** you may need to remember the place where you got on so that the driver knows what to charge you when you reach your destination.

Simply say **desde** . . . (*from* . . . destination), **¿Cuánto es?** (*How much is it?*) A **pesero** is much faster and more expensive than a **camión** but a lot cheaper than a taxi.

Destination Mexico

Every year, thousands of tourists come to Mexico, and many of them start their holiday in Mexico City. Overleaf there is a brief description of Mexico D.F. taken from a holiday brochure from a tour operator in Spain, followed by some key words and phrases to help you understand the text. Try to get the gist of what it says rather than translating it word for word. After you have read the passage, answer the questions that follow.

rodeada *surrounded*	**ciudad** (f) *city*
montaña (f) *mountain*	**mezcla** (f) *mixture*
valle (m) *valley*	**amplia** *wide*
goza de *it enjoys*	**barrio** (m) *district*
se encuentran *are situated*	**mercado** (m) *market*
como *such as*	**edificio** (m) *building*
mundialmente *world* (adj)	**iglesia** (f) *church*

MÉXICO D.F.

La capital de México, rodeada de montañas, está situada en un valle de 2.240 m. de altitud. Goza de una intensa vida cultural y artística, es el centro intelectual de toda Hispanoamérica. Aquí se encuentran lugares históricos como el Zócalo, el Palacio Nacional, la Catedral Metropolitana, la capital azteca de Tenochtitlán o el mundialmente famoso Museo Nacional de Antropología.

Esta ciudad de 21 millones de habitantes es una mezcla del pasado y del presente. Una ciudad moderna, con amplias avenidas y plazas animadas, barrios elegantes, mercados populares, edificios futuristas, residencias coloniales e iglesias barrocas.

Responda en inglés

(a) Where is the capital of Mexico situated?
(b) What does the text say about the city's cultural and artistic life?
(c) How does the text describe the city itself?

3

ABREN A LAS OCHO

They open at eight

In this unit you will learn how to

- ask and tell the time
- ask and say what time places open and close
- ask and say what time meals are served

Diálogos

1 ¿Qué hora es?

Anne Barker, an English visitor who has just arrived in Mexico, wants to set her watch by the local time. She asks the hotel receptionist what time it is.

Anne Barker	Buenos días.
Recepcionista	Buenos días, señora.
Anne Barker	¿Qué hora es, por favor?
Recepcionista	Son las ocho y media.
Anne Barker	Gracias.
Recepcionista	De nada.

¿Qué hora es?   *What time is it?*
Son las ocho y media.   *It's half past eight.*

Nota explicativa

Asking the time

¿Qué hora es? (*What time is it?*) is the standard phrase you will hear in most countries when asking the time. But in some parts of Latin America, including Mexico, you will also hear the phrase **¿Qué horas son?**

2   ¿Qué hora tiene usted?

Another visitor is asking the time.

Señora	Perdón, ¿qué hora tiene usted?
Recepcionista	Son diez para las nueve.
Señora	Gracias.
Recepcionista	Para servirle.

¿Qué hora tiene usted?   *What time do you make it?*
Son diez para las nueve.   *It's ten to nine.*

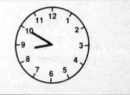

Nota explicativa

Son diez para las nueve (*It is ten to nine*)

This form is heard in Mexico and some other Latin American countries, for example Colombia and Chile. In Spain and some parts of Latin America people say **Son las nueve menos diez**. (*It is ten to nine*).

3 Abren a las ocho

A hotel guest has come down for breakfast, but the restaurant is closed.

Señorita	¿Dónde está el restaurante, por favor?
Recepcionista	(*pointing*) Está ahí, señorita, pero está cerrado.
Señorita	¿A qué hora abren?
Recepcionista	Abren a las ocho. Dentro de cinco minutos.
Señorita	Gracias. Muy amable.

ahí *there*	**Abren a las ocho.** *They open at eight.*
Está cerrado. *It's closed.*	
¿A qué hora abren? *What time do they open?*	**dentro de cinco minutos** *within five minutes*

——— Notas explicativas ———

Asking what time a place opens

¿A qué hora abren?   *What time do they open?*

— **47** —

An alternative to this question is

¿A qué hora abre?   *What time does it open?*

4 En la tienda de regalos

A visitor needs to buy some presents to take home. He asks the shop
assistant in the gift shop what time they close.

Cliente   Perdón, ¿a qué hora cierran?
Dependienta   Hoy cerramos a las siete y cuarto.
Cliente   Gracias.

tienda (f) *shop*	**cerramos** *we close*
regalo (m) *gift, present*	**a las siete y cuarto** *at a quarter*
cierran *you close*	*past seven*

5 ¿A qué hora es la cena?

Another visitor is inquiring about dinner time.

Señorita   Buenas tardes
Recepcionista Buenas tardes, señorita.
Señorita   ¿A qué hora es la cena, por favor?
Recepcionista Es a las nueve.
Señorita   ¿Y el restaurante, dónde está?
Recepcionista Está al fondo del pasillo.
Señorita   Muchas gracias.
Recepcionista Para servirle.

¿A qué hora . . .? *At what time . . .?*	**Es a las nueve.** *It's at nine.*
cena (f) *dinner*	**al fondo** *at the end, at the bottom*

——— Nota explicativa ———

La cena (*dinner*)

In some parts of Latin America, Colombia and Chile for example, **la**

cena refers to a special late-night dinner to celebrate something. The word normally used for dinner in these countries is **la comida**.

6 ¿A qué hora desayunas?

Raúl and Rosa, two Mexicans, talk about their meals.

Raúl ¿A qué hora tomas el desayuno normalmente?
Rosa A las ocho y media. ¿Y tú?
Raúl Yo tomo el desayuno a las siete.
Rosa ¡Qué temprano! ¿Y a qué hora almuerzas?
Raúl Entre las doce y media y la una.
Rosa Yo almuerzo a las dos.
Raúl ¿Almuerzas en casa?
Rosa Normalmente sí, ¿y tú?
Raúl Yo no, yo como en la universidad.

tomar el desayuno *to have breakfast*	**almorzar (o → ue)** *to have lunch*
normalmente *normally*	**en casa** *at home*
¡Qué temprano! *How early!*	**comer** *to eat*
	universidad (f) *university*

Responda en inglés

(*a*) What time does Rosa normally have breakfast?
(*b*) And Raúl?
(*c*) What time does Raúl normally have lunch?
(*d*) Where does Rosa normally have lunch?

——— Nota explicativa ———

Tomar el desayuno, desayunar (*to have breakfast*)

In some Latin American countries, and in Spain, you will hear the word **desayunar** instead of **tomar el desayuno** (*to have breakfast*).

🔧– Frases y expresiones importantes –

- Asking and telling the time

¿Qué hora es?	*What time is it?*
¿Qué hora tiene?	*What time do you make it?*
Es la una.	*It's one o'clock.*
Son las siete y cuarto.	*It's a quarter past seven.*
Son las ocho y media.	*It's half past eight.*
Es un cuarto para las tres.	*It's a quarter to three.*
Son las tres menos cuarto.	*It's a quarter to three.*
Son diez para las nueve.	*It's ten to nine.*
Son las nueve menos diez.	*It's ten to nine.*
Son las diez y veinte.	*It's twenty past ten.*

- Asking and saying what time places open and close

¿A qué hora abren?	*What time do they open?*
Abren a las ocho.	*They open at eight.*
¿A qué hora cierran?	*What time do you close?*
Cerramos a las siete y cuarto.	*We close at quarter past seven.*

- Other phrases related to opening and closing

El supermercado está abierto.	*The supermarket is open.*
La panadería está abierta.	*The baker's is open.*
El mercado está cerrado.	*The market is closed.*
La farmacia está cerrada.	*The chemist's is closed.*
Las tiendas están abiertas / cerradas.	*The shops are open / closed.*

- Asking and saying what time meals are served

¿A qué hora es la cena?	*What time is dinner?*
Es a las nueve.	*It's at nine o'clock.*

- Other phrases used when asking about meal times

¿A qué hora es el desayuno / el almuerzo?	*What time is breakfast / lunch?*
¿A qué hora sirven el desayuno / el almuerzo / la cena?	*What time do you serve breakfast / lunch / dinner?*

Notas gramaticales

1   Asking and telling the time with ser

To ask and tell the time, as in **¿Qué hora es?** (*What time is it?*), **Son las diez** (*It's ten o'clock*), Spanish uses the verb **ser**. To say the time, start with **es** if it is one o'clock and **son** with all other times.

Es la una y cuarto.	*It's quarter past one.*
Son las nueve.	*It's nine o'clock.*

For more examples refer to **Frases y expresiones importantes**.

2   At what time?

Notice also the use of **ser** in the following examples:

¿A qué hora es el desayuno?	*What time is breakfast?*
Es a las ocho.	*It's at eight o'clock.*

When we inquire about the time a place opens or closes or, more generally, about the time something takes place, the phrase **¿qué hora?** must always be preceded by the preposition **a**: **¿A qué hora ...?**

3   The days of the week

Días de la semana	*Days of the week*
lunes	*Monday*
martes	*Tuesday*
miércoles	*Wednesday*
jueves	*Thursday*
viernes	*Friday*
sábado	*Saturday*
domingo	*Sunday*

Notice that in Spanish the days of the week are written with small letters. To say *on Monday, on Tuesday*, etc., use the word **el** (*the*, m/sing): **el lunes**, **el martes**. To say *Mondays, Tuesdays*, etc., use the word **los** (*the*, m/pl): **los lunes**, **los martes**. To say *Today /*

Tomorrow is Friday / Saturday, etc., use phrases like these: **Hoy es viernes**, **Mañana es sábado**. To ask what day it is today, say **¿Qué día es hoy?**

4 Three kinds of verbs

According to the ending of the infinitive (or dictionary form of the verb), Spanish verbs may be grouped into three main categories or conjugations: -**ar** (or first conjugation), -**er** (or second conjugation) and -**ir** (or third conjugation). For example:

tom**ar**	*to take*
com**er**	*to eat*
abr**ir**	*to open*

In Spanish, there are regular and irregular verbs. Regular verbs are those that follow a fixed pattern, which varies only according to certain grammatical categories, such as the ending of the infinitive (see above), *person*, for instance **yo** (*I*), **tú** (*you*, fam), **él** (*he*) (see **Notas gramaticales,** Unit 1) or *tense*, for example present tense, future tense.

5 The present tense

-ar verbs

In the present tense, all regular -**ar** verbs follow this pattern:

tomar	to take
tom**o**	*I take*
tom**as**	*you take* (fam, sing)
tom**a**	*you take* (pol, sing)
tom**a**	*he, she, it takes*
tom**amos**	*we take*
tom**an**	*you take* (pl), *they take*

¿A qué hora tomas el desayuno?	*What time do you have breakfast?*
Tomo el desayuno a las ocho.	*I have breakfast at eight.*

-er verbs

Regular -**er** verbs are conjugated in the following way:

comer	*to eat*
com**o**	*I eat*
com**es**	*you eat* (fam, sing)
com**e**	*you eat* (pol, sing)
com**e**	*he, she, it eats*
com**emos**	*we eat*
com**en**	*you eat* (pl), *they eat*

Como en la universidad.	*I eat in the university.*
Rosa come en casa.	*Rosa eats at home.*

-ir *verbs*

Regular -**ir** verbs are conjugated like this:

abrir	*to open*
abr**o**	*I open*
abr**es**	*you open* (fam, sing)
abr**e**	*you open* (pol, sing)
abr**e**	*he, she, it opens*
abr**imos**	*we open*
abr**en**	*you eat* (pl), *they open*

¿A qué hora abren?	*What time do they open?*
Abrimos a las ocho.	*We open at eight.*

Notice that the endings for -**er** and -**ir** verbs are the same, except in the first person plural **nosotros**. Note also that the plural familiar form corresponding to **vosotros** (*you*) has been omitted, as this is not normally used in Latin America (see **Notas gramaticales**, Unit 1).

6   Stem-changing verbs: e → ie *and* o → ue

Certain verbs undergo a change in the stem (the infinitive minus its ending). Stem-changing verbs (also known as radical-changing verbs) have the same endings as regular verbs. **Cerrar** (*to close*) is a stem-changing verb, in which -**e** changes into -**ie**. Notice that this change occurs only when the stem is stressed, therefore verb forms corresponding to **nosotros** (*we*) (**cerramos**, *we close*) are not affected by it.

cierro	*I close*
cierras	*you close* (fam, sing)
cierra	*you close* (pol, sing), *he, she, it closes*
cierran	*you close* (pl), *they close*

In later units you will encounter other verbs which change in the same way as **cerrar**.

Almorzar (*to have lunch*) is also a stem-changing verb, in which -**o** changes into -**ue**.

almuerzo	*I have lunch*
almuerzas	*you have lunch* (fam, sing)
almuerza	*you have lunch* (pol, sing), *he, she has lunch*
almuerzan	*you have lunch* (pl), *they have lunch*

In later units you will encounter other verbs which change in the same way as **almorzar**.

 ———————— **Actividades** ————————

1 Ask and say the time, following the example below.

¿Qué hora es? Son las seis y veinte.

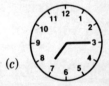

(*a*)   (*b*)   (*c*)

(*d*)   (*e*)   (*f*)

2 You are in Chile on business and want to make several phone calls abroad, so you need to be aware of time differences. Look at the information below and then answer the questions giving the correct time.

En Chile es mediodía (*midday*).

(a) ¿Qué hora es en la Ciudad de México?
(b) ¿Qué hora es en Londres?
(c) ¿Qué hora es en Buenos Aires?
(d) ¿Qué hora es en París?

3 On your next visit to Mexico, don't miss the **Ballet Folklórico Mexicano**, a well-known group which presents the best of

Mexican music and dance. Look at this advertisement for the ballet and the vocabulary which follows. Then answer the questions below.

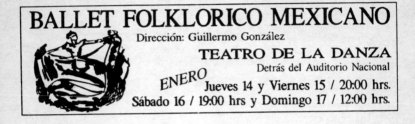

BALLET FOLKLORICO MEXICANO

Dirección: Guillermo González

TEATRO DE LA DANZA

Detrás del Auditorio Nacional

ENERO Jueves 14 y Viernes 15 / 20:00 hrs.

Sábado 16 / 19:00 hrs y Domingo 17 / 12:00 hrs.

In advertisements such as the one above, at railway stations, airports, on the radio, and so on, Spanish uses the 24-hour clock. Colloquially, however, people use phrases like the following to distinguish between a.m. and p.m.: **Son las dos de la tarde** (*It's two o'clock in the afternoon*), **A las diez de la noche** (*At ten o'clock at night*).

teatro (m) *theatre*	**enero** *January*
danza (f) *dance*	

Responda en español

(*a*) ¿Dónde está el Teatro de la Danza?
(*b*) ¿Cuántas funciones (*performances*) hay el viernes 15 (quince)?
(*c*) ¿A qué hora es la función el viernes?
(*d*) ¿A qué hora es la función el domingo 17 (diecisiete)?

4 Ask what time these places open and close.

la tienda *shop*	**el correo** *post office*
el supermercado *supermarket*	**el museo** *museum*

(*a*) Ask what time shops open.
(*b*) Ask what time the supermarket opens.
(*c*) Ask what time the post office closes.
(*d*) Ask what time museums close.

5 Jorge Vera from Mexico was asked what time shops open in Veracruz, his home town. Listen to what he says, or read the transcript on page 267, then answer the questions below. Here are some key words used by Jorge:

mañana (f)	*morning*	**para trabajar**	*to work*
entonces	*then*	**hasta**	*until*
trabajan	*they work*		

¿Verdadero o falso? (*True or false?*)

(*a*) Las tiendas abren a las ocho y media de la mañana.

(*b*) Las tiendas cierran entre una y cuatro.

(*c*) En la noche cierran a las siete.

——— Nota explicativa ———

En la mañana (*in the morning*), **en la tarde** (*in the afternoon*), **en la noche** (*at night*), (see (*c*) above). In some parts of Latin America and in Spain, people say **por la mañana / tarde / noche**. In phrases which carry a time, such as *at half past eight in the morning*, Spanish always uses **de** instead of **por**: **a las ocho y media de la mañana**.

6 You are on holiday in a South American country and you need to change some money. It is 2.30 p.m. and the nearest bureau de change (**casa de cambio**), La Internacional, which is two blocks from your hotel, on the left, does not open until 4.00. Use the information to write a dialogue similar to the one below between yourself and a hotel receptionist.

Señorita	Disculpe, ¿qué hora tiene, por favor?
Recepcionista	Es un cuarto para las nueve. / Son las nueve menos cuarto.
Señorita	¿A qué hora abren los bancos?
Recepcionista	Abren a las nueve.
Señorita	¿Hay un banco por aquí?
Recepcionista	Sí, el Banco de la Nación está en la esquina.

| **Señorita** | Muchas gracias. Muy amable. |
| **Recepcionista** | Para servirle. ¡Que le vaya bien! |

> **en la esquina**   *on the corner*

7 A Spanish-speaking friend is asking you what time you have your meals. Answer his questions.

(a) ¿A qué hora tomas el desayuno / desayunas normalmente?
(b) ¿Y a qué hora almuerzas?
(c) ¿Dónde almuerzas?
(d) ¿Cenas muy tarde? ¿A qué hora?

> **cenar**   *to have dinner*   **muy tarde**   *very late*

8 Jorge Vera and Clotilde Montalvo (Coty) were asked about the main meals and their times in Mexico, their country. Listen to both conversations, or read the transcripts on page 267, and note the differences in the information given by each of them. Then answer the questions below. These key words and phrases will help you to understand:

> **dime**   *tell me*
> **comida** (f)   *meal*
> **¿Cuál es el horario?**   *What are the times?*
> **cada**   *each*
> **opcionalmente**   *alternatively*
>
> **podríamos llamarle**   *we could call it*
> **poscena**   *after-dinner snack*
> **que puede ser**   *which can be*
> **si nos acostamos tarde**   *if we go to bed late*

Responda en inglés

(a) What are the times of the three main meals, according to Jorge?
(b) What time is the optional after-dinner snack?

> **la de mediodía** (m)   *the midday one*   **en adelante**   *onwards*
> **que varía**   *which varies*   **temprano**   *early*
> **en que se toma**   *which is when it is taken*

Complete these sentences with the information given by Coty.

(c) La comida principal es la de _____ .
(d) El almuerzo es entre _____ y _____ .
(e) La cena es _____ .

── Imágenes de Hispanoamérica ──

Shopping hours

As in Spain, shops in most of Latin America usually close for lunch for about two or three hours. This old custom makes perfect sense in a warm climate, where the midday heat is not conducive to work. Shops re-open again about 4.00 or 4.30 p.m. and remain open until 7.30 or 8.00 o'clock. In large cities, some shops, especially department stores, do not close for lunch.

Banking hours

Banking hours differ from country to country in Latin America, but they open between 9.00 and 9.30 a.m. and close between 1.00 and 2.00 p.m. In the afternoon, they normally remain closed. If you find yourself short of local currency at an odd hour, try a **casa de cambio** (*bureau de change*). These are usually open until late afternoon or early evening. You can also change money at large hotels.

Main meals

Most Latin Americans have a light **desayuno** (*breakfast*) before going to work, normally consisting of **café** (*coffee*) and **tostadas** or **pan tostado** (*toast*), **con mantequilla y mermelada** (*with butter and jam*), not very different from what you might have at home. But in some countries, especially Mexico, **el desayuno** is often a more substantial meal. Hotels and restaurants usually provide a selection of fresh fruit and hot dishes, where **tortillas**, **huevos** (*eggs*), cooked in a variety of ways, and of course **chile** (*chilli*) are never missing. Coffee is often good in most Latin American countries, but if you think you will miss your cup of tea, you should take some tea bags with you. The quality of tea in Latin America is far from good. In Mexico, ask for **té negro** (lit. *black tea*) if you want normal tea rather than herbal. If you are travelling in Chile, beware of coffee, as you will normally be given instant coffee. If you want to be sure you are getting proper coffee, just say **¿Tiene café-café?** or **Quiero café-café**. If it is any consolation, food shops in Chile usually stock a large selection of good teas.

El almuerzo (*lunch*) is the main meal in Latin America and it normally consists of a two- or even a three-course meal. Families usually have lunch together at home. In big cities, restaurants sometimes offer quick, inexpensive lunches for working people. If this is what you want, ask for **el menú del día** or **el plato del día** (the day's menu or the day's dish) or **la comida corrida** in Mexico. The alternative is to eat **a la carta**, which will obviously be more expensive.

La cena (*dinner*) is a light meal, sometimes only consisting of **una sopa** (*soup*), **una ensalada** (*salad*) or perhaps some sandwiches. Unless, of course, you are going out for dinner, in which case this will be similar to lunch.

Those travelling in Chile should become familiar with the word **la once** or **las onces** (lit. *eleven* or *elevenses*). This is a light meal taken about 5.00 p.m., which consists of tea or coffee and sandwiches, cake (**torta**) or fruit pie (**küchen**). In some countries, including Spain, this afternoon snack or tea is called **la merienda**.

4

¿QUÉ HACES?

What do you do?

In this unit you will learn how to

- introduce people
- say where you live and what work you do
- talk about daily and spare-time activities
- ask and say how old people are

Diálogos

1 Te presento a mi hermana

Jorge, a Mexican from Veracruz, introduces his friend Juan, a Chilean, to his sister.

Juan   Hola, Jorge.

Jorge   Hola, Juan. Pasa. ¿Cómo te va?

Juan   Bien, gracias, ¿y tú, cómo estás?

Jorge   Pues, un poco cansado. Tengo mucho trabajo. Mira, te presento a mi hermana Luisa, que está aquí de vacaciones. Luisa, éste es Juan, mi amigo chileno.

Luisa   Encantada.

Juan Mucho gusto.
Luisa ¿De qué parte de Chile eres?
Juan Soy de Santiago. ¿Y tú no vives en Veracruz?
Luisa No, vivo en Cancún. Trabajo en una agencia de viajes. ¿Y tú, qué haces?
Juan Soy arquitecto. Trabajo en una empresa constructora.

---

pasa *come in* (fam)	**mi** *my*
pues *well*	**de vacaciones** *on holiday*
un poco *a little*	**vivir** *to live*
cansado/a *tired* (m/f)	**trabajar** *to work*
éste *this*	**hacer** *to do*
tengo *I have*	**arquitecto** (m) *architect*
trabajo (m) *work*	**empresa constructora** (m)
mira *look* (fam)	*construction company*
te presento a *let me introduce* *you to* (fam)	

Responda en inglés

(*a*) Where does Luisa live?
(*b*) What work does she do?
(*c*) What does Juan do?

Notas explicativas

Tengo (*I have*)

Notice the irregular form **tengo** (*I have*), from **tener** (*to have*), in:

Tengo mucho trabajo.   *I have a lot of work.*

More on this under **Notas gramaticales**.

Introducing people

Te presento a mi hermana.   *Let me introduce you to my sister.* (fam)

Le presento a mi hermano.   *Let me introduce you to my brother.* (pol)

Te and **le** (*you* or *to you*) refer to the person you are speaking to and does not vary for masculine and feminine.

Éste, ésta (*this*)

Éste es Juan.   *This is Juan.*

Éste (*this*) is a masculine form. If you are introducing a woman, use the feminine form **ésta**:

Ésta es Luisa.   *This is Luisa.*

More on this under **Notas gramaticales**.

2 Empiezo a las nueve

Juan asks Luisa about her work.

Juan   ¿Estás contenta de vivir en Cancún?
Luisa   Sí, es un lugar muy bonito y tiene un clima muy bueno.
Juan   Y tu trabajo, ¿qué tal?
Luisa   Es un trabajo interesante, aunque a veces pienso que trabajo demasiado.
Juan   ¿Cuál es tu horario de trabajo?
Luisa   Empiezo a las nueve de la mañana y termino a las siete de la tarde.
Juan   ¿Sin interrupción?
Luisa   No, cerramos al mediodía entre las dos y las cuatro.

---

estar contento/a *to be happy* (m/f)	**interesante** *interesting*
lugar (m) *place*	**aunque** *although*
muy bonito *very pretty*	**a veces** *sometimes*
tiene *it has*	**pensar (e → ie)** *to think*
clima (m) *weather, climate*	**demasiado** *too much*
muy bueno *very good*	**empezar (e → ie)** *to begin*
tu *your* (fam)	**terminar** *to finish*
¿Qué tal? *What is it like?*	**sin** *without*

Responda en inglés

(*a*) Why does Luisa like Cancún?
(*b*) What time does she start and finish work?

Notas explicativas

The linking word que (*that*)

Notice the use of the linking word **que** (*that*) in: **Pienso que trabajo demasiado** *I think (that) I work too much*. In this context, **que** functions as a relative pronoun. **Que** may also refer to people, in which case it translates into English as *who*. Consider this example from dialogue 1 above:

Mi hermana Luisa, que está aquí de vacaciones.	*My sister Luisa, who is here on holiday.*

Stem-changing verbs

Pensar (*to think*) and **empezar** (*to begin*) are stem-changing verbs (see **Notas gramaticales**, Unit 3) in which the **-e** of the stem changes into **-ie**. From now on, changes in the stem will be indicated in brackets next to the verb (e.g. **e → ie, o → ue**).

3 ¿Qué haces los fines de semana?

Luisa asks Juan about his spare-time activities.

Luisa ¿Qué haces los fines de semana?

Juan Por lo general, me levanto bastante tarde. A veces salgo fuera de Santiago, voy a la playa o al campo. Cuando me quedo en Santiago voy al cine o salgo a comer con mis amigos. Generalmente me acuesto muy tarde. ¿Y tú, qué haces?

Luisa No hago nada especial. Normalmente veo la televisión, leo o escucho música.

fines de semana (m, pl) *weekends*	**cuando** *when*
por lo general *usually*	**me quedo** *I stay*
me levanto *I get up*	**cine** (m) *cinema*
bastante *quite*	**con** *with*
tarde *late*	**generalmente** *usually, generally*
salgo fuera *I go out*	**me acuesto** *I go to bed*
voy *I go*	**no hago nada** *I don't do anything*
playa (f) *beach*	**veo la televisión** *I watch television*
o *or*	**leo** *I read*
campo (m) *countryside*	**escucho música** *I listen to music*

Responda en inglés

(a) What does Juan do at the weekend?

(b) What does Luisa do?

———— Nota explicativa ————

Reflexive verbs

Verb forms like **me levanto** (*I get up*), **me acuesto** (*I go to bed*) and **me quedo** (*I stay*) are known as reflexive verbs. For an explanation see **Notas gramaticales**.

4 Tiene doce años

Luisa tells Juan about her family.

Juan ¿Eres casada?

Luisa Sí, soy casada. Tengo dos hijos.

Juan ¿Cuántos años tienen?

Luisa Mi hijo mayor, José, tiene doce años, y la menor, Cristina, tiene diez. Tú eres soltero, ¿no?

Juan Sí, soy soltero. ¿Y tu esposo, qué hace?

Luisa Es maestro.

ser casado/a *to be married*	**menor** *younger*
ser soltero/a *to be single*	**Tiene doce años.** *He is twelve years old.*
¿Cuántos años tienen? *How old are they?*	**¿Qué hace?** *What does he do?*
hijos (m, pl) *children*	**esposo/a** *husband / wife*
hijo (m) *son*	**maestro** (m) *school teacher*
mayor *elder*	

Responda en inglés

(*a*) How many children does Luisa have?
(*b*) What are their ages?

--- **Nota explicativa** ---

Expressing marital status

To express marital status, you can use either **ser** or **estar**, e.g. **soy casado/a** (m/f) or **estoy casado/a** (*I am married*). The first seems more common in Latin America, while the second is more frequent in Spain.

– Frases y expresiones importantes –

- Introducing people
  Te presento a mi hermana. *Let me introduce you to my sister.* (fam)
  Éste es Juan. *This is Juan.*

- Saying where you live and what work you do
  ¿Tú no vives en Veracruz? *You don't live in Veracruz?*
  Vivo en Cancún. *I live in Cancún.*
  ¿Qué haces? *What do you do?*
  Trabajo en una empresa constructora. *I work in a construction company.*

- Other ways of asking people where they live and what work they do

¿Cuál es su / tu dirección?	*What is your* (pol / fam) *address?*
¿En qué trabaja Ud.?	*What work do you do?* (pol)
¿En qué trabajas (tú)?	*What work do you do?* (fam)

- Talking about daily and spare-time activities

¿Cuál es tu horario de trabajo?	*What are your working hours?*
Empiezo a las nueve de la mañana.	*I begin at nine in the morning.*
Termino a las siete de la tarde.	*I finish at seven in the evening.*
¿Qué haces los fines de semana?	*What do you do at weekends?*
Voy al cine.	*I go to the cinema.*
Salgo a comer.	*I go out for dinner.*

- Saying how often you do something

generalmente / por lo general	*generally / usually*
normalmente	*normally*
a veces	*sometimes*
de vez en cuando	*from time to time*
siempre	*always*
nunca	*never*
Generalmente me levanto tarde.	*I usually get up late.*
Normalmente voy al cine.	*I normally go to the cinema.*

- Asking and saying how old people are

¿Cuántos años tiene José?	*How old is José?*
José tiene doce años.	*José is twelve years old.*

Notas gramaticales

1   My, your, his . . .

To say *my*, *your*, *his*, *her*, etc. in Spanish, use the following set of words.

mi	*my*
tu	*your* (fam, sing)
su	*your* (pol, sing), *his, her, its*
nuestro/a	*our* (m/f)
su	*your* (pl), *their*

These words, which are called possessives, agree in number (sing/pl) with the noun that they accompany, but only **nuestro** (*our*) agrees in gender (m/f).

Consider these examples:

Mi hermana se llama Luisa.   *My sister is called Luisa.*
Mis hermanas se llaman Luisa   *My sisters are called Luisa*
y María.   *and María.*
¿Dónde está **nuestro** hotel?   *Where is our hotel?*
¿Dónde está **nuestra** habitación? *Where is our room?*

Note that the form **vuestro** (*your*, pl/fam), corresponding to **vosotros** (*you*, pl/fam) used in Spain, is not normally used in Latin America.

2   *This and these*

To say *this* and *these* in Spanish, use the following set of words, which vary for number (sing/pl) and gender (m/f).

este señor (m)   *this gentlemen (next to you)*
esta señora (f)   *this lady (next to you)*
estos señores (m)   *these gentlemen (next to you)*
estas señoras (f)   *these ladies (next to you)*

In these examples, **este, esta**, etc. have been followed by nouns (e.g. **señor, señora**), in which case they are written without an accent. If they are not followed directly by a noun, they are normally written with an accent.

Ésta es mi hermana.   *This is my sister.*
Éste es mi hermano.   *This is my brother.*

For *that* and *those*, see Unit 6.

3 Irregular verbs

There are many verbs in Spanish which do not follow a fixed pattern, i.e. they are irregular. In the present tense, some verbs are irregular only in the first person singular. Here are some examples:

hacer	*to do, to make*	**hago**	*I do, I make*
salir	*to go out*	**salgo**	*I go out*
ver	*to watch, to see*	**veo**	*I watch, I see*

For other irregular verbs, see page 276.

No hago nada especial.	*I don't do anything special.*
Salgo a cenar.	*I go out for dinner.*
Veo la televisión.	*I watch television.*

4 Tener (*to have*) *in the present tense*

Tener (*to have*), which is irregular in the first person singular of the present tense, is also a stem-changing verb (see Unit 3):

tengo	*I have*
tienes	*you have* (fam, sing)
tiene	*you have* (pol, sing), *he, she, it has*
tenemos	*we have*
tienen	*you have* (pol), *they have*

| Tengo mucho trabajo. | *I have a lot of work.* |
| ¿Qué hora tiene? | *What time do you make it?* |

5 Using tener *to ask and say how old people are*

Tener is also used to refer to age, in which case it translates into English as *to be*. Here is how to ask someone's age in a polite and familiar way:

| ¿Cuántos años tiene usted? | *How old are you?* (pol) |
| ¿Cuántos años tienes? | *How old are you?* (fam) |

(**Nota**: **¿Cuántos?** means literally *How many?*)

To say how old someone is, use **tiene**:

> Tiene doce años. *He / she is 12 years old.*

To say your own age use **tengo**:

> Tengo treinta y cinco años. *I am thirty-five years old.*

6 Ir (*to go*)

Here are the present tense forms of **ir** (*to go*), a verb which is very irregular.

voy	*I go*
vas	*you go* (fam, sing)
va	*you go* (pol, sing), *he, she, it goes*
vamos	*we go*
van	*you go* (pl), *they go*

> Voy a la playa. *I go to the beach.*
> ¿Vas al cine? *Do you go to the cinema?*

7 Reflexive verbs

A reflexive verb is one that has -se added to the infinitive, e.g. **levantarse** (*to get up*). Normally, **se**, as in this example, is not expressed at all in English, but it sometimes translates into English as *oneself*, for example **mirarse** (*to look at oneself*). Many verbs in Spanish are reflexive where their English equivalents are not.

In the examples from dialogue 3 (**me levanto** (*I get up*), **me acuesto** (*I go to bed*), **me quedo** (*I stay*)) **me** can be said to correspond to the English word *myself*. Words like **se** and **me** are called reflexive pronouns and these precede the conjugated verb. Here is a verb fully conjugated:

levantarse *to get up*	
me levanto	*I get up*
te levantas	*you get up* (fam, sing)
se levanta	*you get up* (pol, sing), *he, she, it gets up*
nos levantamos	*we get up*
se levantan	*you get up* (pl), *they get up*

The plural familiar form **os levantáis** (*you get up*) has been omitted, as this is not normally used in Latin America.

Remember that in a dictionary, reflexive verbs are listed with -**se** on the end of the infinitive, for example: **divertirse** (*to enjoy oneself*), **quedarse** (*to stay*), **acostarse** (*to go to bed*).

8 Personal a

Observe the use of **a** after the verb:

Te presento **a** mi hermana.   *Let me introduce my sister to you.*

When a verb is followed by a word or phrase which is a definite person, as in **mi hermana**, Spanish requires the use of the preposition **a**. Look at these examples:

Veo la televisión.   *I watch television.*
Veo **a** Luisa.   *I see Luisa.*

9 Formation of adverbs

An adverb is a word that tells you something about the action of the verb, for example how often or how frequently something is done.

Words like *normally*, *generally* and *usually* are adverbs, and in Spanish these are normally formed by adding -**mente** to the adjective.

normal	*normal*
normalmente	*normally*
general	*general*
generalmente	*generally*
usual	*usual*
usualmente	*usually*

If the adjective ends in -**o**, change the -**o** to -**a** and add -**mente**.

rápido	*rapid, quick*
rápidamente	*rapidly, quickly*

Notice that if the adjective carries an accent, the adverb must carry the same accent. For general information on the use of accents see page 254.

🕊 ———————— **Actividades** ————————

1 An informal introduction
Raúl Riveros, from Mexico, is introducing his father to his friend
María Elena.

Raúl	Hola, María Elena. ¿Cómo te va?
María Elena	Muy bien, ¿y tú, cómo estás?
Raúl	Bien, gracias. Te presento a mi papá. (*Addressing his father*) Ésta es María Elena.
Señor Riveros	Encantado.
María Elena	Mucho gusto.

Nota: Latin Americans normally use **papá** (*father*) and **mamá**
(*mother*) in this context. Spaniards would normally use **padre**
and **madre** instead.

Raúl is now visiting María Elena, who introduces him to Señora
de García, her mother (**su mamá**). Rewrite the dialogue above
making the necessary adaptations.

2 A formal introduction
You are on business in Latin America, and after greeting señor
Molina, manager of Hispanometal, you introduce your colleague
John Evans to him. After exchanging greetings with John Evans,
señor Molina offers you a seat. Write a dialogue based on this
situation. Then compare your version with the model dialogue in
the **Key to the exercises**.

> **el gerente de . . .** *the manager of . . .*
> **mi colega** *my colleague*
> **siéntense** *sit down* (pl)

3 Latin Americans tend to be more direct in their questions when
they meet people for the first time. For instance, they often ask
people about their work, so here is your chance to practise.

(*a*) On a train journey in Latin America you meet Carlos, a
student from Uruguay. He uses the familiar form to address you,
so you do likewise.

Ud.	*Ask Carlos where he lives.*
Carlos	Vivo en Montevideo. ¿Y tú?

Ud.	*Say where you live and then ask him what work he does.*
Carlos	Soy estudiante. Estudio ingeniería en la Universidad de Montevideo. ¿Y tú?
Ud.	*Say what you do.*

estudiar	*to study*	**ingeniería** (f)	*engineering*

(b)   During an excursion you meet María and her husband José. They use the polite form to address you.

Ud.	*Ask them where they are from.*
María	Somos de Colombia. ¿Y usted, de dónde es?
Ud.	*Say what country you are from and then ask them where they live.*
José	Vivimos en Medellín.
Ud.	*Ask them what work they do.*
María	Mi esposo es médico y yo soy periodista.
Ud.	*Don't wait to be asked! Say something about your own work or occupation.*

médico (m)	*doctor*	**periodista** (m/f)	*journalist*

4   Listen to Coty Montalvo, from Mexico, talking about her work. If you are not using the cassette, use the transcript on page 267 for reading comprehension. The key words which follow will help you to understand what Coty says, while the questions below will help you check comprehension.

regresar	*to come back*	**seguir laborando**	*to continue working*

¿Verdadero o falso?

(a)   Coty empieza a trabajar a las nueve de la mañana.
(b)   Sale a almorzar a la una.
(c)   Termina de trabajar a las siete.

5 Imagine you are writing in Spanish to someone about your own activities. Use the following guidelines to express these ideas:

Say what you do.
Say what days you work or what days you go to school or university.
Say what time you start and what time you finish.
Say where you normally have lunch.
Say what you usually do after work / school.
Say what you usually do at the weekend.

soy estudiante *I am a student*	**después de trabajar / de clases**
estudiar *to study*	*after work / school*
ir al colegio / a la universidad	**salir a caminar / correr** *to go*
to go to school / university	*out and walk / run*
salir de compras *to go out*	**regar (e → ie) el jardín** *to water*
shopping	*the garden*
limpiar la casa *to clean the house*	**leer el periódico** *to read the*
ir al teatro / a conciertos *to go*	*newspaper*
to the theatre / concerts	**cocinar** *to cook*

6 Clotilde (Coty), from Mexico, was asked how she normally spends her holidays. Listen to what she says or, alternatively, read the transcript on page 268, then answer the questions below. First, look at this new vocabulary:

aprovecho *I take the opportunity*	**largo** *long*
sobrinos (m, pl) *nephews and*	**hasta allá** *to there*
nieces	**lo disfruto** *I enjoy it*
frontera (f) *border*	**veo** *I see*
Estados Unidos (m, pl) *United*	**muy de vez en cuando** *very*
States	*rarely*
viaje (m) *journey*	

Responda en inglés

(*a*) Where does Coty normally go on holiday?
(*b*) Why does she enjoy the long journey?

7 Read this information about Luisa Alvarez, then use the information in the box on page 75 to write a similar passage about Antonio Fernández, his children and his wife (**su esposa**).

Luisa Alvarez es mexicana y trabaja como secretaria en una agencia de viajes. Luisa es casada y tiene dos hijos, José y Cristina. Su hijo José tiene doce años y su hija Cristina tiene diez. El marido de Luisa se llama Pablo. Pablo es maestro.

Nombre:	Antonio Fernández
Nacionalidad:	nicaragüense
Profesión:	técnico, empresa textil
Estado civil:	casado
Nº de hijos:	3
Edades:	Adela (24 años), Mario (21), Domingo (19)
Casado/a con:	María Rosa Poblete
Profesión:	ama de casa

nicaragüense (m/f) *from Nicaragua*
técnico (m) *technician*
empresa textil (f) *textile company*

estado civil (m) *marital status*
edad (f) *age*

8 Clotilde Montalvo, from Mexico, talks about herself and her family. Listen to what she says, or read the transcript on page 268, and as you do so, fill in the box overleaf with the information given by her. First, look at these key words:

Centro Cultural de Lenguas Modernas *a languages school in Veracruz, Mexico*
manejar *to drive*

carretera (f) *highway*
chofer de carretera (m) *coach or lorry driver*

Name:	Clotilde Montalvo Rodríguez
Age:	_____
Marital Status:	_____
Profession:	_____
Husband's Profession:	_____
Nº of children:	_____
Age(s):	_____

9 During a stay in a Latin American country you meet someone. Like many Latin Americans often do, he/she asks you about yourself and your family. Answer the relevant questions.

(a) ¿Es usted casado/a o soltero/a?
(b) ¿Tiene hijos? ¿Cuántos?
(c) ¿Tiene hermanos? ¿Cuántos?
(d) ¿Cuántos años tiene(n) su(s) hijo(s) o hermano(s)?
(e) ¿Dónde vive usted?

—— Imágenes de Hispanoamérica ——

Free Trade Agreement

In December 1992, the presidents of Mexico, the United States and Canada, signed a Free Trade Agreement for the creation of the largest trade market in the world, **el Tratado de Libre Comercio de América del Norte**: 363 million people, bigger than the European Economic Community. The problem with this market, however, is the tremendous differences which exist between Mexico and the other two partners. Mexico, a Third World country, has a per capita income of U.S. $1.945, which contrasts sharply with that of the United States, which is U.S. $21.806 (1992). A Mexican worker earns an average of U.S. $1.80 per hour compared with the U.S. $14.77 an hour earned by his American counterpart.

Supporters of the Free Trade Agreement think that foreign investment and the establishment of American and Canadian companies in Mexico will help economic growth and bring new jobs to millions of Mexicans. Those against the Agreement argue that Mexico is going to provide cheap labour for its richer neighbours in the north, and that certain sectors of the Mexican economy will not be able to compete on an equal footing with the United States and Canada.

Whatever the advantages or disadvantages which this Agreement may bring, the truth is that, in spite of economic growth and the generally healthy state of the Mexican economy in comparison with most other Latin American countries, the differences between the rich and the poor in Mexico seem to have widened. About half the Mexican population, according to recent statistics, live in poverty. In contrast to this, economic expansion seems to have brought wealth and a new way of life, not unlike that of the United States, to a sector of the society. This last point is illustrated in the extract, overleaf, from an article published by the magazine **Cambio 16 América**.

Study the key words before you read the text. Then check your comprehension by answering the questions that follow.

una joven ama de casa *a young housewife*	**hacer** *to make*
después de leer *after reading*	**unas cervezas** *a few beers*
escuchar las noticias *to listen to the news*	**dejar** *to leave*
sale *she goes out*	**ropa** (f) *clothes*
le encanta pasear *she loves to walk*	**limpiar** *to clean*
nueva *new*	**cadena** (f) *chain*
colonia (f) *eau de cologne*	**lavandería** (f) *dry cleaners*
adquiere *she buys*	**llamar** *to call*
harina (f) *flour*	**creen** *they believe*
	sello (m) *seal*
	garantía de calidad (f) *quality guarantee*

HA NACIDO UN GIGANTE
ROMÁN OROZCO, MÉXICO

Guadalupe Chávez es una joven ama de casa que vive en la zona residencial Lomas de Chapultepec, del Distrito Federal. Después de leer el periódico *The News* y escuchar las noticias en inglés de la CBS, sale a la calle en su Ford Taunus. Le encanta pasear por las avenidas de Polanco, la nueva zona comercial chic de la capital mexicana. En Calvin Klein compra una colonia para su marido y en Shirley unos pantalones vaqueros (*jeans*) para su hijo. En el Mr. Price Supermarket, de la avenida Masarick, adquiere harina Aunt Jemina para hacer *hot cakes*, y unas cervezas Miller Light.

En la paralela calle de Horacio deja ropa para limpiar en Supreme/USA, una moderna cadena de lavanderías computerizadas. Desde el automóvil llama con su teléfono celular IUSAcell a su amiga Chelita . . . Guadalupe es una de la muchas personas que en este país creen que el sello *Made in USA* es garantía de calidad.

(Cambio 16 América, Nº 1.101, Spain)

Responda en inglés

(a) What does Guadalupe do before going out in her car?
(b) What does she buy in Calvin Klein?
(c) What does she buy at Mr. Price Supermarket?
(d) What does Guadalupe think of the seal *Made in USA*?

5

UNA MESA PARA DOS

A table for two

In this unit you will learn how to

- express wants and preferences
- order food and drink
- say how you want your food
- inquire about wishes and intentions
- request something

Diálogos

1 En el avión

James Parker is flying from London to Bogotá with a South American airline. Lunch is now being served and James has to choose from the menu overleaf.

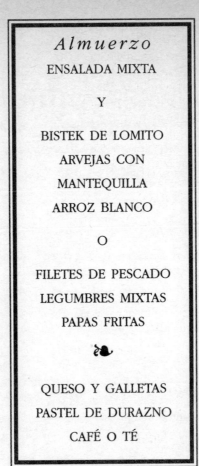

Almuerzo

ENSALADA MIXTA

Y

BISTEK DE LOMITO

ARVEJAS CON

MANTEQUILLA

ARROZ BLANCO

O

FILETES DE PESCADO

LEGUMBRES MIXTAS

PAPAS FRITAS

QUESO Y GALLETAS

PASTEL DE DURAZNO

CAFÉ O TÉ

ensalada mixta (f)   *mixed salad*
bistek de lomito (m)   *fillet steak*
arvejas con mantequilla (m)
 buttered green peas
arroz blanco (m)   *plain rice*
filetes de pescado (m)   *fish fillets*
legumbres mixtas (f)   *mixed*
 vegetables

papas fritas (f)   *fried potatoes*
queso (m)   *cheese*
galletas (f)   *biscuits*
pastel de durazno (m)   *peach cake*
café (m)   *coffee*
té (m)   *tea*

Azafata	¿Qué menú prefiere, señor?
James	Prefiero el filete de lomito.
	(*The stewardess hands James his food tray.*) Gracias.
Azafata	¿Qué va a tomar?
James	Quiero vino tinto, por favor.
	(*The stewardess gives James a small bottle of red wine.*) Gracias.
Azafata	De nada.
	(*After lunch, the stewardess comes round with coffee.*) ¿Va a tomar café?
James	Sí, por favor.

Responda en inglés

prefiere *you prefer* (pol)	**quiero** *I want*
prefiero *I prefer*	**vino tinto** (m) *red wine*
¿Qué va a tomar? *What are you going to drink?*	**¿Va a tomar café?** *Are you going to have coffee?* (pol)

(a) What does James order for lunch?
(b) What does he drink?

Notas explicativas

Colombian pronunciation

Units 5 and 6 are set in Colombia, and most of the speakers in the introductory dialogues are Colombian. Colombians claim they speak the best Spanish in Latin America. Even if we are reluctant to accept adjectives such as *good* or *bad* regarding different dialects of the same language, one must admit that the Spanish spoken in many areas of Colombia seems, to foreign ears at least, clearer than that of some other Latin American countries. For untrained foreign ears, it is probably easier to understand than dialectal forms whose main characteristic is the weakening of vowel sounds (e.g. in Mexico) or of final consonants (e.g. in Venezuela). However, within Colombia, there are wide differences between the Spanish spoken in places like Bogotá or Cali, for example, usually associated with 'good, clear

Spanish', and that spoken around the Caribbean, which bears some of the characteristics of Caribbean Spanish in general, that is, weakening or even disappearance of consonants in certain positions, e.g. **do**[h], **tre**[h], instead of **dos**, **tres** or **pe**[h]**cao** instead of **pescado**.

Certain areas of Colombia have kept old Spanish forms such as the use of **vos** for **tú**.

Expressing wants and preferences

Quiero (*I want*), **prefiero** (*I prefer*). The infinitives of these two verbs are **querer** (e → ie) and **preferir** (e → ie), respectively. Notice that both are stem-changing verbs (see Unit 3).

Asking someone what he or she wants or prefers

To ask someone what he or she wants in a familiar way, you can use **querer**:

    ¿Qué quieres comer?   *What do you want to eat?*

To ask someone what he or she wants in a polite way, avoid **querer** as this may sound a little abrupt. Instead, you can use the verb **desear** (lit. *to wish*):

    ¿Qué desea comer?   *What would you like to eat?*

To ask someone what he or she prefers, use **preferir**:

    ¿Qué prefiere Ud.?   *What do you prefer?* (pol)
    ¿Qué prefieres?   *What do you prefer?* (fam)

Tomar (*to drink*)

To offer someone a drink or to say what they are going to drink, Latin Americans normally use the verb **tomar** (lit. *to take*) instead of **beber** (*to drink*): **¿Qué va a tomar?** (*What are you going to drink?*), **Voy a tomar café** (*I am going to drink coffee*). But if you use **beber**, this will also be understood.

Fruit and vegetables

Differences in vocabulary between Latin America and Spain and within Latin America itself are more common when talking about fruit and vegetables than most other contexts. Here are some examples:

Latin America	**Spain**	
la papa	la patata	*potato*
el durazno	el melocotón	*peach*
las arvejas (los chícharos (Mex))	los guisantes	*peas*

See also Unit 6 and the Glossary of Latin American terms on pages 281–87.

2 Una mesa para dos

James Parker is visiting a firm in Bogotá. Today he is going to have dinner with señor Julio Donoso, a Colombian associate. As they come into the restaurant, a waitress approaches them.

Mesera	Buenas noches.
Señor Donoso	Buenas noches. ¿Tiene una mesa para dos?
Mesera	(*Pointing to a table*) Sí, pueden sentarse aquí si desean.
Señor Donoso	Sí, está bien. Nos trae la carta, por favor. (*The waitress brings them the menu.*) Gracias.
Mesera	¿Van a tomar un aperitivo?
James	Para mí no, gracias.
Señor Donoso	Para mí tampoco.
Mesera	Bien, ya regreso.

mesero/a	*waiter, waitress*	**nos trae**	*will you bring us*
mesa (f)	*table*	**carta** (f)	*menu*
para dos	*for two*	**aperitivo** (m)	*apéritif*
pueden	*you can*	**para mí**	*for me*
sentarse	*to sit*	**tampoco**	*neither*
si desean	*if you wish*	**ya regreso (regresar)**	*I'll be right back (to come back)*
está bien	*it's all right*		

——— Notas explicativas ———

El mesero, la mesera (*waiter, waitress*)

These words are used in Colombia, Mexico and most other Latin

American countries. In the southern countries of South America you will hear the word **el mozo** (*waiter*). A waitress is referred to as **la señorita**. In Spain, the word is **el camarero / la camarera**.

Poder (*to be able to, can, may*)

Notice the use of **poder** (o → ue) followed by an infinitive:

Pueden sentarse aquí.   *You can sit here.*

To ask someone if he or she can do something use **¿Puede (usted) . . .?** (pol) or **¿Puedes . . .?** (fam), followed by an infinitive:

¿Puede estar aquí a las 5.00?   *Can you be here at 5.00?*

To say that you can or cannot do something, use **puedo / no puedo**, followed by an infinitive:

Puedo estar aquí a las 7.00.   *I can be here at 7.00.*
No puedo venir mañana.   *I can't come tomorrow.*

3   ¿Cómo lo quiere?

The waitress comes back to their table.

Mesera	¿Qué van a pedir?
James	Yo quiero una sopa de verduras para empezar.
Mesera	Una sopa de verduras . . . ¿Y qué más?
James	Quiero pollo.
Mesera	El pollo, ¿cómo lo quiere?
James	Lo quiero asado.
Mesera	¿Con qué lo quiere? ¿Con arroz, con puré . . .?
James	Con arroz. Y me trae una ensalada mixta también, por favor.
Mesera	¿Y para usted, señor?
Señor Donoso	Para mí, crema de espárragos, y carne guisada con papas.
Mesera	¿Las papas, las quiere fritas, doradas . . .?
Señor Donoso	Fritas.
Mesera	¿Y qué van a tomar?
Señor Donoso	Una botella de vino tinto.
Mesera	Tenemos un vino chileno muy bueno.
Señor Donoso	Sí, tráiganos un vino chileno.

¿Qué van a pedir? *What are you going to order?* (pl)	**también** *also*
sopa de verduras (f) *vegetable soup*	**para usted** *for you (pol)*
para empezar *to start*	**crema de espárragos** (f) *asparagus soup*
pollo (m) *chicken*	**carne guisada** (f) *stewed meat*
¿Cómo lo quiere? *How do you want it?* (pol)	**¿Las quiere fritas?** *Do you want them fried?* (pol)
asado *roast*	**papas doradas** (f, pl) *golden potatoes*
¿Con qué lo quiere? *What do you want with it?* (pol)	**una botella** (f) *a bottle*
me trae *will you bring me* (pol)	**tráiganos** *bring us*

Responda en inglés

(*a*) What is James going to have first?

(*b*) What does he want as a second course?

—— Notas explicativas ——

Saying how you want your food

Notice how to say *it* and *them*:

¿Cómo lo quiere?	*How do you want it?* (pol)
¿Las quiere fritas?	*Do you want them fried?* (pol)

More on this under **Notas gramaticales**.

Requests

Y me trae una ensalada mixta.	*And will you bring me a mixed salad.*

Notice that in the previous sentence, the Spanish verb is in the present tense.

Tráiganos un vino chileno.	*Bring us a Chilean wine.*

Traiga is an imperative form from **traer** (*to bring*), to which the pronoun **nos** (*us*) has been added. For the formation of imperatives, see Unit 12.

4 ¿Qué van a comer de postre?

Señor Donoso and señor Parker have finished their meal. The waitress now offers them a dessert.

Mesera	¿Qué van a comer de postre?
Señor Donoso	¿Qué tiene?
Mesera	Tenemos helados, fruta, flan, pastel de queso . . .
James	Yo quiero una ensalada de fruta.
Señor Donoso	Para mí un helado de chocolate.
Mesera	¿Van a tomar café?
James	Yo no, gracias.
Señor Donoso	Sí, yo quisiera un café.

¿Qué van a comer? *What are you going to eat?* (pl)		**flan** (m) *caramel*	
de postre *for dessert*		**pastel de queso** (m) *cheesecake*	
helado (m) *ice-cream*		**ensalada de fruta** (f) *fruit salad*	
fruta (f) *fruit*		**quisiera** *I would like*	

Responda en inglés

(*a*) What does James order for dessert?
(*b*) What does señor Donoso order?

Nota explicativa

Ordering food

Notice the two alternative forms **yo quiero** (*I want*) and **yo quisiera** (*I would like*). When ordering food and drink, the first seems to be much more frequently used, while the second is often used in more polite requests.

5 Nos trae la cuenta, por favor

Señor Donoso and James are ready to leave and they ask the waitress for the bill.

| **Señor Donoso** | Nos trae la cuenta, por favor. |
| **Mesera** | Sí, un momento señor. Enseguida se la traigo. |

cuenta (f) *bill*	**se la traigo** *I will bring it to you*
enseguida *straight away*	

Notas explicativas

A polite request

Nos trae la cuenta, por favor.   *Will you bring us the bill, please.*

Note that in this sentence the Spanish verb is in the present tense.

Replying to a request

Enseguida se la traigo.   *I will bring it to you right away.*

In this construction, **se** stands for *to you* (sing/pl) while **la** stands for *it* (**la cuenta**, *the bill*). Notice also that the Spanish verb is in the present tense: **traigo** (*I bring*).

Frases y expresiones importantes

- Expressing wants and preferences
  Quiero vino blanco / tinto.   *I want white / red wine.*
  Prefiero el filete de lomito.   *I prefer the fillet steak.*
  Quisiera un café.   *I would like a coffee.*

- Ordering food and drink
  Para mí, crema de espárragos. *Asparagus soup for me.*
  Yo quiero una sopa de   *I want vegetable soup.*
  verduras.

- Saying how you want your food
  ¿Cómo lo quiere? (el pollo).   *How do you want it?*
                                       (chicken) (pol)

  Lo quiero asado.   *I want it roasted.*

¿Con qué lo quiere?	*What do you want it with?* (pol)
(Lo quiero) con arroz.	*(I want it) with rice.*

- Inquiring about wishes and intentions

¿Qué va a tomar?	*What are you going to drink?* (pol)
¿Va a tomar café?	*Are you going to have coffee?* (pol)

- Requesting something

Nos trae la carta, por favor.	*Will you bring us the menu, please.*
Me trae una ensalada.	*Will you bring me a salad.*
Tráiganos un vino chileno.	*Bring us a Chilean wine.*

- Other useful words and phrases used in the context of food and restaurants.

¿Hay algún restaurante por aquí?	*Is there a restaurant nearby?*
¿Puede recomendarme un restaurante?	*Can you recommend a restaurant?*
Quisiera reservar una mesa para tres.	*I would like to reserve a table for three.*
¿Qué me / nos recomienda?	*What do you recommend?*
¿Puede traerme/nos (más) pan / agua?	*Can you bring me / us some (more) bread / water?*
Por favor, me trae un vaso / un plato / un cuchillo / un tenedor / una cuchara.	*Can you bring me a glass / plate / knife / fork / spoon, please.*
Tráigame/nos mantequilla, por favor.	*Bring me / us some butter, please.*
¿Tiene algún plato vegetariano?	*Have you got a vegetarian dish?*
Soy vegetariano/a.	*I'm a vegetarian.*
¿Puede enviarme/nos el desayuno a la habitación?	*Can you send breakfast to my / our room?*

Notas gramaticales

1 Voy a . . . (*I am going to . . .*)

To inquire about wishes and intentions, and to express intentions, as in *What are you going to drink?*, *We are going to eat*, we use the present tense of **ir** (*to go*) (**voy, vas, va, vamos, van**), followed by **a** and an infinitive (words like **tomar** (*to have*) and **comer** (*to eat*)).

Voy a tomar café.	*I am going to have coffee.*
¿Vas a tomar vino?	*Are you going to have wine?* (fam)
¿Qué va a tomar?	*What are you going to drink?* (pol)
	What is he / she going to drink?
Vamos a comer.	*We are going to eat.*
¿Qué van a comer?	*What are you* (pl) /
	they going to eat?

2   Lo, la, los, las (*it, them*)

To say *it* or *them*, as in *How do you want it?*, *Do you want them fried?* we use the following set of words:

Singular	**Plural**
lo (m)	los (m)
la (f)	las (f)

These words, which are called object pronouns, vary in number (singular and plural) and gender (masculine and feminine), according to the word they refer to. For example:

¿Cómo quiere el pollo?	*How do you want the chicken?*
¿Cómo **lo** quiere?	*How do you want it?*
¿Cómo quiere las papas?	*How do you want the potatoes?*
Las quiero fritas.	*I want them fried.*
¿Con qué quiere la carne?	*What do you want the meat with?*
La quiero con papas.	*I want it with potatoes.*

Notice the position of **lo, las,** etc. before the verb. However, if the sentence has a main verb followed by an infinitive (e.g. **voy a comer**), the pronoun may either precede the main verb or be attached to the infinitive. For example:

Lo voy a comer con arroz.	*I am going to eat it with rice.*
Voy a comer**lo** con papas.	*I am going to eat it with potatoes.*

In contexts other than the one above, **lo(s)** and **la(s)** may also refer to people:

| Voy a invitarlo. | *I am going to invite you* (m) / *him.* |
| Quisiera invitarla. | *I would like to invite you* (f) / *her.* |

3 Me, nos . . . (*me, to me, us, to us . . .*)

(*a*) To say *me, to me, us, to us,* etc. as in *Will you bring me a salad, Will you bring us the menu,* use the following set of words followed by a verb in the present tense.

me	*me, to me, for me*
te	*you, to you, for you* (fam, sing)
le	*you, to you, for you* (pol, sing)
le	*him, to him, for him*
le	*her, to her, for her*
nos	*us, to us, for us*
les	*you, to you, for you* (pl)
les	*them, to them, for them*

Me trae una ensalada.	*Will you bring me a salad.*
¿**Te** traigo un café?	*Shall I bring you coffee?* (fam)
¿**Le** traigo el postre?	*Shall I bring you* (pol) / *him* / *her the dessert?*
Nos trae la cuenta.	*Will you bring us the bill.*
Enseguida **les** traigo la cuenta.	*I will bring you* (pl) / *them the bill right away.*

Notice that in the examples above, **le** and **les** is used for both masculine and feminine. Note also that the plural familiar word **os** (*you, to you, for you*) used in Spain is not used in Latin America, where **les** applies to both familiar and formal contexts.

(*b*) Some sentences have two object pronouns, for example:

Me la trae, por favor.   *Will you bring it to me, please.*

Notice that in Spanish *to me* (**me**) comes before *it* (**la**).

(*c*) When **le(s)** precedes **lo(s)** or **la(s)**, **le(s)** becomes **se**:

| Ahora **le** traigo la cuenta. | *I will bring you the bill now.* |
| Ahora **se la** traigo. | *I will bring it to you now.* |

4 Para

(a) **Para mí, para usted** ... (for me, for you ...)

To say for me, for you, for him, etc use **para** followed by **mí** (me) and **ti** (you, fam) for the first and second person singular, and **usted, él, ella, nosotros, ustedes, ellos/as** with all other persons.

Para mí, pescado con papas fritas.	For me, fish and chips.
¿Y para ti?	And for you? (fam)
¿Y para usted, señor?	And for you, sir? (pol)

With the exception of **con** (with) (see **Notas gramaticales**, Unit 11) other prepositions (words like from, in, without, to, etc.), follow the same rule as **para**.

Él va sin mí.	He is going without me.
Ellos vienen sin ella.	They are coming without her.

(b) Notice the use of **para** in these sentences:

¿Tiene una mesa para dos?	Have you got a table for two?
Quiero una sopa para empezar.	I want a soup to start with.

5 Agreement of adjectives

In Spanish, adjectives (words like big, small, long) must agree in gender (masc/fem) and number (sing/pl) with the word they refer to. Here are some examples taken from this unit.

una ensalada mixta	*a mixed salad*
legumbres mixtas	*mixed vegetables*
un pollo asado	*a roast chicken*
pollos asados	*roast chickens*

Actividades

1   You are on business in Bogotá, and today you are having lunch with a Colombian colleague at Casa Brava, so you decide to telephone the restaurant to make a reservation. Complete your part of the conversation, overleaf, with the restaurant manager.

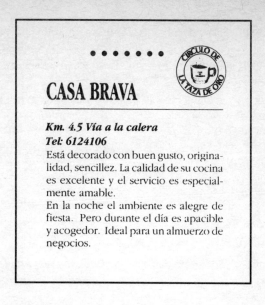

CASA BRAVA

Km. 4.5 Vía a la calera
Tel: 6124106

Está decorado con buen gusto, origina-lidad, sencillez. La calidad de su cocina es excelente y el servicio es especial-mente amable.

En la noche el ambiente es alegre de fiesta. Pero durante el día es apacible y acogedor. Ideal para un almuerzo de negocios.

Jefe	(*Al teléfono*) Restaurante Casa Brava, buenos días.
Ud.	*Answer the greeting and say you would like to book a table for two.*
Jefe	Para hoy, ¿verdad?
Ud.	*Yes, for today.*
Jefe	¿Y para qué hora?
Ud.	*For half past one.*
Jefe	¿A nombre de quién?
Ud.	*Say in what name you want the reservation.*

¿A nombre de quién?	*In whose name?*

2 You arrive at Restaurante Casa Brava with your colleague and you are met by the head waiter.

Mesero	Buenas tardes.
Ud.	*Answer the greeting and say you have a reservation for half past one.*

Mesero	¿Cómo se llama usted?
Ud.	*Give your name.*
Mesero	Sí, su mesa es ésa, la que está junto a la ventana.

junto a *next to*	**ventana** (f) *window*

3 The waiter brings you the menu. The choice is limited at lunch time but it seems all right. First, study the key words in the menu on page 94, then write a dialogue between the waiter, yourself and your colleague, using some of these key phrases. After preparing your own conversation, check it against the main dialogues on pages 81–86 and compare it with the model dialogue in the **Key to the exercises** on page 259.

El mesero	**Usted y su colega**
¿Qué desean comer?	Para empezar . . .
¿Y qué más?	Para mí . . .
¿Con qué lo / la quiere?	Quiero . . .
¿Y para usted, señor?	Lo / La quiero con . . .
¿Algo más?	Tráigame . . .
¿Qué van a tomar?	Quiero una ensalada de . . .
¿Qué desean de postre?	Una botella de vino tinto / blanco
¿Van a tomar café?	Una cerveza / un agua mineral

camarones (m) *shrimps*	**pollo asado** (m) *roast chicken*
aguacate relleno (m) *stuffed avocado*	**a la plancha** *grilled*
empanada (f) *turnover, pie*	**pescado frito** (m) *fried fish*
sopa de zapallo (f) *pumpkin soup*	**durazno** (m) *peach*
chuleta (f) *chop*	**en almíbar** *with syrup*
ternera (f) *veal*	**fresa** (f) *strawberry*
cerdo (m) *pork*	**crema** (f) *cream*
carne asada (f) *roast meat*	**pastel** (m) *cake*
	cerveza (f) *beer*

Nota: Most of the dishes listed in the menu are standard and should be understood in most countries. Many common Colombian dishes have been excluded, as these may not be understood in other countries.

<u>Restaurante</u>
<u>Casa Brava</u>

PARA EMPEZAR
Cocktail de camarones
Aguacate relleno
Empanadas

SOPAS Y CREMAS
Sopa de verduras
Sopa de tomate
Crema de espárragos
Crema de zapallo
Sopa o crema del día

CARNES Y PESCADO
Chuletas de ternera
Chuletas de cerdo
Carne asada
Pollo asado
Filete de pescado
 a la plancha
Pescado frito

POSTRES
Duraznos o mangos
 en almíbar
Flan de vainilla
Fresas con crema
Pastel de fresas
Helados

4 At a table next to you, a Colombian is ordering food. What food has she ordered? Listen to her conversation with the waiter, or read the transcript on page 268, then complete the order below, as the waiter might have done. First, look at these new words.

champiñones (m, pl) *mushrooms* **pollo en salsa de mostaza** (m) *chicken in mustard sauce*	**soufflé de calabaza** (m) *pumpkin soufflé (a baked dish containing squash, beaten eggs and seafood, served with sauce)* **no queda** *we don't have any left* **jugo** (m) *juice*

5 You are going out for a meal with an English-speaking colleague who is travelling in Latin American with you. Your colleague has spotted the advertisement, overleaf, for a restaurant and would like to know a bit about it. Look at the key words before you read the advertisement, then answer your colleague's questions.

sabor (m) *taste*	**a cuerpo de rey** *like a king*
atención (f) *service*	**ser atendido** *to be served*
precio (m) *price*	**como un príncipe** *like a prince*
acogedor *warm, welcoming*	**pagar** *to pay*
sabrá *you will know*	**plebeyo** (m) *plebeian*

(Revista Wikén de El Mercurio Chile.)

Responda en inglés

(*a*) Why is **Sebastián** the 'perfect combination'?

(*b*) What sort of food do they serve?

—— Imágenes de Hispanoamérica ——

Latin American food and diet

The two passages which follow (below and overleaf), both in Spanish, are related to food and diet. The first touches on the contribution of the New World (**el Nuevo Mundo**) to the European diet, while the second deals with Latin American staple food.

Look at the key words first, before you read each passage, then check your comprehension by answering the questions which follow the texts.

algunos *some*	**frijol** (m) *bean*
que hoy en día *which nowadays*	**haba** (f) *broad bean*
en realidad *actually*	**cacahuete** (m) *peanut*
son originarios de *they come from*	**damasco** (m) *apricot*
otros *others*	**difícil** *difficult*
entre ellos *among them*	

La contribución del Nuevo Mundo a la dieta europea

Algunos productos que hoy en día son esenciales en la dieta europea, son en realidad originarios de las Américas. Los más importantes son la papa y el tomate. Pero hay muchos otros, entre ellos los frijoles, las habas, el chile, los aguacates, los cacahuetes, los damascos, las papayas, el chocolate, etcétera. Es difícil imaginar la cocina europea sin algunos de estos productos, especialmente la papa y el tomate.

Responda en inglés

(a) Which two main products came to Europe from the Americas?
(b) According to the text, what is difficult to imagine?

variada *varied*	**base** (f) *basis*
basada *based*	**plato** (m) *dish*
cada *each*	**se come** *people eat*
por ejemplo *for example*	**como en** *as in*
quizás *perhaps*	**mayoría** (f) *majority*
tortilla (f) *corn bread*	**Caribe** (m) *Caribbean*
pan (m) *bread*	**mar** (m) *sea*
maíz (m) *maize*	**carne de vaca** (f) *beef*

LA COCINA HISPANOAMERICANA

La cocina hispanoamericana es inmensamente variada y está basada fundamentalmente en los productos típicos de cada país o región. La dieta de los mexicanos, por ejemplo, es muy diferente a la de los colombianos o a la de los argentinos. Lo más típico de México, quizás, son las tortillas, una especie de pan de maíz, que constituye la base de muchos platos mexicanos. Otro ingrediente básico en la dieta mexicana es el chile. México es un país muy grande y existen platos típicos de cada región, muchos de ellos a base de carne. En la costa se come mucho pescado y mariscos.

En los países centroamericanos, como en la mayoría de los países de la región, se comen muchos platos a base de maíz. El arroz con pollo es un plato típico en muchos países del Caribe y de América del Sur, entre ellos Colombia. Pero en Colombia, como en otros países sudamericanos, la cocina es muy variada y los restaurantes presentan una gran variedad de platos nacionales e internacionales. En el Perú y Chile, por ejemplo, se comen muchos productos del mar. En la Argentina y el Uruguay se come preferentemente carne de vaca.

Preparando tortillas

Responda en inglés

(*c*)   What is the most typical food in Mexico?
(*d*)   What is the staple food in Central America?
(*e*)   Name a typical dish in many Caribbean and South American countries.
(*f*)   What do Argentinians and Uruguayans prefer to eat?

Tips for the traveller

As you travel in Latin America, you will discover that the same or similar dish or product has different names in different countries. This is why it is impossible to give a full list of products or common dishes here. A couple of examples will illustrate this. Beans, for instance, which are known as **judías** in Spain, are called **frijoles** in many Latin American countries, but you will also hear the words **caraotas** in Venezuela and **porotos** in Peru, Chile and Argentina. Avocados are called **aguacates** in most countries, but in Peru, Chile and Argentina, they are called **paltas**. In the tourist resorts and international restaurants in the capital cities, waiters sometimes know some basic English, but away from the tourist track you will have to rely on your own knowledge of Spanish. Try learning some basic words for food which can be understood everywhere, for example: **carne de cerdo** (*pork*), **carne de vaca** (*beef*), **pollo** (*chicken*), **pescado** (*fish*), **arroz** (*rice*), **papas** (*potatoes*) and **ensalada de lechuga / tomate** (*lettuce / tomato salad*). With the help of a dictionary or phrase book, try making a list of these basic words and add others and different variants as you travel. If you are in a market, use the phrase **¿Qué es esto?** (*What is this?*) or **¿Cómo se llama esto?** (*What is this called?*) to inquire about the name of a product. In a restaurant, you may want to know the main ingredients of a dish, in which case ask **¿Qué contiene?** (*What does it contain?*) or **¿En qué consiste?** (*What does it consist of?*).

As for drinks, you will be able to get **una cerveza** (*a beer*) or **un agua mineral** (*a mineral water*) almost anywhere, but wine, **el vino**, is more expensive and, with the exception of good restaurants, not many places will have it. Chile and Argentina are wine-producing countries and you will find plenty of good red and white wines, **vino**

tinto and **vino blanco**. In Colombia try beer, which is excellent, or if you want something stronger, go for rum, which is good and inexpensive. And of course coffee, which in most Latin American countries is of good quality. If you want it black, simply ask for **un café**, but in Colombia ask for **un tinto**, a word which in other countries means *red* as in *red wine*. Coffee with a dash of milk is usually known as **un café cortado**, or **un café con crema** in Mexico and **un perico** in Bogotá, Colombia, while a milky coffee is **un café con leche**.

Your restaurant bill

Restaurants in some countries add **IVA** (VAT) to the bill (**la cuenta**). The percentage varies from country to country, but bear in mind that this is a tax and not a tip. Service (**el servicio**) is sometimes included, but even then, waiters usually expect a tip (**una propina**). There is no standard percentage here, it simply varies with the size of your bill. Between five and ten per cent should be sufficient.

6

¿CUÁNTO VALE?
How much does it cost?

In this unit you will learn how to

- ask for something in a shop
- describe things
- express comparisons
- say that you like or dislike something
- ask and say how much something costs

Diálogos

1 ¿Cuánto vale?

Mario, a Colombian, would like to buy a briefcase (**un maletín**). He asks the shop assistant in a leather shop to show him one.

Mario	Buenos días. Quisiera ver ese maletín que está en la vitrina.
Vendedora	¿Éste?
Mario	Sí, ése, el negro.
	(*Mario examines the briefcase.*)

Vendedora	Es un maletín muy bonito y muy elegante.
Mario	¿Es de cuero?
Vendedora	Sí, todos los artículos que vendemos son de cuero.
Mario	Me gusta mucho. ¿Cuánto vale?
Vendedora	Doscientos cincuenta mil pesos.
Mario	Es un poco caro. ¿No tiene otro más barato?
Vendedora	Sí, ése de color café es más barato. Vale ciento veinte mil pesos.
Mario	Ése no me gusta mucho.
Vendedora	No tenemos otro.
Mario	Bueno, voy a llevar el negro. ¿Puedo pagar con tarjeta de crédito?
Vendedora	Claro que sí.

¿Verdadero o falso?

(*a*) A Mario le gusta el maletín café (marrón).
(*b*) Mario paga con cheque.

¿Cuánto cuesta? *How much does it cost?*	**peso** (m) *Colombian currency*
ése *that one* (m)	**un poco caro** *a little expensive*
el negro *the black one*	**otro** *another, other*
bonito *nice*	**más barato** *cheaper*
cuero (m) *leather*	**ése de color café** *that brown one*
artículo (m) *article*	**voy a llevar** *I am going to take*
vendemos (vender) *we sell (to sell)*	**¿Puedo pagar . . .?** *Can I pay . . .?*
Me gusta mucho. *I like it very much.*	**tarjeta de crédito** (f) *credit card*
	claro que sí *certainly*
	vendedora (f) *saleswoman*

Notas explicativas

El maletín (*briefcase*)

This is a Latin American term. In Spain the word is **la cartera**. In some Latin American countries, for example Peru and Argentina, you will hear the word **el portafolio**.

Asking and saying how much something costs

¿Cuánto vale? *How much does it cost?*

An alternative phrase, also very common, but less frequent in Colombia, is **¿Cuánto cuesta?** The infinitive here is **costar** (o → ue) (*to cost*). To say *How much do they cost?*, use the third person plural of the verb: **¿Cuánto valen?** or **¿Cuánto cuestan?**

La vitrina

A shop window in Latin America is **la vitrina** or **la vidriera.** In Spain, it is **el escaparate.**

Asking and saying what something is made of

Observe the use of the preposition **de** to indicate what something is made of:

¿Es de cuero?	*Is it made of leather?*
Son de cuero.	*They are made of leather.*

Todo(s) (*the whole, all*), otro(s) (*another, other, others*)

Todo and **otro** change according to number (sing/pl) and gender (masc/fem), for example:

todo el día	*the whole day*
todos los artículos	*all the articles*
otro color	*another colour*
otras tiendas	*other shops*

2 ¿Me lo puedo probar?

Clara, a Colombian, goes into a clothes shop (**una tienda de ropa**) to buy a sweater (**un suéter**).

Vendedor	A la orden.
Clara	(*Pointing to some sweaters*) Quisiera ver esos suéteres, por favor.
Vendedor	¿Qué talla tiene usted?
Clara	Talla ocho.
Vendedor	Bueno, tenemos en blanco, azul, verde, rojo y amarillo.
Clara	El verde me gusta más. Es muy bonito. ¿Me lo puedo probar?
Vendedor	Claro que sí.
	(*Clara tries the sweater on.*)

Clara	Éste me queda un poco pequeño. ¿Tiene uno más grande?
Vendedor	Sí, aquí tiene uno en la talla diez, en el mismo color. (*Clara tries on the other sweater*).
Clara	Sí, éste me queda bien. ¿Cuánto vale?
Vendedor	Cuarenta mil pesos.
Clara	Sí, lo voy a llevar.
Vendedor	¿Va a pagar en efectivo?
Clara	Sí, en efectivo.

A la orden. *Can I help you?*		**más grande** *bigger*	
probar *to try on*		**mismo/a** *same*	
suéter (m) *sweater (pullover)*		**me queda bien** *it fits me well*	
esos *those*		**lo** *it* (m)	
talla (f) *size (clothes)*		**pagar en efectivo** *to pay cash*	
me gusta más *I like it more*		**vendedor** (m) *shop assistant*	
pequeño *small*			

los colores (*colours*)			
amarillo	*yellow*	naranja	*orange*
azul	*blue*	negro	*black*
blanco	*white*	rojo	*red*
gris	*grey*	rosa	*pink*
café	*brown*	verde	*green*

Nota: In some countries, including Spain and Argentina, brown is called **marrón**. In certain countries, for example Argentina and Chile, red is also known as **colorado**. Another word for **rosa** is **rosado**.

Complete estas frases (*Complete these sentences*)

(*a*) Clara prefiere un suéter de color _____ .
(*b*) Clara paga en _____ .

——— Notas explicativas ———

Can I help you?

The phrase **A la orden** is the standard way of saying *Can I help you?* in Colombia. In other parts of Latin America you are more likely to hear **¿A sus órdenes?** (very frequent in Mexico), **¿Qué desea?**, **¿Dígame?**, **¿Diga?** or **¿En qué le puedo servir?**.

El suéter

The word **suéter**, from the English *sweater* (pullover), will be understood almost everywhere in Latin America. Other words used in Latin America with a similar meaning are **el saco** and **el buzo**, also in Colombia, **la chomba** in Chile, **la chompa** in Peru and Ecuador. Some countries, for example Argentina, use the word **el pullover**.

Asking if you can try something on

¿Me lo puedo probar?   *Can I try it on?*

An alternative phrase for *Can I try it on?* is **¿Puedo probármelo?**, while the shop assistant might say **¿Quiere probárselo?** or **¿Se lo quiere probar?** (*Do you want to try it on?*). The infinitive here is **probarse** (*to try on*). **Me** is the reflexive pronoun for the first person singular (see Unit 4 for reflexive verbs), while **lo** stands for **el suéter** (*it*, masc).

Saying how clothes fit

Me queda bien.   *It fits me well.*

The infinitive here is **quedar** (*to fit*), while **me** means *me*. Similar phrases with this construction are:

No me queda bien.   *It doesn't fit me well.*
Me quedan grandes/pequeños.   *They are too big/small for me.*

Forms of payment

Pagar en efectivo means to pay with ready money as opposed to by cheque (**pagar con cheque**) or credit card (**pagar con tarjeta de crédito**). If you are going to pay the whole amount at once rather than paying in instalments (**pagar a plazos**), then the phrase is **pagar al contado**.

3   En el mercado

Silvia, a Colombian, is buying some fruit and vegetables in the market.

Vendedor	A la orden, señora.
Silvia	¿Cuánto valen las papas?
Vendedor	Doscientos cincuenta pesos la libra.
Silvia	Deme tres libras.
	(*The stallholder weighs the potatoes and puts them in a bag.*)
Vendedor	¿Algo más?
Silvia	Sí, ¿qué precio tienen las lechugas?
Vendedor	Treinta pesos cada una.
Silvia	Quiero dos. Y los tomates, ¿cuánto valen?
Vendedor	Doscientos cincuenta pesos la libra.
Silvia	Deme libra y media.
Vendedor	¿Algo más?
Silvia	No, eso es todo. ¿Cuánto es?
Vendedor	Son mil ciento ochenta y cinco pesos.
Silvia	Hasta luego, gracias.
Vendedor	Hasta luego.

mercado (m)	*market*	**cada una**	*each one*
libra (f)	*pound*	**medio/a**	*half*
deme	*give me*	**eso es todo**	*that's all*
¿Algo más?	*Anything else?*	**hasta luego**	*goodbye*
precio (m)	*price*		

Responda en inglés

(*a*) How much are the potatoes?
(*b*) How many lettuces does Silvia buy?
(*c*) How much does she pay in total?

Notas explicativas

Libras y kilos (*pounds and kilos*)

Most Latin American countries use kilos, but Colombians use **libras** (*pounds*): **una libra** (*one pound*), **media libra** (*half a pound*) instead of **un kilo** or **medio kilo**.

Tener (*to have*)

Notice the use of **tener** (*to have*) in the following:

¿Qué precio tienen las luchugas?   *What is the price of the lettuces?*

¿Cuánto es? (*How much is it?*)

Once you have done your shopping, the question to ask is **¿Cuánto es?** (*How much is it?* or *How much does it all come to?*).

4 En el correo

Silvia goes to the post office to send a postcard (**una postal**).

Silvia	¿Cuánto vale mandar una postal a Inglaterra?
Empleado	Mil doscientos pesos.
Silvia	Quiero dos estampillas de mil doscientos y cinco de seiscientos pesos.
	(*The clerk gives Silvia the stamps and she pays for them.*)
	Gracias. ¿Dónde está el buzón?
Empleado	Está afuera.

mandar *to send*		**buzón** (m) *postbox*	
estampilla (f) *stamp*		**afuera** *outside*	

Responda en inglés

(*a*) How many stamps does Silvia buy, and for what value?

(*b*) Where is the postbox?

――――――― **Nota explicativa** ―――――――

la estampilla *stamp*

The Latin American word for **el sello**, which is used in Spain.

Frases y expresiones importantes

- Asking for something in a shop

  Quisiera ver (esos suéteres).   *I would like to see (those sweaters).*

  Quiero (dos lechugas).   *I want two lettuces.*

  Deme tres libras / kilos.   *Give me three pounds / kilos.*

- Describing things

  Es muy bonito.   *It's very nice.*

  ¿Es de cuero?   *Is it made of leather?*

  Son de cuero.   *They are made of leather.*

- Expressing comparisons

  Ése es más barato.   *That one is cheaper.*

  ¿Tiene uno más grande?   *Have you got a bigger one?*

- Saying that you like or dislike something

  Me gusta mucho.   *I like it very much.*

  Ése no me gusta mucho.   *I don't like that one very much.*

- Asking and saying how much something costs

  ¿Cuánto vale(n)?   *How much does it / do they cost?*

  ¿Cuánto cuesta(n)?   *How much does it / do they cost?*

  Vale(n) / cuesta(n) mil pesos.   *It costs / they cost a thousand pesos.*

  ¿Qué precio tiene(n)?   *What is the price?*

- Other useful words and phrases used in the context of shopping

¿Hay alguna farmacia por aquí?	*Is there a chemist's nearby?*
¿Dónde está el supermercado más cercano?	*Where is the nearest supermarket?*
¿Dónde hay una panadería / librería / tintorería / lavandería / tienda de artículos fotográficos . . .?	*Where is there a baker's / bookshop / dry cleaner's / launderette / camera shop . . .?*
Estoy mirando solamente.	*I am just looking.*
¿Tiene usted . . .?	*Have you got . . .?*
¿Tiene algo mejor?	*Have you got something better?*
Es demasiado caro/a / grande / pequeño/a / corto/a / largo/a	*It is too expensive / big / small / short / long*
¿Puede usted mostrarme / enseñarme . . .?	*Can you show me . . .?*
¿Aceptan ustedes dólares?	*Do you accept dollars?*
¿Puedo pagar con cheques de viajero / tarjeta de crédito?	*Can I pay with traveller's cheques / by credit card?*
Voy a pagar al contado / en efectivo.	*I am going to pay cash.*
¿Dónde está la caja?	*Where do I pay?*

◙ ———— Notas gramaticales ————

1 *That and those*

To say *that* and *those* in Spanish we use the following set of words:

that	**those**
ese (m)	esos (m)
esa (f)	esas (f)

Quisiera ver ese maletín.	*I would like to see that briefcase.*
Quisiera ver esos suéteres.	*I would like to see those sweaters.*

When **ese, esa**, etc. are used instead of a noun, they are normally written with an accent.

Ése de color negro.	*That black one.* (masc)
Me gusta ésa.	*I like that one.* (fem)

To say *that*, as in *That is all*, *What is that?*, we use the word **eso**, which is neuter:

Eso es todo.	*That is all.*
¿Qué es eso?	*What is that?*

2   Me gusta, te gusta . . . (*I like (it), you like (it). . .*)

To express likes and dislikes in Spanish, we use the verb **gustar** (*to like*), preceded by a pronoun (words like *me*, *you*, *him*, *her*).

me gusta	*I like (it)*
te gusta	*you like (it)* (fam, sing)
le gusta	*you like (it)* (pol, sing)
	he, she likes (it)
nos gusta	*we like (it)*
les gusta	*you like (it)* (pl)
	they like (it)

These phrases translate literally into English as *it pleases me*, *it pleases you*, *it pleases him*, etc. Therefore the verb remains in the third person singular. To say *I like them*, *you like them*, *he likes them*, use the third person plural of the verb (**gustan**):

me gustan	*I like them*
te gustan	*you like them*
le gustan	*you, he, she, likes them*

To say what you like to do, use the appropriate form of **gustar** followed by the infinitive. Look at these examples:

Me gusta viajar.	*I like to travel.*
Nos gusta jugar al tenis.	*We like playing tennis.*

3   *Expressing comparisons*

To express comparisons in Spanish (e.g. cheaper, bigger), we simply place the word **más** (*more*) before the adjective. Here are some examples:

Ése es más barato.	*That is cheaper.*
Ésos son más caros.	*Those are more expensive.*
Esos suéteres son más grandes.	*Those sweaters are bigger.*

4 Using ser to describe things

To describe things, we normally use the verb **ser** (*to be*):

Es un maletín muy bonito.	*It's a very nice briefcase.*
Es muy elegante.	*It is very elegant.*
Son bonitos.	*They are nice.*
Es de cuero / fibra sintética.	*It is made of leather / synthetic fibre.*

Actividades

1 You are on holiday in Bogotá and before going back home you decide to buy a present for someone. Choose one of these articles and then play your part in this conversation with a shop assistant.

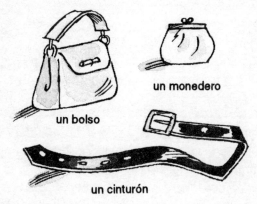

un bolso

un monedero

un cinturón

Ud.	*Tell the shop assistant which article you would like to see from the shop window.*
Vendedora	¿Cuál? ¿Éste?
Ud..	*That one, the brown one.*
Vendedora	Aquí tiene usted.
Ud.	*Say it is very nice and ask if it is made of leather.*
Vendedora	Sí, es de cuero. Sólo vendemos artículos de cuero.
Ud.	*Ask how much it costs. The price given by the shop assistant seems a bit high, so ask if they have a cheaper one.*

Vendedora	No, éste es el más barato que tenemos. Es muy fino. Es un cuero de muy buena calidad.
Ud.	*Say you like it very much.*
Vendedora	Sí, es precioso.
Ud.	*Say you are going to take it and ask if you can pay with a credit card.*
Vendedora	Sí, por supuesto. ¿Lo quiere para regalo?
Ud.	*Yes, it is for a present.*

sólo *only*		**precioso** *very nice*	
el más barato *the cheapest one*		**por supuesto** *certainly, of course*	
fine *good quality*			
calidad (f) *quality*		**regalo** (m) *present*	

———— Nota explicativa ————

Another word for **un bolso**, used in some Latin American countries, including Colombia where they use both words, is **una cartera**. In Spain, **una cartera** is a wallet or a briefcase.

2 Clothes seem to be cheaper in Colombia than back home, so you decide to buy something for yourself. Choose from one of these items and then play your part in the conversation, overleaf, with the shop assistant.

una blusa

una camisa

una falda   una chaqueta

---

blusa (f)	*blouse*	**falda** (f)	*skirt*
camisa (f)	*shirt*	**chaqueta** (f)	*jacket*

Ud.	*Tell the shop assistant what you would like to see.*
Vendedor	¿Qué talla tiene usted?
Ud.	*Say what size you are.*
Vendedor	¿En qué color la prefiere?
Ud.	*Ask what colours they have.*
Vendedor	Las tenemos en negro, gris, blanco, beige y naranja.
Ud.	*Say you prefer it in white.*
Vendedor	Aquí tiene usted una blanca.
Ud.	*Say you don't like the style (**el modelo**) very much. Ask if they have others.*
Vendedor	(*Showing you other items*) Sí, éstas son diferentes. ¿Le gustan?
Ud.	*Yes, you like those more.*
Vendedor	Aquí tiene una en blanco.
Ud.	*Ask if you can try it on.*
Vendedor	(*Pointing to the fitting room*) Sí, allí está el probador.
Ud.	*Say it fits very well and ask how much it costs.*
Vendedor	Ésa cuesta treinta y cinco mil pesos.
Ud.	*Yes, you are going to take it.*
Vendedor	¿Cómo va a pagar?
Ud.	*Say you are going to pay cash (with ready money).*

¿En qué colores ...?   *What colours ...?*

Nota explicativa

La chaqueta, in Colombia, is a short jacket. A man's jacket, as for a suit, is **un saco**. The word **saco** is also known in other Latin American countries, such as Argentina.

3 You go out shopping again. This time you buy several things, and while waiting to have them wrapped, you overhear a conversation between a Colombian customer buying shoes (**unos zapatos**) and a shop assistant. Listen to the conversation, or read the transcript on page 269, and as you do so, complete the box below with details of the purchase. First look at these new words:

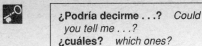

¿Podría decirme . . .? *Could you tell me . . .?*	s/ (sin) *without*
¿cuáles? *which ones?*	c/ (con) *with*
descuento (m) *discount*	número (m) *size (of shoes)*

artículo	precio s/descuento	precio c/descuento	color	número
zapatos				

4 'Next time you want to buy men's clothes, why don't you try Almacenes García. They have big discounts for you.' Listen to this radio advertisement, or read the transcript on page 269, and try to understand what discounts are being offered and on what articles of clothing. First look at these key words, then answer the questions below.

almacenes (m, pl) *department store*	manga corta (f) *short sleeve*
calidad (f) *quality*	caballero (m) *gentleman*
por fin de temporada *for end of season*	descuento (m) *discount*
manga larga (f) *long sleeve*	pantalones (m, pl) *trousers*
	promociones (m, pl) *special offers*

Responda en inglés

(a) What sort of shirts are on offer?

(b) What discounts are they giving on men's trousers?

(c) What phrases have been used in the advertising to express the following: *all men's trousers* and *special offers are not included?*

5 You are in a market buying some fruit and vegetables. Study these key words first and then do the exercise overleaf.

los aguacates *avocados*	las zanahorias *carrots*
los mangos *mangoes*	las lechugas *lettuces*
los duraznos *peaches*	los repollos *cabbages*

How would you express the following in Spanish?

(a) How much are the avocados?
(b) Have you got mangoes?
(c) What is the price of the peaches?
(d) I would like a kilo of carrots.
(e) Give me one lettuce.
(f) I want two cabbages.
(g) That is all.
(h) How much is it?

6 Here is an incomplete dialogue between a Colombian post-office clerk and a customer who is sending a letter (**una carta**) to the United States. Fill in the missing words.

Cliente ¿Cuánto cuesta ____ una carta ____ los Estados Unidos?

Empleado Mil ____

Cliente Deme una ____ de mil y cuatro ____ seiscientos.

Empleado ¿Algo más?

Cliente ____ es todo. ¿Cuánto ____?

Empleado Son ____ pesos.

Cliente ¿Dónde está el ____?

Empleadop Está afuera, ____ la derecha.

7 Understanding figures in Spanish may not be easy at first, so here is a chance to practise. First, look at the advertisement for furniture and try reading each of the prices a few times until you feel sure that you can say them fluently. Luis Nuñez, from Bogotá bought several pieces of furniture from the shop, and now the shop assistant is adding up the price. As you listen to the figures, make a list of the items bought by Luis and write down the total amount he paid. If you are not using the cassette, read the transcript on page 269. First, look at this new vocabulary:

saldo (m) *sale, bargain*	**nevera** (f) *refrigerator*
feria (f) *trade fair*	**lavadora** (f) *washing machine*
oferta (f) *special offer*	**equipo sonido** (m) *stereo*
sofacama (m) *sofabed*	*equipment*
juvenil *for young people*	**cama** (f) *bed*

── Imágenes de Hispanoamérica ──

Latin American currency

The currency used in Colombia is **el peso**. **El peso** is also used in Mexico, Bolivia, Cuba, Chile, Dominican Republic, Uruguay and Argentina. The unit of currency in Ecuador is **el sucre**, in Paraguay **el guaraní**, in Peru **el sol**, in Venezuela **el bolívar**, in Costa Rica and El Salvador **el colón**, in Nicaragua **el córdoba**, in Guatemala **el quetzal**, in Honduras **la lempira**, in Panama **el balboa** and in Puerto Rico **el dólar**.

The word for money is **el dinero** (standard), but many Latin Americans use the more informal word **la plata** (lit. *silver*) for example **No tengo plata** (*I have no money*).

Pesos and dollars

Latin American currency is strongly linked to the American dollar, and if you are travelling on the continent it is best to take dollars rather than pounds or any other European currency, as in smaller towns you may find it difficult to have these accepted.

The rate of exchange of the **peso** in relation to the dollar is not the same in all countries which use this currency. At the time of writing this passage, for instance, one American dollar was worth 800 Colombian **pesos**, 400 Chilean **pesos** and 3.5 Mexican **nuevos pesos**. At times, some Latin American countries have very high rates of inflation, and exchange rates may vary substantially within a short period of time.

Oddly enough, in some countries you may get less for your traveller's cheques (**los cheques de viaje** or **los cheques de viajero**) than for your cash, but for safety reasons it is best to carry traveller's cheques (preferably in American dollars), for which you can always get a refund if they are lost or stolen. Avoid carrying a lot of cash with you and, if possible, never change money in the street.

It is not unusual in Latin America to see people outside banks (**bancos**) or bureaux de change (**casas de cambio**) offering tourists a better rate of exchange for their currency, but this may be dangerous as you may be cheated or robbed.

Shopping in Latin America

Shopping in Latin America can be great fun, and in many countries prices are generally cheaper than in Europe or the United States. Handicrafts are a good buy almost everywhere in the continent, especially in market places, where you will find a large selection of items. Latin American markets are fascinating, and stall holders normally expect you to bargain, so don't heistate to use phrases like: **Es demasiado caro** (*It's too expensive*), **Se lo compro en** . . . (*I'll buy it for . . .*) or **¿Cuál es el último precio?** (*What is your bottom price?*). In shops in town, and in hotels, you may pay a lot more for the same goods. Countries like Mexico, Guatemala, Colombia, Ecuador, Bolivia and Peru, among others, have wonderful handicrafts of many different kinds, ranging from pottery to woodcraft, rugs and wall hangings, leather articles, silver and gold jewellery and other artifacts.

7

PLANES DE
VACACIONES
Holiday plans

In this unit you will learn how to

- talk about the future
- express intentions
- describe places
- describe the weather

Diálogos

1 Vamos a ir en tren

On her way to work, Elisa, a Chilean, meets her friend Antonio, also from Chile. Elisa and Antonio talk about their holiday plans.

Elisa	Hola, ¿qué tal?
Antonio	Hola, ¿cómo te va?
Elisa	No muy bien. Estoy muy cansada. ¡Tengo mucho trabajo!
Antonio	Bueno, ya saldrás de vacaciones y podrás descansar. ¿Tienes algún plan para este verano?
Elisa	Bueno sí, iré con Alfonso al sur por un par de semanas. Pensamos llegar hasta Chiloé. Es la primera vez que voy. Yo no conozco nada del sur.

Antonio	Te va a gustar mucho. Chiloé es precioso. ¿Van en auto?
Elisa	No, vamos a ir en tren y pensamos volver en bus. ¿Y tú, qué piensas hacer?
Antonio	Bueno, yo tomaré mis vacaciones en febrero. Voy a ir a México y Ecuador.
Elisa	¡Estupendo! ¿Vas solo?
Antonio	No, voy con dos amigos de la oficina.
Elisa	¿Y por cuánto tiempo van?
Antonio	Bueno, es un tour, vamos a estar ocho días en México y cuatro días en Quito.
Elisa	¡Te felicito! Dicen que México es un país muy lindo. Espero que lo pases muy bien.
Antonio	Gracias. Tú también.
Elisa	Adiós.
Antonio	Chao.

---

estar cansado/a   *to be tired*
ya saldrás de vacaciones   *you'll soon be on holiday*
podrás   *you will be able to*
descansar   *to rest*
verano (m)   *summer*
iré   *I will go*
sur (m)   *south*
par (m)   *couple*
semana (f)   *week*
pensamos llegar hasta   *we're thinking of going as far as*
primera vez (f)   *first time*
conozco   *I know*
te va a gustar   *you are going to like it*

precioso   *very beautiful*
auto (m)   *car*
¿Qué piensas hacer?   *What are you thinking of doing?*
tomaré   *I will take*
voy a ir   *I am going to go*
solo   *on your own, alone*
¿Por cuánto tiempo van?   *How long are you going for?*
vamos a estar   *we are going to be*
¡Te felicito!   *Congratulations!*
dicen (decir) (e → i)   *they say (to say)*
Espero que lo pases muy bien.   *I hope you have a very good time*
tú también   *you too*

---

los meses del año   *the months of the year*

enero   *January*
febrero   *February*
marzo   *March*
abril   *April*
mayo   *May*
junio   *June*

julio   *July*
agosto   *August*
septiembre   *September*
octubre   *October*
noviembre   *November*
diciembre   *December*

Notice that in Spanish, months are written with small initial letters.

---

las estaciones *the seasons*

el otoño *autumn*　　　　**la primavera** *spring*
el invierno *winter*　　　　**el verano** *summer*

¿Verdadero o falso?

(*a*)　Elisa irá al sur de Chile con Alfonso.
(*b*)　Antonio va a ir a Chiloé.

--- **Notas explicativas** ---

Chilean pronunciation

All the introductory dialogues in Units 7, 8 and 9 are set in Chile and have been recorded by Chileans, with the exception of dialogue 3, Unit 8, which features a Venezuelan speaker. As in southern Spain, Argentina, Venezuela and generally around the Caribbean, Chileans tend to pronounce final -s (e.g. **días**) and s- before a consonant (e.g. **está**), like an aspirated **h**, with the result that **días** and **está** sound more like **día**[h] and **e**[h]**tá**. A common greeting such as **¿Cómo está usted?** usually becomes **¿Cómo e**[h]**tá u**[h]**ted?**. In deliberate and more careful speech, however, and when influenced by adjoining sounds, the s sound tends to be restored. If you pay special attention to the speakers on the cassette, you will notice that the same speaker may at times substitute the s by an aspirated **h** or pronounce it fully. Like Mexicans and other Latin Americans, Chileans do not differentiate between the pronunciation of **ll**, as in **calle**, and **y**, as in **yo**. And as in the rest of Latin America, c and z, as in **gracias** and **plaza**, are pronounced like the s in **casa**.

Talking about the future

Saldrás (*you will go*), **podrás** (*you will be able to*), **iré** (*I will go*) and **tomaré** (*I will take*) are future forms of **salir**, **poder**, **ir** and **tomar** respectively. The future tense is covered under **Notas gramaticales**.

Expressing intentions

One way of expressing intentions in Spanish is by using the verb **pensar** (e → ie) (*to think*), followed by the infinitive:

Pensamos llegar hasta Chiloé.	*We are thinking of going as far as Chiloé.*
¿Qué piensas hacer?	*What are you thinking of doing?*

To say what you are thinking of doing use **pienso**:

Pienso ir a México.	*I am thinking of going to Mexico.*

Double negative

No conozco nada del sur.	*I don't know the south at all.*

Notice the double negative in this sentence, where **nada** means literally *nothing*, a construction which is standard in Spanish. Note also that **conocer** (*to know*) is irregular in the first person singular of the present tense: **conozco, conoces, conoce, conocemos, conocen**.

El bus (*bus*), el auto (*car*)

Chileans, like some other Latin Americans, for example Colombians, use the word **el bus**, short for **el autobús** (*bus*). A car is normally referred to as **un auto**, short for **un automóvil**. The word **auto** is also used in other countries, for example Mexico and Argentina.

Referring to future plans with ir a *followed by the infinitive*

Voy a ir.	*I am going to go.*
Vamos a estar diez días en México.	*We are going to be in Mexico for ten days.*

As in English, future plans may be expressed in Spanish by using the future tense (see **Notas gramaticales**) or with the construction **ir a** followed by the infinitive. For a revision of this, see Unit 5.

Use of por *to refer to a period of time*

¿Por cuánto tiempo van?	*How long are you going for?*
Por un par de semanas.	*For a couple of weeks.*

Lindo (*beautiful*)

This word is quite frequently used in Latin America, perhaps more so than **bonito**, which is the word normally used in Spain.

Describing places with ser

Notice the use of **ser** (*to be*) in the description of places:

Chiloé es precioso.	*Chiloe is very beautiful.*
Es un país muy bonito / lindo.	*It is a very beautiful country.*

Chiloé

Chiloé is a region in southern Chile, about 1200 km from Santiago, the capital city. It includes an island which is 250 km long and 50 km wide.

Leave-taking

¡Adiós! and **hasta luego** (*goodbye*) are standard terms and are used in all Spanish-speaking countries, in formal and familiar contexts. **¡Chao!** (*bye-bye!*), derived from the Italian **ciao!**, is informal and is very common in many Latin American countries. You may occasionally hear diminutives of these words, for example **¡adiosito!**, **¡chaíto!**.

2 No hace frío

Alfonso describes the weather in Chiloé to his wife Elisa.

Elisa	¿Qué tal el tiempo en Chiloé? ¿Crees que hará frío?
Alfonso	No, en esta época del año no hace frío, pero sí puede llover. En el sur llueve mucho, especialmente en Chiloé.
Elisa	Tendremos que llevar algo para la lluvia, por si acaso.
Alfonso	Sí, creo que sí.

---

no hace frío *it's not cold*
¿Qué tal el tiempo? *What's the weather like?*
¿Crees que hará frío? *Do you think it will be cold?*
creer *to think, to believe*
época (f) *time*

llueve (llover) (o → ue) *it rains (to rain)*
tendremos que *we will have to*
llevar *to take, to carry*
algo *something*
lluvia (f) *rain*
por si acaso *just in case*
creo que sí *I think so*

Responda en inglés

(a) Does Alfonso think it may be cold in Chiloé?
(b) What does Elisa propose to take with them?

Notas explicativas

Describing the weather

To describe the weather, Spanish normally uses the verb **hacer** (lit. *to do, to make*). Notice these two examples from the dialogue:

No hace frío.   *It is not cold.*
¿Hará frío?   *Will it be cold?*

Sí

Notice the emphatic use of **sí** in the following:

Pero sí puede llover.   *But it may rain.*

Frases y expresiones importantes

- Talking about the future

  ¿Tienes algún plan para este verano?   *Do you have any plans for this summer?*
  Iré con Alfonso al sur.   *I am going to the south with Alfonso.*

  Voy a ir a México y Ecuador.   *I am going to Mexico and Ecuador.*

- Other words and phrases used to refer to the future

  mañana   *tomorrow*
  mañana por la mañana / tarde / noche   *tomorrow morning / afternoon / night*
  pasado mañana   *the day after tomorrow*
  dentro de una semana   *within a week*
  la próxima semana / la semana próxima   *next week*
  el próximo mes / el mes próximo   *next month*
  la semana / el mes / el año que viene   *next week / month / year*

- Expressing intentions

Pensamos llegar hasta Chiloé.	*We are thinking of going as far as Chiloe.*
¿Y tú, qué piensas hacer?	*And what are you thinking of doing?*

- Describing places

Chiloé es precioso.	*Chiloe is very beautiful.*
México es muy lindo.	*Mexico is very beautiful.*

- Other ways of describing places

Tiene una iglesia muy interesante.	*It has a very interesting church.*
Al lado de la iglesia hay un museo colonial.	*Next to the church there is a colonial museum.*

- Describing the weather

(No) hace frío.	*It is (not) cold.*
Llueve mucho.	*It rains a lot.*

- Other ways of describing the weather

Hace (mucho) calor.	*It is (very) warm.*
Hace (mucho) viento.	*It is (very) windy.*
Hace buen / mal tiempo.	*The weather is good / bad.*
Hace sol.	*It is sunny.*
Nieva. (nevar)	*It snows. (to snow)*
Está nublado.	*It is overcast.*
Está despejado.	*It is clear / cloudless.*
Está lloviendo.	*It is raining.*

Notas gramaticales

1 Looking ahead

To refer to the future you can use:

(i) the future tense:

Iré con Alfonso al sur.	*I am going to the south with Alfonso.*
¿Hará frío?	*Will it be cold?*

(ii) the construction **ir a** with an infinitive:

Voy a ir a México.	*I am going to Mexico.*
Vamos a estar diez días	*We are going to be in Mexico*
en México.	*for ten days.*

(iii) the present tense, particularly with verbs which indicate movement:

¿Van en auto?	*Are you going by car?*
¿Por cuánto tiempo van?	*How long are you going for?*

Of these three ways of referring to the future, the future tense is the least common, particularly in Latin America, where **ir a** + the infinitive is far more frequently used, especially in colloquial speech. However, you will hear the future tense in some contexts and with certain verbs, for instance when there is an implication of inevitability, e.g. **Tendremos que llevar algo para la lluvia** (*We'll have to take something for the rain*), or when there is uncertainty, e.g. **¿Crees que hará frío?** (*Do you think it will be cold?*), or simply for reasons of economy, e.g. **iré con él** instead of **voy a ir con él**. In formal spoken language, the future tense is more frequent (e.g. a tourist guide outlining plans for an excursion: **Saldremos del hotel a las 7.00**, *We'll leave the hotel at 7.00*). In the press, the future tense is the standard form used to refer to future events.

2 The future tense

To form the future tense, you use the infinitive followed by the appropriate ending, which is the same for the three conjugations (**-ar**, **-ir**, and **-er**). Here is an example of a fully conjugated regular verb.

tomar *to take*	
tomar**é**	*I will take*
tomar**ás**	*you will take* (fam, sing)
tomar**á**	*you will take* (pol, sing), *he, she, it will take*
tomar**emos**	*we will take*
tomar**án**	*you will take* (pl), *they will take*

Nota: Notice that the **vosotros** (*you*, pl, fam) form **tomaréis**, which is used in Spain, has been omitted, as this is not normally used in Latin America.

Here are some more examples of the use of the future tense:

Tomaremos una semana de vacaciones.	*We will take a week's holiday.*
Veremos qué podemos hacer.	*We'll see what we can do.*
¿Adónde irás este verano?	*Where will you go this summer?*

Irregular future forms

Some verbs have an irregular stem in the future tense but the endings are the same as for regular verbs. Here is a list of the most important.

decir	*(to say, to tell)*	diré, dirás, dirá, diremos, dirán
hacer	*(to do, to make)*	haré, harás, hará, haremos, harán
poder	*(can, to be able to)*	podré, podrás, podrá, podremos, podrán
salir	*(to go out)*	saldré, saldrás, saldrá, saldremos, saldrán
tener	*(to have)*	tendré, tendrás, tendrá, tendremos, tendrán
venir	*(to come)*	vendré, vendrás, vendrá, vendremos, vendrán

Here are some examples of the future tense with irregular verbs:

El avión saldrá a las 7.00 de la mañana.	*The plane will leave at 7.00 in the morning.*
Tendrán que estar en el aeropuerto dos horas antes.	*You'll have to be at the airport two hours earlier.*
El autobús vendrá a las 4.30.	*The bus will come at 4.30.*

For other irregular future forms see pages 276–80.

3 Conocer *and* saber (*to know*)

In dialogue 1 above you encountered the verb **conocer** (*to know or to be acquainted with something, a person or a place*). **Saber**, above, also translates into English as *to know*, but it is used to refer to knowledge of a fact or the ability to do something. Like **conocer**, the first person singular of **saber** in the present tense is irregular: **sé** (*I know*). Compare the following:

Conozco México.	*I know Mexico.*
Conozco a Isabel.	*I know Isabel.*

No sé dónde está Quito.   *I don't know where Quito is.*
No sé manejar.   *I don't know how to drive.*

Actividades

1   You have been posted by your company to Chile, and during your first holiday there you decide to visit other parts of Latin America with a local friend. The following holiday advertisement in a Chilean newspaper catches your attention, and one of the destinations – Quito, Mexico – seems to be what you want. The following day in your office you talk about it with a Chilean colleague.

(Revista del Domingo, El Mercurio, Chile)

Colega	¿Qué piensas hacer este verano?
Ud.	*Say you are thinking of going to Mexico and Quito.*
Colega	¡Qué interesante! México es un país muy lindo y Quito también me gusta mucho. ¿Vas por mucho tiempo?
Ud.	*No, you are going to be there 12 days in all (**en total**).*
Colega	¿Es un tour?
Ud.	*Yes, it is a tour and it's not very expensive. It costs 949 dollars.*
Colega	No está caro. ¿Incluye el pasaje aéreo?
Ud.	*Yes, it includes the flight, 4-star hotels, excursions and transfers.*
Colega	Me parece muy barato. ¿Vas a ir solo/a?
Ud.	*No, you are going to travel with a friend. Ask your colleague what he is going to do in the summer.*
Colega	Voy a ir a la playa con mi familia. Pensamos ir a Viña del Mar.

pasaje aéreo (m)	*plane ticket, flight*	**traslado** (m)	*transfer*
estrella (f)	*star*	**c/u (cada uno)**	*each one*

2 You decide to take the tour advertised above, but before you travel you write to a Mexican acquaintance to tell him of your visit to Mexico. In his reply, your Mexican correspondent suggests some places to visit together during your stay in Mexico City. Read what he says, then check your understanding by answering the questions which follow. First study these key words and phrases.

me alegro mucho de que vengas		**lugar** (m)	*place*
I am glad you are coming		**barrio** (m)	*district*
aunque	*although*	**así que**	*so*
estoy seguro	*I am sure*	**juntos**	*together*
como tendrás	*as you will have*	**si te interesa**	*if it interests you*

Me alegro mucho de que vengas a México. Aunque la ciudad es enorme, estoy seguro de que te gustará. Como tendrás algunos días libres, te llevaré en el coche a conocer algunos de los lugares más interesantes de la ciudad. Podremos ir a Coyoacán, que es un barrio típico, con buenos restaurantes y algunos monumentos importantes. Allí está el Museo de Frida Khalo. Yo no lo conozco, así que lo visitaremos juntos.

Si te interesa, podremos ir a Cuernavaca y Taxco, dos ciudades muy interesantes que no están muy lejos de México...

Nota: The word **México** in the passage refers to Mexico City. That is the word most Mexicans use to refer to the capital city.

Responda en inglés

(a) What is Coyoacán?
(b) What museum will you be able to visit there?
(c) What cities will your friend take you to?
(d) Are they far from Mexico City?

3 In his reply, your Mexican acquaintance also gives you information about the weather in Mexico City. Read it through, then check your understanding by answering the questions below.

En general, el clima es bastante agradable, aunque en invierno a veces hace un poco de frío, especialmente entre diciembre y enero, que es cuando tú vendrás. Pero en esta época del año no llueve mucho. El invierno este año ha sido muy suave, con mucho sol y algunos días de bastante calor. En todo caso, tendrás que traer un suéter para las mañanas y para la noche...

Responda en inglés

(a) What is the weather generally like in Mexico City?
(b) Is it cold in winter?
(c) Does it rain in December and January?
(d) What does your acquaintance suggest you bring?

4 In Mexico you are going to stay at the Hotel Ana Luisa, a 4-star hotel. In this description of the hotel, all the verbs are missing. Complete the passage with the appropriate verb, then check your answers in the **Key to the exercises**.

El hotel Ana Luisa es un hotel de 4 estrellas que ____ situado frente al Monumento de la Revolución, a pocos pasos del Paseo de la Reforma. Este elegante hotel ____ 250 habitaciones, todas con baño privado, TV a color, teléfono y mini-bar. En el hotel Ana Luisa ____ dos restaurantes de comida internacional, dos bares y una cafetería. Para su confort durante los meses de verano, el hotel ____ aire acondicionado.

a pocos pasos de *a few steps away from*	**meses de verano** (m, pl) *summer months*
baño privado (m) *private bath*	**aire acondicionado** *air conditioning*

5 While in Mexico, you might have a chance to visit Veracruz. A friend back home went on holiday there and he liked it very much. He has recommended somewhere to stay: **Motel Miraflores**. Listen to this advertisement from Mexican radio, or read the transcript on page 270, and pay special attention to the facilities they announce at **Motel Miraflores**. Then make a list of them in English. The vocabulary which follows includes some new words you will hear in the advertisement. You should be able to guess the meanings of other new words.

paraíso (m) *paradise*	**cama** (f) *bed*
para que usted disfrute *so that you may enjoy*	**alberca** (f) *swimming pool* (Mex)
cómodamente *comfortably*	**siempre deseará volver** *you will always want to come back*
estancia (f) *stay*	**sin número** *without number*
antena parabólica *satellite dish*	

6 In Quito, Ecuador, you will stay at the Hotel Quito. Listen to how someone from Quito describes the hotel or, alternatively, read the transcript on page 270, then answer the questions below. First study these new words and phrases:

piscina (f) *swimming pool*	**salones** (m, pl) *room, hall*
en la parte trasera *at the back*	**se hacen** *are held*
espacio verde (m) *green area*	**convenciones** (m, pl) *conferences*
bien grandes *very large*	**aparte** *besides*
Techo del Mundo *roof of the world*	

Responda en inglés

(a) How many rooms has the hotel got?
(b) How many restaurants does it have?
(c) What other facilities does it have?

7 It is your last day in the office before your departure for Mexico and you are very busy. A colleague is trying to set up an urgent meeting with you. Answer his questions by looking at the diary notes overleaf.

√√√   **VIERNES 31**   √√√

10.00   Entrevista con el Sr. Valdés.

11.00   Ir al banco y comprar cheques de viajero.

12.00

   12.30-Reunión con el director de producción.

13.00   Almuerzo con el gerente.

14.00   ―

15.00   Llamar a la agencia de viaje para reconfirmar hora del vuelo.

vuelo (m)   *flight*

Responda en español

(a) ¿Qué vas a hacer a las 11.00?
(b) ¿Y a las 12.30?
(c) ¿Vas a almorzar solo/a?
(d) ¿Estarás libre por la tarde? ¿A qué hora?

8 You are already thinking about your next holiday, which may be in Panama or Peru. They sound like good places to escape to in winter. Listen first to what Elizabeth from Panama City says about the weather in her country. Then listen to Karina Tomas, a Peruvian, describing Lima, the capital of Peru. If you do not have the cassette, use the transcript on page 270 for reading comprehension. First, look at this new vocabulary, then check your comprehension by answering the questions below.

clima (m) *climate* **temperatura promedio** (f) *average temperature* **todo el año** *the whole year*	**netamente** *essentially* **lluviosa** *rainy* **seca** *dry*

¿Verdadero o falso?

(a) La temperatura promedio en Panamá es de dieciocho grados centígrados.

(b) En invierno llueve mucho.

(c) En verano no llueve.

aún *still* **se conservan** *they are retained* **época colonial** (f) *colonial times* **zoológico** (m) *zoo*	**en cuanto a** *as regards* **cálido** *warm* **lluvias** (f, pl) *rains*

Responda en inglés

(d) How does Karina describe Lima?

(e) What does Lima have to offer, according to her?

(f) What is the weather like?

9 The people you will meet in Mexico and Ecuador will probably ask you about your own city. How would you answer the following questions:

(a) ¿Cómo es la ciudad?

(b) ¿Cuántos habitantes tiene?

(c) ¿Cómo es el clima?

10 On the seat next to you on the plane you find a newspaper giving information on the weather in different capital cities, including Mexico, your destination. Study the table overleaf and then answer these questions.

Responda en español

(a) ¿Hace sol en México?

(b) ¿Cómo está el tiempo en Londres?

(c)   ¿Está lloviendo en París?
(d)   ¿Cómo está el tiempo en Madrid?

El tiempo en el mundo

Ciudades	Mín	Máx	Estado
Amsterdam	9	25	despejado
Asunción	18	30	despejado
Atenas	17	25	despejado
Berlín	13	18	nublado
Bruselas	18	27	despejado
Buenos Aires	12	20	lluvioso
Caracas	18	28	despejado
Ginebra	8	23	despejado
La Habana	19	30	despejado
La Paz	2	19	despejado
Lima	17	23	variable
Londres	16	23	despejado
Los Angeles	16	26	nublado
Madrid	12	22	lluvioso
México	12	26	nublado
Miami	22	29	despejado
Montevideo	14	20	lluvioso
Moscú	12	15	nublado
Nueva York	17	25	nublado
París	12	25	despejado
Pekín	16	28	despejado
Río de Janeiro	20	26	despejado
Roma	11	23	despejado
San José	15	26	nublado
Seúl	14	24	despejado
Tokio	18	22	nublado
Varsovia	17	22	despejado
Viena	10	16	despejado
Washington	16	27	nublado

—— Imágenes de Hispanoamérica ——

Summertime

It is December, and in Chile, Argentina and other countries in the southern hemisphere people start making plans for their summer holidays. Most Latin Americans spend their holidays in their own country, although more and more people are travelling to neighbouring countries. A two-hour flight will take Chileans across the Andes to Buenos Aires, to enjoy the excitement of the big and modern Argentinian capital. Argentinians will travel hundreds of kilometres, many of them by car, to reach the Chilean coastal resorts on the Pacific. The flow is at its peak during January and February, although there can be great variations depending on the economic conditions and the cost of living in different countries.

A look at Chile

People spending their summer holidays in their own country usually have a wide choice. Chile, for instance, a country 4,200 km. long, situated between the Andes and the Pacific, offers tremendous variations of climate and landscape. From Peru, in the north, you can cross the border into Chile, travelling along the Panamerican Highway (**la carretera Panamericana**) and experience the climate of the Atacama desert, where it never rains. Travelling 2,000 km. further south, along the same route, you will reach Santiago, the Chilean capital, lying in a fertile valley, where agriculture is highly developed. The city, lying at the foot of the Andes, is surrounded by farms and vineyards. Chile's fine export wines are produced in this central valley, which extends for several hundred kilometres. The majority of Chileans live in this region, which has rainy winters but dry warm summers.

The Panamerican Highway continues south until it reaches the city of Puerto Montt, about 1,000 km. from the capital. Puerto Montt is the centre of one of the most beautiful regions in Chile, an area of huge lakes, volcanoes, forests, rivers and waterfalls. There is abundant rain in this part of the country during most of the year. Until the middle of the 19th century, much of this region was inhabited by Araucanian Indians, who never submitted to Spanish domination. But in the second half of the 19th century, the Chilean government brought European immigrants, mainly Germans, to settle this land. Nowadays, the Indian population is relatively small and their living conditions are generally poor compared to those of **mestizos** (mixture of Indian and white) or whites.

About 1,600 km. separate Puerto Montt from Cape Horn (**Cabo de Hornos**) in the far south. The population is scarce in this region of

Puerto Montt, Chile

torrential rains, heavy winds and extreme cold. It is a land of islands, channels, fjords and glaciers. In the southern-most part of this region is Patagonia and the city of Punta Arenas. Patagonia stretches east towards Argentina. Beyond Patagonia, across the Magellan Strait, to the south, is the island of Tierra del Fuego, shared by Chile and Argentina. On the Chilean side, the only town is Porvenir, with a population of about 5,000 people, many of them descendants from old Yugoslav settlers.

There is no road linking Puerto Montt to Punta Arenas, although one – **la carretera austral** – is presently being built. The best way to reach the far south, other than by plane or by road via Argentina, is by boat from Puerto Montt or from the island of Chiloé, a voyage which is highly recommended for its beautiful scenery.

8

DE VIAJE
Travelling

In this unit you will learn how to

- ask and answer questions about departure and arrival times
- book in at a hotel
- ask and answer questions regarding duration

Diálogos

1 Sale a las dieciocho treinta

Elisa and her husband Alfonso are travelling to Puerto Montt in southern Chile, and from there to the island of Chiloé. Today Elisa is buying train tickets.

Elisa	Buenos días. ¿A qué hora hay trenes a Puerto Montt?
Empleado	Tiene el rápido, que sale a las dieciocho treinta, y el expreso, que sale a las veintiuna treinta.
Elisa	¿A qué hora llega el rápido?
Empleado	A las catorce horas del día siguiente.
Elisa	¿Y el expreso?
Empleado	El expreso llega a las diecinueve diez del día siguiente. El rápido demora diecinueve horas y media y el expreso veintiuna horas con cuarenta minutos.

Elisa	Bueno, en ese caso prefiero el rápido. Lleva coche dormitorio, ¿verdad?
Empleado	Sí, lleva departamentos sencillos, para dos personas, y departamentos grandes, para cuatro.
Elisa	¿Cuánto cuesta el departamento sencillo?
Empleado	El sencillo vale cuarenta y cinco mil pesos ida y vuelta.
Elisa	Quiero de ida solamente.
Empleado	De ida le sale a veinticinco mil pesos.
Elisa	¿Por persona?
Empleado	No, ése es el precio del departamento.
Elisa	Muy bien, deme dos boletos para el sábado 15 de febrero.
Empleado	Aquí tiene. Son veinticinco mil pesos.
Elisa	Gracias.

tren (m) *train*	**coche** (m) *car (train)*
rápido (m) *fast train*	**departamento sencillo** *single*
que sale a las 18.30 *which leaves*	*compartment*
at 6.30 p.m.	**(boleto) de ida y vuelta** (m) *return*
llegar *to arrive*	*(ticket)*
día siguiente (m) *following day*	**(boleto) de ida** (m) *single (ticket)*
llevar *to carry, to have*	**solamente** *only*

Complete estas frases

(a) El rápido sale de Santiago a las _____ .
(b) El rápido llega a Puerto Montt a las _____ .

——— Notas explicativas ———

Saying how long something takes

Demora diecinueve horas y media.   *It takes nineteen and a half hours.*

Demorar (*to take* (*time*)) is heard frequently in Latin America, more so than **tardar**, which is the word used in Spain. Both verbs may be used in other contexts, e.g. **¿Por qué demoras / tardas tanto?** (*Why do you take so long?*).

El coche-dormitorio (*sleeping car*)

In Spain the word is **el coche-cama**.

Un departamento sencillo (*a single compartment*)

In Spain, the word for *compartment* is **un compartimiento**.

Expressing cost with salir a (*to come to, to work out . . .*)

Le sale a 25.000 pesos.   *It comes to / will cost you 25.000 pesos.*

Notice this use of **salir** to refer to cost. This is standard Spanish, used also in Spain. Note also:

Sale caro / barato.   *It is / works out expensive / cheap.*

Deme dos boletos (*Give me two tickets*)

El boleto (*ticket*) is used in Latin America. In Spain, the word is **el billete**. The ticket office is **la boletería** in most parts of Latin America. Another word you will hear in some places is **la taquilla**, which is also used in Spain.

2 Una habitación para dos

Elisa and Alfonso are spending two nights at a hotel in Puerto Montt, before they continue their journey to Chiloé.

Alfonso	Buenas tardes.
Recepcionista	Buenas tardes.
Alfonso	¿Tiene una habitación para dos personas?
Recepcionista	Sí, sí tenemos.
Alfonso	¿Cuánto cuesta?
Recepcionista	Dieciocho mil pesos.
Alfonso	¿Con desayuno?
Recepcionista	No, sin desayuno. El desayuno es aparte.
Alfonso	Bueno, está bien.
Recepcionista	¿Cuántos días van a quedarse?
Alfonso	Dos días solamente. Nos vamos el martes.
Recepcionista	De acuerdo. Me da su nombre, por favor.
Alfonso	Alfonso Abucadís.
Recepcionista	¿Cómo se escribe el apellido?
Alfonso	A-b-u-c-a-d-i-s. Abucadís.
Recepcionista	¿Y la dirección?
Alfonso	Calle Las Acacias 731, departamento D, Santiago.
Recepcionista	Bien, aquí tienen la llave. Es la pieza veinticuatro, en el segundo piso, al final del pasillo. Allí está la escalera.
Alfonso	Gracias.

---

aparte *separate*
quedarse *to stay*
nos vamos (irse) *we are leaving*
  (to leave)
de acuerdo *fine*
Me da su nombre *Will you give me your name*

¿Cómo se escribe? (escribir)
  How do you spell it? (to write)
llave (f) *key*
escalera (f) *stairs*

Responda en inglés

(a) How much is a double room?
(b) Is breakfast included in the price?

Notas explicativas

Asking for a room

A room, in Chile, is **una pieza**, or the standard **una habitación**. The first is more frequent, especially in a home, while the second is more often heard in a phrase such as **¿Tiene una habitación?** (*Have you got a room?*).

Spelling names

Many Latin Americans have non-Spanish surnames or names which are fairly uncommon and which need to be spelled. **¿Cómo se escribe?** (*How do you spell it?*, lit. *How do you write it?*) is the standard phrase to use. A less frequent phrase is **¿Puede / podría deletrearlo?** (*Can / could you spell it?*). The verb here is **deletrear** (*to spell*). For the Spanish alphabet, see page 255.

¿Cómo se pronuncia? (*How do you pronounce it?*)

To ask somebody how to pronounce a name or any other word simply say:

¿Cómo se pronuncia su nombre / apellido?	*How do you pronounce your name / surname?*
¿Cómo se pronuncia esta palabra?	*How do you pronounce this word?*

Asking somebody to repeat a word or phrase

If you have not heard properly, you may say **¿Cómo?** or **¿Perdón?** (*Pardon?, Sorry?*) or **¿Puede / podría repetir, por favor?** (*Can / could you repeat, please?*). In some parts of Latin America, for example Mexico and Ecuador, you will hear the word **¿mande?** for *pardon?*

Asking somebody to speak more slowly

If the speaker is talking too fast for you, simply say: **Más despacio, por favor** (*More slowly, please*) or **¿Podría hablar más despacio, por favor?** (*Could you speak more slowly, please?*).

Apologising for your Spanish!

If you are not too confident about your Spanish, use one or more of these phrases:

Disculpe, pero no hablo muy
  bien español.
I am sorry, but I don't speak
  Spanish very well.

Hablo muy poquito español.
I speak only a little Spanish.

Disculpe, pero no entiendo.
I am sorry, but I don't understand.

¿Qué significa . . .?
What does . . . mean?

In an emergency, you might want to add:

¿Habla usted inglés?
Do you speak English?

¿Alguien habla inglés?
Does anybody speak English?

3 ¿Tiene agua caliente?

A tourist from Venezuela arrives at a hotel in Puerto Montt. If you are using the cassette, pay attention to her accent, especially the intonation, which is different from that of the hotel receptionist, who is a Chilean. Notice in her accent the substitution of final **s** by an aspirated **h**, for example in **bueno(h) día(h)** which occurs in many parts of South America and the Caribbean.

Turista	Buenos días.
Recepcionista	Buenos días.
Turista	¿Tiene un cuarto individual?
Recepcionista	Sí, sí tenemos.
Turista	¿Cuánto vale?
Recepcionista	Doce mil pesos.
Turista	¿Tiene baño?
Recepcionista	No, es con baño compartido, pero también hay una habitación con baño. Pero ésa cuesta quince mil pesos.
Turista	¿Sabe?, pero yo prefiero una con baño. ¿Tiene agua caliente?
Recepcionista	Sí, sí, tiene agua caliente, sí.
Turista	¿Y ustedes sirven desayuno?
Recepcionista	No, no señora. El desayuno se paga aparte.
Turista	Bueno, bueno.

| **Recepcionista** | Bien, por favor, ¿puede escribir su nombre y dirección aquí? Y su firma también. |
| **Turista** | De acuerdo. |

---

baño compartido (m)   *shared bathroom*
agua (f)   *water*
caliente   *hot*
¿Sirven desayuno? (servir) (e → i)
  Do you serve breakfast? (to serve)

se paga aparte   *it is paid separately*
¿Puede escribir . . .?   *Can you write . . .?*
firma (f)   *signature*

Responda en español

(a) ¿La turista quiere una habitación individual o doble?
(b) ¿Ella prefiere una habitación con baño o sin baño?

Notas explicativas

El cuarto (*room*)

Notice that the Venezuelan speaker uses the word **el cuarto** for *room*, which is more frequent in her country, while the Chilean speaker uses the word **la habitación**.

¿Sabe?

Observe the use of **¿sabe?** (*you know?*) at the beginning of a statement in:

¿Sabe?, pero yo prefiero una   *You know, (but) I prefer one*
con baño.   *with a bathroom.*

This use of **¿sabe?** is quite frequent in Latin America.

4 ¿Cuánto tiempo llevan aquí?

On their second day in Puerto Montt, Elisa meets a colleague of hers.

Elisa   Andrés, ¡qué sorpresa! ¿Qué haces aquí?

Andrés	Estoy aquí de vacaciones con mi señora y los niños. Ellos están en el hotel ahora.
Elisa	Te presento a Alfonso, mi marido. *(addressing Alfonso)* Éste es Andrés, un compañero de trabajo.
Alfonso	Mucho gusto.
Andrés	Hola, encantado.
Elisa	¿Cuánto tiempo hace que están aquí?
Andrés	Hace una semana, pero nos vamos pasado mañana.
Elisa	¿Por qué se van tan pronto?
Andrés	Porque Carmen tiene que volver al trabajo.
Elisa	¡Qué lástima!
Andrés	Y ustedes, ¿cuánto tiempo llevan aquí?
Elisa	Llevamos dos días solamente, pero pensamos estar dos semanas. Vamos a ir a Chiloé.

¡Qué sorpresa! *What a surprise!*	**¿por qué?** *why*
marido (m) *husband*	**tan pronto** *so soon*
compañero de trabajo (m) *colleague*	**porque** *because*
¿Cuánto tiempo hace que están aquí? *How long have you been here?*	**¡Qué lástima!** *What a pity!*
pasado mañana *the day after tomorrow*	**¿Cuánto tiempo llevan aquí?** *How long have you been here?*

Responda en inglés

(*a*) What is Elisa's colleague Andrés doing in Puerto Montt?
(*b*) How long have Andrés and his family been in Puerto Montt?

Nota explicativa

Mi señora, mi esposa, mi mujer   *my wife*

All three words are standard but usage varies in different countries and in different contexts. Chileans, for example, normally use the phrase **mi señora**, while in Argentina, as in Spain, people prefer to use **mi mujer**. Other countries show preference for the phrase **mi esposa**.

— Frases y expresiones importantes —

- Asking and answering questions about arrival and departure times

¿A qué hora hay trenes a Puerto Montt?	*What time are there trains to Puerto Montt?*
Sale a las 18.30.	*It leaves at 6.30 p.m.*
¿A qué hora llega?	*What time does it arrive?*
Llega a las 14.00 horas.	*It arrives at 2.00 p.m.*

- Booking in at a hotel

¿Tiene una habitación para dos?	*Have you got a room for two?*
Quiero una habitación (or **cuarto**) **individual** (or **sencillo/a**) **/ doble.**	*I want a single / double room.*
Prefiero una habitación con / sin baño.	*I prefer a room with / without a bathroom.*
¿Tiene agua caliente?	*Does it have hot water?*
¿Cuántos días van a quedarse?	*How long are you going to stay?*
Dos días (solamente).	*Two days (only).*
Con / sin desayuno.	*With / without breakfast.*
¿Sirven desayuno?	*Do you serve breakfast?*

- Asking and answering questions regarding duration

¿Cuánto tiempo hace que están aquí?	*How long have you been here?*
Hace una semana (que estamos aquí).	*(We have been here) for a week.*
¿Cuánto tiempo llevan aquí?	*How long have you been here?*
Llevamos dos días solamente.	*We have only been here for two days.*

- Other useful words and phrases used in the context of travel

¿A qué hora hay buses para . . .?	*What time are there buses for . . .?*
¿Cuándo hay vuelos a . . .?	*When are there flights to . . .?*
¿A qué hora sale el próximo tren / bus / vuelo para . . .?	*What time does the next train / bus / flight for . . . leave?*
¿Dónde está la boletería / la taquilla?	*Where is the ticket office?*
Quiero un boleto de ida y vuelta para . . .	*I want a return ticket for . . .*

Quiero dos boletos de ida.	*I want two single tickets.*
Quisiera hacer una reservación para el (domingo 20 de marzo).	*I would like to make a reservation for (Sunday, 20th March).*
En primera / segunda clase.	*In first / second class.*
Fumador / no fumador.	*Smoker / non smoker.*
¿De qué andén sale?	*What platform does it leave from?*
¿Hay que cambiar de tren / avión?	*Do I have to change trains / planes?*
¿Lleva coche comedor?	*Is there a dining car?*

Notas gramaticales

1 Impersonal sentences

Notice the use of **se** in impersonal sentences such as the following:

¿Cómo se escribe?	*How do you spell it?*
¿Cómo se pronuncia?	*How do you pronounce it?*
¿Cómo se dice?	*How do you say it?*

2 Expressing duration

(a) Hace + *time phrase* + que + *present tense*

The construction is used to express the duration of an action which began in the past and is still in progress. Look at these sentences:

¿Cuánto tiempo hace que están aquí?	*How long have you been here?*
Hace una semana que estamos aquí.	*We have been here for a week.*
Estamos aquí desde hace una semana.	*We have been here for a week.*

¿Cuánto tiempo hace que trabajas en Santiago?	*How long have you been working in Santiago?*
Hace dos años que trabajo allí.	*I have been working there for two years.*
Trabajo allí desde hace dos años.	*I have been working there for two years.*

(b) Llevar + *time phrase*

To ask how long someone has been in a place and to reply to a question like this, you can use the present tense of **llevar** followed by a time phrase:

¿Cuánto tiempo llevan aquí?	*How long have you been here?*
Llevamos dos días solamente.	*We have only been here for two days.*
¿Cuánto tiempo llevas en en este trabajo?	*How long have you been in this job?*
Llevo tres años.	*For three years.*

3 Para *and* por

Observe the uses of **para** and **por** in the following examples:

Para el sábado 15 de febrero.	*For Saturday, 15th February.*
Una pieza para dos.	*A room for two.*
Cinco mil pesos por persona.	*Five thousand pesos per person.*

✔ ——————— **Actividades** ———————

1   You are in Chile, and you want to travel from Santiago to Concepción, one of the largest cities in Chile, in the region of BíoBío, about 500 km. south of Santiago. You go to the railway station to get information about trains. Follow the model (dialogue 1) to ask the questions, then use the information overleaf to fill in the answers.

RÁPIDO DEL BÍOBÍO: Sale a las 22:30 horas para llegar a las 7:30 horas a Concepción (sólo se detiene en San Rosendo para conectar con Los Angeles).
Departamento gran dormitorio: 34.200 pesos (ida y vuelta)
Departamendo sencillo: 27.900 pesos (ida y vuelta)
Cama baja: 13.500 pesos (ida y vuelta)
Cama alta: 9.900 pesos (ida y vuelta)
Salón: 3.900 pesos (ida)
Económica: 3.150 pesos (ida)
Primera: 2.350 (ida)
No tiene segunda

(Revista del Domingo, diario El Mercurio, Chile.)

| **se detiene (detenerse)** *it stops* | **cama** (f) *bed, birth* |
| (to stop) | |

Ud.	*Ask what time there is a train to Concepción.*
Empleado	_____.
Ud.	*Ask what time it arrives in Concepción.*
Empleado	_____.
Ud.	*Ask if it has a sleeping car.*
Empleado	_____.
Ud.	*You are travelling on your own, so ask how much a berth is.*
Empleado	_____.
Ud.	*Ask if that is the single or return price.*
Empleado	_____.
Ud.	*Say it is all right, and ask for a return ticket for Monday, 20th July. Say you prefer a bottom berth.*
Empleado	Aquí tiene. Son trece mil quinientos pesos.

2   You are telling a Chilean friend about your planned journey to Concepción.

Ud.	*Say you are going to travel to Concepción.*
Amigo	¿Cuándo piensas viajar?
Ud.	*Say you are leaving on July 20th.*

Amigo	¡Qué bien! Concepción es una ciudad muy bonita. Te va a gustar. Hace mucho tiempo que no voy allí. ¿Vas en bus?
Ud.	*No, you are going to travel by train.*
Amigo	Pero el tren demora bastante, ¿no?
Ud.	*It takes nine hours.*
Amigo	¿Va directo?
Ud.	*No, it stops in San Rosendo.*
Amigo	Sí, conozco muy bien San Rosendo. Tengo una amiga allí a quien no veo desde hace mucho tiempo. Se llama Carmela. Estudiamos juntos en la universidad.

a quien *whom*		**¡qué bien!** *great!*	
estudiamos juntos	*we studied*		
together			

3 Someone has recommended the Hotel Arauco in Concepción to you, and you decide to get a room there. Write the conversation you might have with the hotel receptionist, using dialogue 2 as a model and some of the words and phrases listed under **Frases y expresiones importantes**. In the **Key to the exercises**, which begins on page 257, you will find another model dialogue to compare with your own version.

dos noches	*two nights*	**¿Cuánto cuesta / vale?** *How much does it cost?*	
cinco días	*five days*		
una semana	*a week*	**¿Está incluído el desayuno?** *Is breakfast included?*	

4 While reading a newspaper in Concepción you notice the advertisement, overleaf, for an adventure holiday down the rapids of the river BíoBío which, in spite of protests in Chile and abroad, is going to be turned into a dam to provide electricity for the region. This is the sort of holiday that might interest one of your friends back home. Make sure you understand what they are offering so that you can tell your friend later on. Here are some key words:

ejecutivo/a (m/f) *executive*	**tiempo libre** (m) *spare time*
a punto de *about*	**carpa** (f) *tent (in Spain **una**
ser represado *to be turned into*	**tienda de campaña**)*
a dam	**guía** (m/f) *guide*
partiendo *departing*	**ambos** *both*
a primera hora *early*	**han descendido** *have*
regresando *returning*	*descended*
ha sido pensado *it has been*	**Stgo.** *short for Santiago*
planned	**$** *pesos (Chilean currency)*
aprovechar *to use*	**balsa** (f) *raft*

BÍO-BÍO para Ejecutivos(as)

DESCENSO EN BALSA

A punto de ser represado, ésta puede ser la última oportunidad para conocer el río BíoBío. Tres días de excitante aventura en los rápidos más extraordinarios del mundo. Partiendo en avión el viernes a primera hora y regresando el domingo por la noche, este programa ha sido pensado para usted, que sabe aprovechar su tiempo libre.

En CASCADA tomamos su diversión en serio.

Valor (*): $199.500/persona enero, febrero, marzo.

Incluye: Pasaje aéreo Stgo-Concepción-Stgo, transporte terrestre, comidas, alojamiento en carpas, equipos y guías profesionales.

(*) Descuentos a grupos sobre 8 personas.

Sergio Andrade y Alejandro Astorga son los experimentados guías de Cascada; ambos han descendido en balsa el río BíoBío por más de seis años.

CASCADA

NATURE EXPEDITIONS

Orrego Luco 054 Fono: 2327214

(Revista del Domingo de El Mercurio, Chile)

Responda en inglés

(*a*) How long does this adventure holiday last?

(*b*) When does the plane leave Santiago?

(*c*) When does it return to Santiago?

(*d*) What does the holiday include?

(*e*) Are there any special discounts?

5 Your friend is flying to Chile from Sao Paulo, Brazil, where he had to do some business. He has asked you to meet him at the airport, so you want to make sure you are there on time. Check the flight details in the box below.

LLEGAN: HOY

PROCEDENCIAS	VUELO	COMPAÑÍA	LLEGA
GUAYAQUIL	041	ECUATORIANA	15.30
MENDOZA	201	LADECO	17.30
MONTEVIDEO-BUENOS AIRES	140	LAN CHILE	19.15
MONTEVIDEO-BUENOS AIRES	350	LADECO	19.30
MIAMI-BOGOTÁ-GUAYAQUIL	301	LADECO	21.30
SAO PAULO	173	LAN CHILE	21.55

(Diario La Segunda, Santiago, Chile)

Responda en español

(*a*) ¿En qué vuelo llega su amigo?

(*b*) ¿En qué compañía viaja?

(*c*) ¿A qué hora llega?

 6 Guillermo, someone you met in Santiago, would like to go to Mendoza in Argentina, across the Andes from Chile. He is not sure how best to travel there, so he asks advice from his friend Carlos. Listen to their conversation, or read the transcript on page 270, then answer the questions below. These key words will help you:

---

me gustaría *I would like*	**veces** *times*
si en bus o . . . *whether by bus or . . .*	**pasaje** (m) *fare*
mira *look*	**te puedo recomendar** *I can recommend to you*
muchísimo más *very much more*	**Te los puedo dar.** *I can give them to you.*

¿Verdadero o falso?

(*a*) Carlos recomienda el bus porque el viaje es más barato.
(*b*) El bus demora dieciséis horas.
(*c*) El pasaje en bus no es caro.
(*d*) El hotel Plaza está en la calle principal.

—— Imágenes de Hispanoamérica ——

El transporte en Hispanoamérica

In the passage which follows, you will read about long-distance transport in Latin America. Study the key words before you read, then check your understanding by answering the questions which follow.

países de habla hispana (m, pl) *Spanish-speaking countries*	**utilizar** *to use*
varía *it varies*	**llevan** *they have*
por carretera *by road*	**asientos reservados** (m, pl) *reserved seats*
suele ser *it is usually*	**cómodo** *comfortable*
por ferrocarril *by railway*	**tiempo de vacaciones** (m) *holiday time*
red ferroviaria (f) *rail network*	
por esta razón *for this reason*	**viajar** *to travel*
viajes de larga distancia (m, pl) *long-distance journeys*	**por lo que** *so*
	con antelación *in advance*
la mayoría de la gente *most people*	**llamado** *called*

América es un gran continente, y el transporte en los países de habla hispana varía entre lo más primitivo y lo más moderno y sofisticado. En general, predomina el transporte por carretera, que suele ser más rápido y más eficiente que el transporte por ferrocarril. La mayoría de los países hispanoamericanos no tiene una red ferroviaria importante. Argentina es una excepción. En otros países, en México y Chile por ejemplo, la red ferroviaria es mucho más reducida y presenta grandes deficiencias. Por esta razón, en los viajes de larga distancia, la mayoría de la gente prefiere utilizar el autobús o el avión.

En algunos países, entre ellos México, Chile, Argentina, existe un excelente servicio de autobuses de larga distancia, a precios bastante económicos. En México, por ejemplo, hay un servicio de autobuses (llamados también **camiones** en México) de primera clase que llevan aire acondicionado y baño (llamado también **lavabo** o **sanitario**). Este servicio, con asientos reservados, es mucho más cómodo que el servicio de segunda clase. En tiempo de vacaciones, mucha gente viaja en autobús, por lo que es necesario reservar los asientos con antelación.

Responda en inglés

(a) How do most people travel in Latin America?

(b) What does the text say about first-class long-distance buses in Mexico.

(c) What do you need to do during holiday time if you want to travel by bus? Why?

Accommodation

The quality of hotels in Latin America varies enormously. In large cities such as Mexico City, Caracas, Bogotá, Santiago de Chile or Buenos Aires, there are hotels of different categories. Some are excellent, although relatively expensive. Three-star hotels are adequate and relatively cheap, and they normally have a bathroom and hot water. In some countries they may also have air-conditioning. In hotels, breakfast is normally not included. If you are not sure what you are getting for your money, don't be afraid to ask, for example: **¿Tiene baño / agua caliente / aire acondicionado la habitación?** (*Has the room got a bathroom / hot water / air conditioning?*), **¿Puedo ver la habitación?** (*Can I see the room?*).

In small towns, the choice is more limited and in some places you may not find medium-priced hotels, in which case you may want to try **una pensión** or **un hospedaje**. These are family-run boarding houses, often clean, safe and inexpensive, although they may not have the comforts you are used to, and you will probably have to share the bathroom with other guests. Sometimes they include breakfast.

One final word of warning. Hotels in Latin America often do not answer letters requesting reservations, although once a reservation has been made, personally or on the phone, this is usually kept. In any case, in the capital cities you will always find an official tourist office which will help you make a reservation, a service which is normally free.

9

UN RECADO
A message

In this unit you will learn how to

- refer to events which are past and complete
- ask to speak to someone on the phone and identify yourself
- leave messages
- say how long ago something happened

Diálogos

1 ¿Cuándo hizo la reserva?

Dennis Clerk has come to Chile on business. He arrives at the hotel Plaza, where his friend Barbara Butler has booked a room for him.

Dennis Clerk   Buenas tardes. Mi nombre es Dennis Clerk. Tengo una habitación reservada.

Recepcionista   Perdone, ¿puede repetir su nombre, por favor?

Dennis Clerk   Dennis Clerk. C-l-e-r-k. Clerk.

Recepcionista   Un momentito por favor. ¿Cuándo hizo la reserva?

Dennis Clerk   Bueno, no la hice yo. Una amiga, la señorita Barbara Butler, reservó la habitación por teléfono, hace una semana más o menos.

Recepcionista   Ah sí, aquí está. Tiene la habitación ochenta y cinco. ¿Podría llenar esta ficha, si es tan amable?

Dennis Clerk   Sí, cómo no.

¿Cuándo hizo . . .? *When did you make . . .?*	**más o menos** *more or less, about*
hice *I made*	**¿Podría llenar . . .?** *Could you fill in . . .?*
una amiga reservó la habitación *a friend booked the room*	**ficha** (f) *registration form*
por teléfono *over the telephone*	**si es tan amable** *if you would be so kind*
hace una semana *a week ago*	**cómo no** *certainly*

Responda en inglés

(a)   When did Barbara book the room for Dennis Clerk?

(b)   Did she book it in person?

Notas explicativas

Talking about the past

Observe the following past tense forms:

hice, from **hacer** (*to do, to make*) *I did* or *I made*; **hizo**, from **hacer** = *you, he, she, it did* or *made*; **reservó**, from **reservar** (*to book, to reserve*) = *you, he, she booked* or *reserved*. More on this under **Notas gramaticales**.

Emphatic use of subject pronouns

Notice the position of **yo** (*I*) in the following example.

No la hice **yo**.   *I didn't make it myself.*

Subject pronouns are sometimes placed at the end of a sentence in order to show emphasis.

Saying how long ago something happened

Una amiga reservó la   *A friend booked the room over the*
habitación por teléfono   *telephone about a week ago.*
hace una semana más o menos.

Compare the use here of **hace** with a verb in the past tense, (**reservó**, *booked*) with the construction you learned in Unit 8: **hace** + time phrase + **que** + verb in the present tense (e.g. **Hace una semana que estamos aquí.** *We have been here for a week.*). With a verb in the present tense, **hace** translates into English as *for*; with a verb in the past tense it translates into English as *ago*.

Expressing approximation

Más o menos   *about, more or less*

This is a frequently used phrase in Spanish, especially in Latin America, where language tends to be less categorical than in English. Approximation is often also expressed with the word **unos**, e.g. **hace unos cinco días** (*about five days ago*).

Llenar una ficha (*to fill in a registration form*)

In Spain, **rellenar** seems to be more frequent in this context.

2 ¿Quiere dejar algún recado?

Dennis Clerk telephones señora Patricia Miranda, a Chilean businesswoman, to make an appointment to see her.

Recepcionista	Seguros Iberoamérica, buenos días.
Dennis Clerk	Buenos días. Quiero el anexo dos cinco cero, por favor.
Recepcionista	Un momentito. (*The receptionist puts him through to extension 250.*)
Secretaria	¿Aló?
Dennis Clerk	Buenos días, quisiera hablar con la señora Patricia Miranda, por favor.
Secretaria	La señora Miranda salió a almorzar con

	un cliente. Va a volver a las cuatro. ¿Quiere dejar algún recado?
Dennis Clerk	Sí, por favor dígale que llamó Dennis Clerk. Llegué ayer a Santiago y estoy en el hotel Santiago Park Plaza. La voy a llamar a las cuatro y media.
Secretaria	Muy bien, señor Clerk. Le daré su recado.

---

seguro (m) *insurance*
anexo (m) *extension* (Chile)
¿Aló? *Hello?* (on the telephone, Chile)
salió *she went out*
almorzar *to have lunch*
¿Quiere dejar algún recado? *Do you want to leave a message?*

dígale que . . . *tell her that . . .*
llamó *he called*
llegué *I arrived*
ayer *yesterday*
llamar *to call*
le daré *I will give her*

Responda en inglés

(a) Where is señora Miranda?
(b) What message does Dennis Clerk leave for her?

Notas explicativas

Dígale . . . (*Tell him/her . . .*)

Por favor dígale que llamó
Dennis Clerk.

Please tell her that
Dennis Clerk called.

Diga (*tell, say*), is an imperative or command form derived from **decir** (*to tell, to say*). Notice that the pronoun **le** (*her* or *him*), is attached to the imperative, and that this adds an accent. For the formation and use of imperatives see Unit 12.

La extensión (*extension*)

Most Latin American countries use the word **la extensión** for a telephone extension. Chileans use **el anexo**. Argentina uses the word **el interno**.

Answering the phone

¿Aló?, *Hello?* (on the telephone). This word is used in some Latin American countries only, for example Chile and Peru. In Mexico, most people answer the phone with the word **¿bueno?** while Argentinians normally say **¿hola?**

Reading telephone numbers

Telephone numbers in Spanish are read out as pairs of figures or as single figures, for example: **extensión** (or **anexo**, in Chile) **dos-cincuenta** or **dos-cinco-cero** (250), **teléfono seis-tres-nueve-seis-nueve-cero-siete** or **seis-treinta y nueve-sesenta y nueve-cero siete** (6396907).

3 Ya volvió

At 4.30 p.m. Dennis Clerk telephones señora Miranda again. The receptionist puts him through to her secretary.

Secretaria	¿Aló?
Dennis Clerk	Buenas tardes. ¿Podría decirme si volvió la señora Miranda?
Secretaria	Sí, ya volvió. ¿De parte de quién?
Dennis Clerk	De parte de Dennis Clerk.
Secretaria	Ah sí, un momentito señor Clerk.

¿Podría decirme . . .?	*Could you tell me . . .?*	**ya**	*yet, already*
si *if*		**¿De parte de quién?**	*Who is calling?*
volvió *she returned*		**de parte de . . .**	*this is . . ., from . . .*

4 Fue muy agradable

On Dennis Clerk's first meeting with señora Miranda, they talk about his journey.

Señora Miranda	Encantada de conocerlo, señor Clerk. Bienvenido a Chile.
Dennis Clerk	Muchas gracias.

Señora Miranda	¿Cuándo llegó?
Dennis Clerk	Llegué el miércoles en la noche.
Señora Miranda	¿Y qué tal el viaje?
Dennis Clerk	Fue muy agradable, aunque un poco largo.
Señora Miranda	¿Es la primera vez que viene a Santiago?
Dennis Clerk	No, estuve aquí hace cinco años y me gustó mucho.
Señora Miranda	Me alegro.

¿Cuándo llegó? *When did you arrive?*
hace cinco años *five years ago*
¿Y qué tal el viaje? *And how was your journey?*
Fue muy agradable *It was very pleasant*

un poco *a little*
estuve aquí *I was here*
me gustó *I liked it*
me alegro (alegrarse) *I am glad (to be glad)*

Responda en inglés

(a) When did Dennis Clerk arrive in Santiago?

(b) Is this the first time he has visited Santiago?

——— Notas explicativas ———

Exchanging greetings with people you meet for the first time

Encantada de conocerlo.   *Pleased to meet you.*

Here a woman speaks to a man. A man speaking to a woman would say: **Encantado de conocerla**. This is a very formal greeting, appropriate for the context. A shortened version of this would be **Encantado/a** or simply **Mucho gusto**, which does not change for masculine or feminine (see Unit 2). An informal greeting, used more often among young people, is **Hola** (*Hello*).

Welcome

Bienvenido, *Welcome* (to a man). To a woman, you would say **Bienvenida**.

🔑 – Frases y expresiones importantes –

- Referring to events which are past and complete

  ¿Cuándo hizo la reserva? *When did you make the booking?*
  No la hice yo. *I didn't make it myself.*
  La Sra. Miranda salió a *Señora Miranda went out for*
  almorzar. *lunch.*
  Llegué ayer a Santiago. *I arrived in Santiago yesterday.*

- Asking to speak to someone on the phone and identifying yourself

  Quisiera hablar con la *I would like to speak to*
  Sra. Patricia Miranda. *señora Patricia Miranda.*
  ¿De parte de quién? *Who is speaking?*
  De parte de Dennis Clerk. *This is Dennis Clerk.*

- Other phrases used when asking to speak to someone on the phone

  ¿Está el señor / la señora *Is señor / señora Torres in?*
  Torres?
  ¿Podría hablar con la *Could I speak to*
  señorita Lara? *señorita Lara?*

- Leaving messages

  ¿Quiere dejar algún recado? *Do you want to leave a message?*
  Por favor, dígale que llamó *Please tell her that Dennis Clerk*
  Dennis Clerk. *called.*

- Saying how long ago something happened

  Una amiga reservó la *A friend booked the room*
  habitación hace una semana. *a week ago.*
  Estuve aquí hace cinco años. *I was here five years ago.*

- Other useful words and phrases used to talk about the past

  ayer *yesterday*
  ayer por la mañana / tarde *yesterday morning / afternoon*
  anteayer / antes de ayer *the day before yesterday* (standard)
  antier *the day before yesterday*
  (used in some Latin American
  countries, e.g. Mexico, Colombia.)

  la semana pasada *last week*
  el mes / año pasado *last month / year*
  el lunes / martes pasado *last Monday / Tuesday*
  anoche *last night*

en 1980 / 1992	*in 1980 / 1992*
hace mucho / poco tiempo	*a long / short time ago*

Notas gramaticales

1 *Looking back*

The simple past tense

To refer to events which happened and were completed in the past, as in *A friend booked the room about a week ago*, we use the simple past tense, also known as the preterite tense.

In Latin America, this tense is also used to refer to events which happened in the recent past, for example:

Ya almorcé.	*I have already had lunch.*
Hoy trabajamos mucho.	*We have worked a lot today.*

In Spain, however, another tense, the perfect tense, is normally used to refer to recent past events:

Ya he almorzado.	*I have already had lunch.*
Hoy hemos trabajado mucho.	*We have worked a lot today.*

This tense is also heard in Latin America but its usage is much more restricted. More on this in Unit 12.

Formation of the simple past

There are two sets of endings for this tense, one for **-ar** verbs and another one for **-er** and **-ir** verbs.

reservar	*to book*
reserv**é**	*I booked*
reserv**aste**	*you booked* (fam, sing)
reserv**ó**	*you booked* (pol, sing), *he, she booked*
reserv**amos**	*we booked*
reserv**aron**	*you booked* (pl), *they booked*

Note that the first person plural, **reservamos**, is the same as for the present tense (see Unit 3). Note also that **vosotros reservasteis**, *you booked* (pl, fam), used in Spain, has been omitted, as this is not normally heard in Latin America.

volver	*to return*
volv**í**	*I returned*
volv**iste**	*you returned* (fam, sing)
volv**ió**	*you returned* (pol, sing), *he, she returned*
volv**imos**	*we returned*
volv**ieron**	*you returned* (pl), *they returned*

Again, the plural familiar form **vosotros volvisteis** (*you returned*) has been omitted here. **-Ir** verbs, e.g. **salir** (*to go out*), have the same endings: **salí, saliste, salió**, etc.

Here are some further examples of the use of the simple past tense with regular verbs:

-ar verbs

Reservé dos boletos.	*I booked two tickets.*
Ellos viajaron al sur.	*They travelled to the south.*

-er and **-ir** verbs

Él volvió ayer.	*He returned yesterday.*
El tren salió a la hora.	*The train left on time.*

Irregular past tense forms

Some verbs form the simple past tense in an irregular way. Here is a list of the most important.

estar	(*to be*)	estuve, estuviste, estuvo, estuvimos, estuvieron
tener	(*to have*)	tuve, tuviste, tuvo, tuvimos, tuvieron
decir	(*to say, to tell*)	dije, dijiste, dijo, dijimos, dijeron
hacer	(*to do, to make*)	hice, hiciste, hizo, hicimos, hicieron
venir	(*to come*)	vine, viniste, vino, vinimos, vinieron
traer	(*to bring*)	traje, trajiste, trajo, trajimos, trajeron
ir	(*to go*)	fui, fuiste, fue, fuimos, fueron
ser	(*to be*)	fui, fuiste, fue, fuimos, fueron

Note that the past tense of **ser** is the same as for **ir**.

Here are some examples of the use of the simple past with irregular verbs, all taken from the previous dialogues.

¿Cuándo hizo la reserva?	*When did you make the reservation?*
No la hice yo.	*I didn't make it myself.*
Fue muy agradable.	*It was very pleasant.*
Estuve aquí hace cinco años.	*I was here five years ago.*

For other irregular past tense forms, see the table starting on page 276.

Actividades

1   Write a dialogue based on this situation, using dialogue 1 as a model.

- You arrive in a hotel in a Latin American country. At the reception desk you identify yourself and say that you have a reservation.
- The receptionist asks you to repeat your name. You do so and spell your surname for him.
- He wants to know when you made the reservation. Explain that this was not made by yourself, but by your secretary who phoned directly from your home town (give the name of the town) about five days ago.
- The receptionist finally finds the reservation. He's given you room 50 on the fifth floor. Before giving you the key, he asks you to fill in the registration form.

mi secretaria	*my secretary*	**desde**	*from*
directamente	*directly*		

2   What would you say, in Spanish, in these situations?

(a)   You are in a hotel in Santiago, Chile, and the telephone rings in your room. You lift up the receiver and say . . .?

(b)   You telephone Viña San Sebastián in Chile, a company you are doing business with, and ask for **extension 2552**.

(c) The secretary on extension 2552 answers the phone. Ask to speak to señor Juan Miguel García.

(d) The secretary asks who is speaking. Identify yourself.

(e) You meet señor Juan Miguel García for the first time. Say how pleased you are to meet him.

(f) Back at your hotel, you telephone señorita Elena Alonso, an acquaintance of yours. She is not at home at the moment, and the person who answers the phone asks if you want to leave a message. Ask them to tell señorita Alonso that you phoned and to inform her that you arrived in Santiago two days ago. Say which hotel you are staying at (**Hotel Plaza**) and give the room number (**habitación 50**).

 3 At the office of señor Solís, a businessman from Santiago, Chile, the receptionist has taken two messages for him. The first is from señora Carmen Puig, from Venezuela and the second from señorita Marilú Pérez, a Chilean. Listen to the two messages, or read the transcripts on page 271, then note down each message in English. First, look at these key words:

mensaje (m)	*message*	**urgentemente**	*urgently*
recado (m)	*message*	**vino**	*he/she came*
reunión (f)	*meeting*		

4 Back in his country, Dennis Clerk receives a postcard from someone he met in Chile. Unfortunately, it got a bit smudged. Here
are the words you need to fill in. Put them in the right order in
the gaps below.

(a)	estuvimos	(e)	gustó
(b)	levanté	(f)	fue
(c)	fui	(g)	tomé
(d)	senté	(h)	entramos

Querido Dennis:

Me alegro mucho de haberte conocido y espero que vuelvas a Chile el año próximo,
como me prometiste. Tengo recuerdos
muy bonitos de tu estadía en Chile. Para
mí _____ muy especial.

Ayer en la tarde _____ con Mónica al
café donde nos conocimos. Allí _____ hasta
las cinco de la tarde. Después Mónica
y yo _____ a un cine a ver una película
inglesa que nos _____ mucho. Hoy me _____
muy tarde, _____ un café y después me
_____ frente a mi escritorio a escribirte
esta tarjeta.

Te abraza

María Soledad

querido/a (m/f) *dear*	**nos conocimos** *we met*
de haberte conocido *to have met you*	**película** (f) *film*
	después *afterwards*
espero que vuelvas *I hope you come back*	**escritorio** (m) *desk*
	tarjeta (f) *postcard*
prometiste *you promised*	**te abraza (abrazar)** *love (to embrace)*
recuerdos (m, pl) *memories*	
estadía (f) *stay* (in Spain, **la estancia**)	

5 What questions would you need to ask to get the following replies?

(a) Llegué ayer en la tarde.

(b) El viaje fue bastante tranquilo.

(c) Sí, la señorita Alonso ya volvió.

(d) No, no es la primera vez que vengo. Estuve en Santiago hace un año y medio.

(e) Sí, me gustó mucho Chile.

(f) Sí, ya cené.

6 Marilú, a Chilean, was asked about her last holiday. Listen to what she says or read the transcript on page 271, then answer the questions below. First, look at this new vocabulary:

costa (f) *coast*	**tan puro** *so clean (pure)*
disfrutamos *we enjoyed it*	**harto** *a lot*
ya que *as*	**nadar** *to swim*
maravillosas *wonderful*	**llenos de energía** *full of energy*
aire (m) *air*	

Responda en inglés

(a) Where did Marilú go during the holidays?

(b) Where did they stay?

(c) How does she describe the place?

(d) How does she express the following: *we went out a lot, we sunbathed, we swam, we played some sports*?

7 A Latin American friend asks you about your last holiday. Answer his questions using real or imaginary information.

(a) ¿Dónde fuiste de vacaciones?
(b) ¿Fuiste solo/a o acompañado/a?
(c) ¿Dónde te quedaste?
(d) ¿Cuánto tiempo estuviste allí?
(e) ¿Qué hiciste durante tus vacaciones?

—— Imágenes de Hispanoamérica ——

The political scene

Ever since independence from Spain in the first half of the nine-teenth century, most Latin American countries have known long periods of political turmoil, and even the most stable and democratic nations, like Chile and Uruguay in South America, have had their share of political instability. In the seventies and eighties, the internal repression exercised by some of Latin America's military dictatorships, especially in countries like Nicaragua, Chile and Argentina, caused great international concern. Internal opposition and pressure from abroad finally brought change to these countries. Chile and Argentina, for instance, were able to elect democratic gov-ernments. But Nicaragua still had a long way to go. The **sandinistas**, a former guerrilla group, which took power after the fall of the dictator **Somoza**, fought a long war with the **contras**, a counter-revolutionary group supported by the United States. Elections in 1990 restored peace to the country, although economic difficulties have prevented this nation from achieving real political stability.

Mexico has been an isolated case in Latin America. After the Revolution of 1910 brought about by repression, poverty and social unrest, the different factions led by the National Revolutionary Party, now known as the Institutional Revolutionary Party (PRI), came together and brought stability to the country. The PRI has governed Mexico to this day and political stability has not been broken.

Guerrilla warfare

At the start of the nineties all Latin American countries, except Cuba, had democratically elected regimes although revolutionary groups are still active in a few countries. Guerrilla warfare in Latin America, which began as a form of pressure to bring about political changes, reached it peak in the sixties, after the revolutionary forces led by Castro came to power in Cuba in 1959. One of the areas most affected by armed struggle was Central America, especially El Salvador, where government-supported forces fought a 12-year war with revolutionary groups, in which thousands of innocent people were killed. Peace negotiations between the guerrillas and the government finally brought peace to El Salvador in December 1992. The brief passage, overleaf, from a Chilean newspaper gives precisely this news. Study the key words before you read the text, then answer the questions which follow.

Che Guevara, símbolo de la revolución en los años sesenta

guerra (f)	*war*	**vida** (f)	*life*
concluyó	*it ended*	**dejó**	*it left*
fecha (f)	*date*	**lisiado**	*disabled*
Naciones Unidas (f, pl)	*United Nations*	**huyó**	*escaped*
cumplimiento (m)	*enforcement*	**al extranjero**	*abroad*
Acuerdos de Paz (m, pl)	*peace agreements*	**iniciar**	*to start*
poniendo fin	*putting an end*	**etapa** (f)	*stage*
		esperanza (f)	*hope*
		alegría	*joy*

El Salvador: La Paz Negociada

LA GUERRA CIVIL EN EL SALVADOR concluyó oficialmente el martes 15 de diciembre, fecha límite determinada por Naciones Unidas para el cumplimiento de los Acuerdos de Paz, poniendo fin a 12 años de violentos conflictos. Costó la vida a más de 75 mil personas, dejó más de 10 mil lisiados de guerra y una economía devastada. Más de medio millón de salvadoreños, en una nación de tan sólo 5 millones de habitantes, huyó al extranjero. El Salvador inicia una nueva etapa de su historia, con 'esperanza y alegría', declararon personalidades de todos los frentes.

(Diario El Mercurio, Chile)

Responda en inglés

(a) When did the civil war officially end in El Salvador?
(b) How many people died in the conflict?
(c) How many people escaped abroad?

The struggle for development

In Europe and the United States, Latin America has been better known for its volatile politics than for its long struggle to develop economically. In recent years however, political stability in certain countries, and the adoption of new economic policies not unlike those applied in Great Britain, Spain or the United States, have helped to open Latin American markets to world trade and have brought a certain degree of economic growth. Chile was the first Latin

American country to apply economic liberalism, later to be followed by Mexico, Argentina and other South American countries. Privatisation, reduction of the state sector, foreign investment and exports have helped these countries to tidy up their economies and create new wealth. However, the gap between the rich and the poor has not closed, and in some cases it seems to have widened. A new class of entrepreneurs seems to be taking over, with little regard for the plight of the poorer sectors of society, who have seen social services reduced or cut to a minimum. But there are those who realise that unless this new accumulated wealth is spread more evenly, Latin America will not be able to achieve real economic growth and political stability. As in other parts of the world, Latin Americans are becoming more pragmatic and less prone to embrace economic or political dogma whole-heartedly.

10

VIVÍA EN ESPAÑA

I used to live in Spain

In this unit you will learn how to

- say what you used to do or were doing
- describe places and people you knew in the past
- say what you are doing now

Diálogos

1 ¿Qué hacías en Barcelona?

Marta Rodríguez is an Argentinian who used to live in Spain. Now she has returned to her native Buenos Aires. At a party she meets José Luis, also from Buenos Aires. In this conversation, Marta tells José Luis about her life in Spain.

José Luis Hola, ¿cómo te **llamás**?
Marta Me llamo Marta, ¿y **vos**?
José Luis Yo me llamo José Luis. ¿**Sos** de Buenos Aires?
Marta Sí, soy de acá, pero recién volví. Vivía en España. Estuve allá varios años.

José Luis	¡No me digas! Yo estuve en España hace un par de años y me gustó mucho. ¿Dónde vivías **vos**?
Marta	En Barcelona. **¿Conocés** Barcelona?
José Luis	Sí, pasé una semana allá. Es una ciudad muy linda. ¿Y **vos**, qué hacías en Barcelona?
Marta	Trabajaba con un colega argentino. Yo soy psicóloga. ¿Y **vos**, qué **hacés**?
José Luis	Recién terminé mis estudios en la universidad. Estudié arquitectura y ahora estoy buscando trabajo.
Marta	¡Qué tengas suerte!
José Luis	Gracias.

¿Cómo te llamás? *What is your name?* (Arg)
vos *you* (fam, sing, Arg)
sos *you are* (fam, sing, Arg)
acá *here*
recién volví *I have just returned*
vivía *I used to live, I was living*
allá *there*
varios *several*
¡no me digas! *you don't say!*
un par de años *a couple of years*
vivías *you used to live, you were living* (fam, sing)
conocés *you know* (fam, sing, Arg)

pasé (pasar) *I spent (to spend)*
¿Qué hacías? *What did you do? What were you doing?* (fam, sing)
trabajaba *I used to work*
psicóloga (f) *psychologist*
¿Qué hacés? *What do you do?* (fam, sing, Argentina)
recién terminé *I have just finished*
estudios (m, pl) *studies*
arquitectura (f) *architecture*
Estoy buscando trabajo. *I am looking for work.*
¡Que tengas suerte! *Good luck!*

Responda en inglés

(*a*) When was José Luis in Barcelona?
(*b*) What did Marta do in Barcelona?

Notas explicativas

Argentinian pronunciation

The introductory dialogues in Units 10 and 11 are set in Argentina and they have been recorded by Argentinians. The Argentinian accent is very distinctive so, if you are using the cassette, pay special attention to it, particularly to the pronunciation of the letters **ll** and **y**, as in **llamas**, **yo**, which are pronounced much like the **j** in *John* or the **s** in *pleasure*. This feature of Argentinian pronunciation is also found in neighbouring Uruguay.

As in Chile, Venezuela, Cuba, and generally in the Caribbean, Argentinians tend to pronounce final **s** (e.g. **buenos**) and **s** before a consonant (e.g. **usted**) like an aspirated **h**, so **buenos** and **usted** become more like **buenoh** and **uhted**. This is not a general rule, however, and you will notice that the same speaker may sometimes substitute the **s** by an aspirated **h** or pronounce it fully. The latter may occur in more deliberate, formal speech.

In parts of Argentina, specially in the west and north, the **r** is not rolled in words such as **río** (*river*) and **perro** (*dog*). What you hear, instead, sounds like **rj**.

In the dialogues, notice the change in the accentuation of verbs in the second person singular of the present tense, for example **llamás**, **trabajás**, instead of the standard **llamas**, **trabajas**. Notice also the non-standard pronoun **vos** instead of **tú**, a feature which is characteristic of Argentinian Spanish. These and other peculiarities of Argentinian usage, most of which can also be heard in neighbouring Uruguay, will be explained in the notes below. You don't have to learn these non-standard forms, but you need to be aware of them, as they are used by all Argentinians. Non-standard forms in the dialogues in this unit are shown in bold, so that you are able to recognise them more easily.

The use of *vos* (*you* (*fam*)) in Argentina

Argentinians do not normally use the subject pronoun **tú** (*you* fam, sing). Instead, they use the word **vos**, which is an old Spanish form, no longer heard in Spain today. **Vos** is used with all tenses and, except in the present tense, verb endings for the second person singular are the same as for **tú**. Here are some examples:

vos fuiste	*you went* (fam, sing)
vos irás	*you will go* (fam, sing)
vos vas a ir	*you are going to go* (fam, sing)

Other subject pronouns, for example **yo**, **usted**, **él**, **ella**, etc. do not change.

The word **vos** is also heard in other parts of Latin America, such as Uruguay, Costa Rica, Colombia and Chile, but its use is restricted to certain regions or to specific social groups. In Argentina, it is more the norm.

Changes in the accentuation of verbs in Argentina

In Argentina, the use of **vos** in the second person singular of the present tense requires a change in the normal accentuation of the verb. Compare the standard on the left with Argentinian usage on the right:

	-ar verbs	
¿Cómo te llamas?	¿Cómo te llamás?	*What is your name?*

	-er verbs	
¿Qué haces?	¿Qué hacés?	*What do you do?*
¿Conoces Barcelona?	¿Conocés Barcelona?	*Do you know Barcelona?*

	-ir verbs	
¿Dónde vives?	¿Dónde vivís?	*Where do you live?*

(See also dialogue 2.)

Sos (*you are* (*fam*)) in Argentina

Eres, as in **¿Eres de Buenos Aires?** (*Are you from Buenos Aires?*), changes in Argentina to **sos**: **¿Sos de Buenos Aires?**

Talking about what you used to do or were doing

In dialogue 1 there are some examples of a new tense, the imperfect, which is used to refer to what you used to do or were doing. Look at the following examples and then consider the explanations under **Notas gramaticales**.

Trabajaba con un colega.	*I used to work with a colleague.*
¿Qué hacías en Barcelona?	*What were you doing in Barcelona?*
Vivía en España.	*I was living / used to live in Spain.*

Acá y allá (*here and there*)

Acá (*here*) is less precise than **aquí**. This word, like **allá** for *there*, is much more frequent in Latin America than in Spain.

Referring to an action which has just finished

Recién volví.   *I have just returned.*
Recién terminé.   *I have just finished.*

This usage of the word **recién**, short for **recientemente** (*recently*), is Latin American. In Spain, **recién** is only used before past participles, e.g. **El pan está recién hecho** (*The bread has just been made*). To say that they have just done something, Spaniards normally use the construction **acabar de** + infinitive, e.g. **acabo de llegar** (*I have just arrived*). This standard construction is also used by Latin Americans, though perhaps less frequently.

Referring to an action which is taking place at the moment of speaking

Estoy buscando trabajo.   *I am looking for work.*

You will find another example of this in dialogue 2 and an explanation under **Notas gramaticales**.

2 Estaba frente a la playa

Marta describes the place where she used to live.

José Luis   ¿En qué parte de Barcelona vivías?
Marta   Bueno, yo no vivía en la ciudad misma. Vivía en Sitges, un lugar muy lindo que está a media hora de Barcelona. Viajaba a Barcelona en tren los días de semana. Los fines de semana los pasaba en Sitges. Compartía un departamento con una amiga catalana. Era una chica bastante joven, y era muy simpática. Nos llevábamos muy bien.
José Luis   ¿No **extrañás** todo eso?
Marta   Bueno, la verdad es que estoy contenta de estar otra vez en Buenos Aires, pero sí, a veces extraño la vida allá. Teníamos un departamento muy agradable. No era muy grande, pero estaba frente a la playa y tenía una vista maravillosa.
José Luis   Y ahora, ¿dónde **vivís**?
Marta   Estoy viviendo en la casa de mis padres en Villa Devoto,

pero pienso alquilar un departamento más cerca del
centro.

José Luis   ¡Ojalá que tengas suerte!
Marta   Gracias.

---

estaba *it was*	**la verdad es que . . .** *the truth is*
misma (f) *itself*	*that . . .*
viajaba (viajar) *I used to travel (to*	**otra vez** *again*
travel)	**teníamos** *we had, we used to have*
días de semana (m, pl) *weekdays*	**tenía** *it had*
pasaba (pasar) *I used to spend (to*	**vista** (f) *view*
spend)	**maravillosa** (f) *wonderful*
compartía (compartir) *I was shar-*	**¿Dónde vivís?** *Where do you live?*
ing (to share)	*(fam, sing, Arg)*
catalana (f) *Catalan, Catalonian*	**estoy viviendo** *I am living*
era *she/he/it was*	**Villa Devoto** *a district of Buenos*
chica (f) *girl*	*Aires*
simpática (f) *nice*	**alquilar** *to rent*
¿no extrañás? (extrañar) *don't*	
you miss? (to miss) (Arg)	

Responda en inglés

(*a*)   How did Marta travel from Sitges to Barcelona?
(*b*)   What was her flatmate like?

Notas explicativas

Referring to what you used to do and describing people and things you knew in the past

There are several examples of the use of the imperfect tense in dialogue 2, referring to what people used to do or simply describing something or somebody known in the past. Here are two of those examples:

Viajaba a Barcelona en tren los días de semana.	*I used to travel to Barcelona by train during the week.*
Era muy simpática.	*She was very nice.*

Look at the explanations under **Notas gramaticales** and then make a list of all imperfect tense verbs in dialogues 1 and 2.

El departamento, el apartamento (*apartment, flat*)

El departamento is used in Argentina and other Latin American countries, for example Uruguay, Chile, Peru and Mexico. Another word you will hear frequently in some Latin American countries, for example Colombia, is **el apartamento**. This and **el piso** are the terms normally used in Spain.

Argentinian accentuation

Notice Argentinian accentuation in ¿**no extrañás** . . .? (*Don't you miss . . .?*). The standard is ¿**no extrañas?**

¡Ojalá! (*Let's hope so!*)

The interjection ¡**ojalá!** can be used by itself or within a phrase:

¡Ojalá que tengas suerte!   *Let's hope you are lucky!*

You will find more information on the use of **ojalá** in Unit 13.

🔑 – Frases y expresiones importantes –

- Saying what you used to do or were doing
  Vivía en España. *I used to live / was living in Spain.*
  ¿Qué hacías en Barcelona? *What were you doing in Barcelona.*
  Trabajaba con un colega. *I used to work with a colleague.*

- Describing places and people you knew in the past
  Estaba frente a la playa. *It was opposite the beach.*
  No era muy grande. *It wasn't very big.*
  Era muy simpática. *She was very nice.*

- Other words and phrases used in the description of people you knew in the past:

  Era alto / bajo / delgado / *He was tall / short / slim /*
  gordo / trigueño / *fat / olive-skinned /*
  moreno / rubio. *dark / blond.*
  Era guapo / agradable / *He was good looking / pleasant /*
  inteligente. *intelligent.*
  Era feo. *He was ugly.*
  Era joven / mayor. *He / she was young / old*

Tenía 20 / 30 años.	*He / she was 20 / 30 years old.*
Tenía ojos cafés /	*He/ she had brown / black /*
negros / verdes / azules.	*green / blue eyes.*
Tenía el pelo negro /	*He / she had black / chestnut /*
castaño / rubio / cano	*blonde / grey hair.*
or **canoso.**	

Nota: For present description, simply use **es** (e.g. **es alto**, *he is tall*) or **tiene** (e.g. **tiene ojos verdes**, *he has green eyes*).

● Saying what you are doing now

Estoy buscando trabajo.	*I am looking for work.*
Estoy viviendo en la casa	*I am living in my parents'*
de mis padres.	*house.*

Notas gramaticales

1 The imperfect tense

The imperfect tense is used to say what you used to do or were doing and to describe people, places and things you knew in the past.

Unlike the preterite tense, which you studied in Unit 9, it denotes actions which were incomplete or whose beginning or end is not specified. Compare for instance:

(preterite tense)
    Viví allí durante un año.   *I lived there for a year.*
(imperfect tense)
    En 1992 yo **vivía** allí.   *In 1992 I was living there.*

The first sentence refers to an event which lasted over a definite period of time and ended in the past, therefore the preterite tense or simple past is used. The second sentence focuses on the action itself, *I was living* or *used to live there*. We don't know when the action was completed, therefore the imperfect tense is used.

In descriptive language in general, for instance *she was nice, the apartment was pleasant*, there is no concern for time (except to show that a past experience is being referred to, e.g. **era simpática** as opposed to **es simpática**), so the imperfect tense is used.

Note, however, that this difference between the two tenses in Spanish is not always expressed in English, as English often uses the simple past where Spanish would use the imperfect tense, for example:

Yo trabajaba con un colega.	*I worked / used to work / was working with a colleague.*
El apartamento era agradable.	*The apartment was nice.*

Formation of the imperfect tense

There are two sets of endings for the imperfect tense, one for -**ar** verbs and another for -**er** and -**ir** verbs.

trabajar	*to work*
trabaj**aba**	*I worked/used to work/was working*
trabaj**abas**	*you worked/used to work/were working* (fam, sing)
trabaj**aba**	*you worked/used to work/were working* (pol, sing) *he, she worked/used to work/was working*
trabaj**ábamos**	*we worked/used to work/were working*
trabaj**aban**	*you worked/used to work/were working* (pl) *they worked/used to work/were working*

Note that the first and third person singular share the same endings. Notice also that the plural familiar form **vosotros trabajabais**, which is used in Spain, has been omitted, as this is not normally used in Latin America.

tener	*to have*
ten**ía**	*I had/used to have*
ten**ías**	*you had/used to have* (fam, sing)
ten**ía**	*you had/ used to have* (pol, sing) *he, she had/used to have/*
ten**íamos**	*we had/used to have*
ten**ían**	*you had/used to have (pl)* *they had/used to have*

Note that the first and third person singular share the same endings. Notice also that the familiar plural form **vosotros teníais**, which is used in Spain, has been omitted, as it is not normally used in Latin America. -**Ir** verbs, e.g. **vivir** (*to live*), have the same endings: **vivía**, **vivías**, **vivía**, etc. Here is another example demonstrating the use of the imperfect tense:

Vivíamos en un departamento muy agradable que **estaba** frente al mar. Los fines de semana **nos levantábamos** muy tarde, **desayunábamos** y después **bajábamos** a la playa. En la playa **había** siempre mucha gente que **venía** de Barcelona a pasar el fin de semana, especialmente durante el verano. A partir de octubre, Sitges **era** un lugar muy tranquilo.

bajar	*to go down*	**a partir de**	*starting in*
había	*there were*	**tranquilo**	*quiet*
gente (f)	*people*		

Irregular imperfect forms

There are only three irregular verbs in the imperfect tense:

ir	*to go*
iba	*I went/used to go/was going*
ibas	*you went/used to go/were going* (fam, sing)
iba	*you went/used to go/were going* (pol, sing)
	he, she, it went/used to go/was going
íbamos	*we went/used to go/were going*
iban	*you went/used to go/were going* (pl)
	they went/used to go/were going

ser	*to be*
era	*I was/used to be*
eras	*you were/used to be* (fam, sing)
era	*you were/used to be* (pol, sing)
	he, she, it was/used to be
éramos	*we were/used to be*
eran	*you were/used to be* (pl)
	they were/used to be

ver	*to see*
veía	*I saw/used to see*
veías	*you saw/used to see* (fam, sing)
veía	*you saw/used to see* (pol, sing)
	he, she, it saw/used to see
veíamos	*we saw/used to see*
veían	*you saw/used to see* (pl)
	they saw/used to see

Note that the **vosotros** forms, **ibais**, **erais**, and **veíais** have been omitted, as these are not normally used in Latin America.

Here is an example demonstrating the use of the imperfect tense with irregular verbs:

Yo **veía** a Carmen todos los días. Carmen **era** alta, delgada, de pelo muy negro y ojos cafés. Carmen y yo **íbamos** a la playa a tomar el sol y nadar. Carmen **era** muy linda e inteligente.

| **tomar el sol** | *to sunbathe* | **nadar** | *to swim* |

Notice that before an **i**, **y** changes to **e**: **e inteligente**.

2   Estar + *gerund*

To refer to events which are taking place at the moment of speaking, you can use the simple present tense, e.g. **¿Qué haces?** (*What are you doing?*) or the present continuous, which is formed with the verb **estar** followed by a gerund (words like **buscando**, *looking for*, and **viviendo**, *living*).

Estoy buscando trabajo.	*I am looking for work.*
Estoy viviendo en la casa de mis padres.	*I am living in my parents' house.*

There are two endings for the gerund in Spanish, one for -**ar** verbs and one for -**er** and -**ir** verbs.

-**ar** verbs form the gerund with -**ando**:
| (trabajar) | Estoy trabaj**ando**. | *I am working.* |

-**er** and -**ir** verbs form the gerund with -**iendo**:
| (comer) | Estamos com**iendo**. | *We are eating.* |
| (escribir) | Ellos están escrib**iendo**. | *They are writing.* |

Actividades

1   In the passage below, which is based on dialogues 1 and 2, all the

verbs are missing. Try to complete it with the verbs from the list, without looking at the dialogues.

(a)	pasaba	(g)	se llamaba
(b)	estaba	(h)	tenía
(c)	compartía	(i)	era
(d)	vivían	(j)	vivía
(e)	trabajaba	(k)	gustaba
(f)	había	(l)	viajaba

En 1990, Marta _____ en Sitges y _____ con un colega argentino en Barcelona. Marta _____ a Barcelona en tren los días de semana. Los fines de semana los _____ en Sitges donde _____ un departamento con una amiga catalana. Su amiga _____ Montserrat. El departamento donde ellas _____ no _____ muy grande, pero_____ una vista maravillosa, ya que _____ frente a la playa. A Marta le _____ mucho Sitges, especialmente a partir de octubre, cuando _____ poca gente en el lugar.

2 Overleaf is an extract from a letter written by María Inés, an Argentinian, to a correspondent. María Inés writes about her life in Bariloche, in southern Argentina, before she came to live in Buenos Aires. Read it through, then check your understanding by answering the questions below. Here are some key words:

preguntar	*to ask*	**plata** (f)	*money*
acerca de	*about*	**temporada** (f)	*season*
vida (f)	*life*	**a pesar de que**	*although*
antes de	*before*	**así fue como ...**	*this was how ...*
te conté (contar)	*I told you (to tell)*	**hice mis valijas**	*I packed my suitcases*
lago (m)	*lake*	**paisaje** (m)	*landscape*
ganaba (ganar)	*I used to earn (to earn)*	**aire puro** (m)	*pure air*

Argentinians use the word **la valija** (*suitcase*). Most other countries use the standard word **la maleta**. Notice also Argentinian accentuation in **preguntás** (*you ask*), instead of the standard **preguntas**.

Querido Paul:

En tu última carta me
preguntás acerca de mi vida antes de
venir a Buenos Aires. Bueno, ya te conté
que llegué aquí hace cinco años. Antes
vivía en Bariloche, una ciudad muy linda que está a unos 1.700 kilómetros de
Buenos Aires.

Bariloche es un lugar de
mucho turismo y yo trabajaba como guía
en una agencia de viajes. Vivía en
un departamento muy agradable, frente al
lago. Durante el verano estaba siempre muy
ocupada y ganaba bastante plata, pero a
partir de marzo, cuando terminaba la
temporada de vacaciones, la vida era
muy tranquila y a veces un poco monótona.

Mi familia vivía en Buenos
Aires y los extrañaba, a pesar de que en
Bariloche tenía algunos amigos. Así fue
como un día hice mis valijas y decidí
volver a la capital. Estoy contenta de estar
aquí otra vez, aunque a veces extraño
el paisaje y el aire puro de Bariloche....

---

me preguntás *you ask me*
(standard, **me preguntas**)

Responda en español

(a) ¿Dónde vivía María Inés?
(b) ¿En qué trabajaba?
(c) ¿Cómo era su departamento?
(d) ¿Dónde estaba su departamento?
(e) ¿Cómo era la vida a partir de marzo?
(f) ¿Por qué decidió volver a Buenos Aires?

3 Look at this plan of the flat where María Inés used to live and then answer the questions which follow.

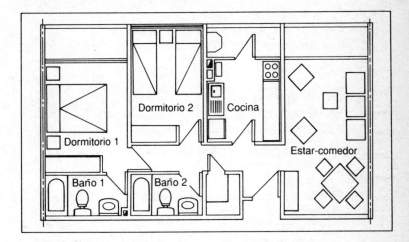

(a) ¿Cuántos dormitorios tenía el departamento?
(b) ¿Cuántos baños tenía?
(c) ¿Dónde estaba la cocina?
(d) ¿Cuántas camas había en el dormitorio uno?

| **estar** (m) | *sitting room* |

4 Now listen to Carlos García, an Argentinian who used to live in São Paulo, Brazil. He talks about his life in that city. If you do not have the cassette, use the transcript on page 272 for reading practice. First look at the key words, then answer the questions below.

¿Siempre has vivido . . . ? *Have you always lived . . . ?*	**casa** (f) *house*
daba clases *I used to teach*	**¿Qué tal eran?** *What were they like?*
pintura (f) *painting*	**extrañaba** *I missed / used to miss*
barrio (m) *district, area*	**como todos los brasileros** *like all Brazilians*
arborizados *with many trees*	
vegetación (f) *vegetation*	**todavía** *still*
vecinos (m, pl) *neighbours*	

¿Verdadero o falso?

(a) Carlos era profesor de pintura.

(b) El barrio de Vila Mariana tenía poca vegetación.

(c) El departamento de Carlos era grande.

(d) Carlos tenía buenos vecinos.

(e) Carlos volvió a Buenos Aires porque no le gustaba San Pablo.

5   Imagine you are asked by a Latin American friend about your life five or ten years ago. Answer these questions giving real or imaginary information.

(a) ¿Dónde vivías tú hace cinco / diez años?

(b) ¿Estabas soltero/a o casado/a?

(c) ¿Con quién vivías?

(d) ¿Qué hacías? ¿Estudiabas / trabajabas?

(e) ¿Dónde estudiabas / trabajabas?

(f) ¿Te gustaba tu trabajo?

(g) ¿Cómo era tu casa?

mi marido *my husband*	**una compañía / empresa** *a company*
mi mujer *my wife*	**el colegio** *school*
mis hijos *my children*	**la universidad de . . .** *the university of . . .*
mis hermanos *my brothers and sisters*	
mis padres *my parents*	

6   At a party you meet Pedro, an Ecuadorean who now lives in your country. Follow the guidelines below to ask him questions, using the familiar form.

(a) Ask where he lived before.

(b) Ask in what part of Ecuador he lived.

(c) Ask what he used to do there.

(d) Ask what he is doing here.

 7 Carlos García, from Argentina, describes his native Buenos Aires. Listen to the description, or read the transcript on page 272, then answer the questions below. First, look at these key words:

¿Cómo describirías . . .? *How would you describe . . .?*	**vida nocturna** (f) *nightlife*
rincones (m, pl) *corners*	**expresarse** *to express oneself*
unidad común (f) *common unity*	**tendencia** (f) *tendency*
movimiento cultural (m) *cultural life (movement)*	**porteños** (m, pl) *name given to the inhabitants of Buenos Aires*
alma (f) *soul*	**entristecer** *to become sad*
	melancolía (f) *melancholy*

Responda en inglés

(a) How does Carlos describe Buenos Aires?

(b) What does he like most about the city?

(c) What doesn't he like about the city?

8 During a holiday in a Latin American country, you meet someone you like very much. When you get back home that evening you describe that person to your Spanish-speaking friend.

Use this description as a guideline, and add further information if you wish.

- He / she was very good-looking, dark, tall and slim.
- He / she had black hair and green eyes.
- He / she was about 25 years old.
- He / she was very nice.

—— Imágenes de Hispanoamérica ——

Latin Americans as migrants

Poor living conditions in rural areas in many parts of Latin America have driven millions of people to the cities in search of work and a better standard of living. Places like Mexico City, Bogotá in Colombia and Lima in Peru, among others, have reached a saturation point and are unable to provide the jobs and services that the new migrants require. Other countries, especially the United States, have absorbed and provided jobs for millions of Latin American migrants, not just from Mexico, but also from other nations in the region. Many of these migrants have entered the country illegally across the Mexican border.

Political repression and civil wars have also driven many Latin Americans out of their countries. Cubans flocked to Miami after the Revolution of 1959 which brought Fidel Castro to power, and this flow has never stopped; at the peak of the civil war in El Salvador, thousands of people sought refuge in the United States; many Nicaraguans also fled to the United States to escape dire economic conditions in their country and the war between the **sandinistas** and the **contras**. In South America, political repression exercised by the military during the seventies and eighties, forced a great number of people from Chile and Argentina to emigrate. Many went to Europe, making their homes in cities like Madrid, Barcelona, Paris and London, among others. Later, the return of democracy brought some of these people, many of them professionals, back to their own countries.

The passage opposite, taken from an article published by a Bolivian newspaper, looks at the increase in the Hispanic population in the United States in the eighties, and compares it with that of other ethnic groups. Study the key words before you read the text, then check your comprehension by answering the questions that follow.

Nota: The term **iberoamericano**, derived from **ibero** (*Iberian*) and **americano** (*American*), is another word to designate Latin Americans.

EE.UU. (Estados Unidos) *United States*	**afronorteamericano** (m) *Afroamerican*
aumentar *to increase*	**crecimiento** (m) *growth*
población (f) *population*	**profundas** (f, pl) *deep*
creció (crecer) *it grew (to grow)*	**próximo siglo** (m) *next century*
asiático *Asian*	**se identifican** *they identify themselves*
se duplicó *it doubled*	
miembro (m) *member*	**mientras** *while*
minoría étnica (f) *ethnic minority*	**se incrementó** *it increased*
siendo *being*	

Población hispana en EE.UU. aumenta más de 50 por ciento

Washington, 11 (AP) – En la década de 1980 la población de origen iberoamericano en Estados Unidos creció más de 50 por ciento, la de origen asiático se duplicó y uno de cada cinco norteamericanos es miembro de una minoría étnica, según el censo de 1990.

La principal minoría continúa siendo la de los negros, o afronorteamericanos. Pero el pronunciado crecimiento de la población hispana, o iberoamericana, y asiática indica una diversificación étnica que tendrá profundas consecuencias políticas y sociales en el próximo siglo.

De los 248,7 millones de habitantes de Estados Unidos, más de 49 millones se identifican como integrantes de una minoría étnica.

Treinta millones son negros y 22,4 millones hispanos. Pero mientras el número de afronorteamericanos creció 13 por ciento en la última década, el de iberoamericanos se incrementó 53 por ciento.

(Diario Los Tiempos, Cochabamba, Bolivia.)

¿Verdadero o falso?

(a) En la década de los ochenta la población de origen hispano en EE.UU. se duplicó.
(b) La principal minoría étnica en EE.UU. es la hispana.
(c) En EE.UU. hay más de veinte millones de hispanos.

This second passage in Spanish, taken from an article published by the international magazine **Cambio 16 América**, looks at illegal immigration into the United States across the Mexican border. Once again, study the key words before you read the text, then check your comprehension by answering the questions that follow.

a patadas con *kicking out at*	**entrar** *to enter*
según *according to*	**lograr** *to succeed*
indocumentado (m) *illegal immigrant*	**los que se empeñan** *those who try*
detenidos *detained*	**frontera** (f) *border*
cada año / mes *each year / month*	**alcanzan** *they reach*
Patrulla Fronteriza (f) *border patrol*	**meta** (f) *goal, objective*
cerca de *nearly*	**tras** *after*
intentan (intentar) *they try (to try)*	**estadounidense** *United States* (adj)

A PATADAS CON LOS ILEGALES

Según Gene McNary, del Servicio de Inmigración y Naturalización de Estados Unidos, un millón de indocumentados, la mayoría de nacionalidad mexicana, son detenidos cada año por la Patrulla Fronteriza y cerca de siete millones de inmigrantes ilegales viven en territorio norteamericano. Cada mes, 150.000 mexicanos intentan entrar ilegalmente en EE.UU. La mayoría lo logra: el 80 por ciento de los que se empeñan en cruzar la frontera alcanzan su meta, aunque muchos de ellos sean finalmente deportados tras su detención en territorio estadounidense.

(Revista Cambio 16 América 1.109, Spain.)

Complete estas frases (*Complete these sentences*)

(*d*) La mayoría de los inmigrantes ilegales son de nacionalidad _____.

(*e*) La Patrulla Fronteriza detiene cada año aproximadamente a _____ de inmigrantes ilegales.

(*f*) El _____ de los que cruzan la frontera ilegalmente logran su objetivo.

11

ME GUSTARÍA
— ALQUILAR UN COCHE —
I would like to hire a car

In this unit you will learn how to

- say what you would like to do
- hire a car
- buy petrol and get your car serviced
- get something repaired
- make a telephone call through the operator

Diálogos

1 Allí alquilan coches

Gonzalo Lira, an Argentinian, has travelled with his family to Bariloche, 1700 kilometres south of Buenos Aires. Gonzalo would like to hire a car and he asks his friend Lucía to recommend a car rental agency.

Gonzalo   Hola Lucía, **buen día**.
Lucía   **Buen día**, Gonzalo.
Gonzalo   ¿Qué vas a hacer hoy?

Lucía	Voy a ir a nadar. ¿**Querés** venir conmigo?
Gonzalo	No, gracias. Me gustaría alquilar un coche para salir con Silvia y los chicos. ¿Me podrías recomendar alguna agencia?
Lucía	Sí, sí, a media cuadra del Centro Cívico está la agencia Nahuelhuapi. Allá alquilan coches.
Gonzalo	¿Cerca del Centro Cívico dijiste?
Lucía	Sí, dos cuadras más abajo, a la derecha.

hoy	*today*	**¿podrías...?**	*could you...?*
conmigo	*with me*	**a media cuadra**	*half a block away*
alquilar	*to hire*	**¿...dijiste?**	*...did you say? (fam)*
chicos (m, pl)	*children*	**más abajo**	*further down*

Responda en inglés

(a) How far is the car rental firm from the **Centro Cívico**?
(b) Where is the **Centro Cívico**?

Notas explicativas

Argentinian usage

Observe that Argentinians say **buen día**, instead of **buenos días**. Notice also non-standard Argentinian usage in ¿**querés**? (*do you want?*, fam), instead of the standard ¿**quieres**?

Alquilar (*to hire*)

Argentinians, like some other Latin Americans, for example Peruvians, use the standard word **alquilar** (*to hire, to rent*). In some parts of Latin America you will hear other words, for example **rentar** in Mexico, and **arrendar** in Chile.

El coche, el auto, el carro (*car*)

Remember that, while Argentinians, like some other Latin Americans, use the word **el coche** or **el auto** for *car*, many other countries use the word **el carro**. To say you would like to hire a car in Colombia or Peru, for example, you need to use the phrase **Me gustaría alquilar un carro**.

Saying what you would like to do

Me gustaría alquilar un coche.   *I would like to hire a car.*

Me gustaría (*I would like*), from **gustar** (*to like*), is in the conditional tense. For an explanation of how to form the conditional see **Notas gramaticales**.

Requesting information

¿Me podrías recomendar . . .?   *Could you recommend, (to me) . . .?*

The word **me** (*to me*) can also be placed after the infinitive: **¿Podrías recomendarme . . .?**. **¿Podrías?** (*could you?*, fam), is an irregular form of the conditional tense. The corresponding infinitive is **poder** (*can, to be able to*). For irregular conditional forms, see **Notas gramaticales**.

2   En la agencia de alquiler de coches

Gonzalo talks to the employee at Agencia Nahuelhuapi.

Empleada	**Buen día**. ¿Qué desea?
Gonzalo	**Buen día**. Quisiera alquilar un coche ¿Qué me recomienda?
Empleada	Bueno, tenemos varios modelos. ¿Quiere un coche chico?
Gonzalo	No demasiado chico. Somos cuatro personas.
Empleada	Bueno, en ese caso le recomiendo el Ford Fiesta, que tiene capacidad para cuatro personas. Es un coche bastante cómodo y económico.
Gonzalo	¿Cuánto cuesta el alquiler?
Empleada	Si es por uno o dos días, cuesta noventa dólares diarios, con kilometraje ilimitado. Por semana, vale cuatrocientos dólares. El impuesto y el seguro están incluidos.
Gonzalo	Bueno, lo quiero por dos días solamente, sábado y domingo.
Empleada	Muy bien. ¿Quiere reservarlo ahora?
Gonzalo	Sí, prefiero reservarlo ahora mismo.
Empleada	Pase por aquí, por favor.

alquiler (m) *rental*	**kilometraje ilimitado** (m) *unlimited*
quisiera *I would like*	*mileage*
capacidad (f) *room*	**ahora mismo** *right now*
cómodo *comfortable*	**pase por aquí** *come this way*
si es por *if it is for*	**chico** *small*

Responda en inglés

(a) How does the employee describe the Ford Fiesta?

(b) How long does Gonzalo want the car for?

Notas explicativas

Use of por

por uno o dos días

pase por aquí

for one or two days

come this way

Prices and currency

In Argentina many prices are quoted in dollars instead of **pesos**, the local currency, although you normally pay the equivalent in pesos.

3 En la estación de servicio

After travelling some distance with his family, Gonzalo stops at a petrol station to fill up.

Empleado ¿Se lo lleno?

Gonzalo Sí, llénelo. Y me revisa la presión de las ruedas también.

Empleado ¿Le miro el aceite?

Gonzalo No, el aceite está bien.

Empleado Listo señor.

Gonzalo ¿Cuánto es?

Empleado Son quince pesos.

Gonzalo Gracias. ¿Me prodría decir si falta mucho para llegar a Esquel?

Empleado Veinte kilómetros más o menos.

Gonzalo Gracias.

estación de servicio (f) *service station*	**rueda** (f) *wheel*
llenar *to fill up*	**aceite** (m) *oil*
revisar *to check*	**listo** *ready*
presión (f) *pressure*	**¿falta mucho?** *(see notes below)*

Responda en inglés

(*a*) What services does Gonzalo request at the service station?

(*b*) How far is Esquel from where he is now?

———— Notas explicativas ————

Petrol

The standard word for *petrol* is **la gasolina**, but Argentinians use the word **la nafta**. For other variations, see the Glossary of Latin American terms.

Making requests and offers

Observe the use of object pronouns in these sentences:

¿Se lo lleno?	*Shall I fill it up for you?*
Me revisa la presión de las ruedas.	*Will you check the air pressure in the wheels for me?*
¿Le miro el aceite?	*Shall I have a look at the oil for you?*

Notice that these sentences express requests or offers of services using the present tense, in which case they translate into English as *Will you . . .?, Shall I . . .?* respectively. Study also the use of object pronouns in the sentences, **se lo** (*for you*), **me** (*for me*), **le** (*for you*).

¿Falta mucho? (Is it a long way off?)

¿. . . falta mucho para llegar a Esquel?	*Is Esquel a long way off?*

Here is another example of the use of **faltar**, this time in the third person pural:

Faltan 200 kilómetros para (llegar a) Mendoza.	*There are 200 km to go before (we get to) Mendoza.*

4 Una rueda pinchada

Bad luck for Gonzalo and his family. Just as they get to Esquel, they have a puncture. Gonzalo gets the spare wheel out and changes the wheel. Then they drive to the nearest garage to have the tyre repaired.

Gonzalo	Buenas tardes. ¿Podrían repararme esta goma?
Mecánico	¿Para cuándo la quiere?
Gonzalo	Para esta misma tarde. Tenemos que volver a Bariloche.
Mecánico	A las tres y media se la puedo tener lista.
Gonzalo	Sí, está bien. Vuelvo a esa hora.

rueda (f)	*wheel*	**esta misma tarde**	*this very*
pinchada	*punctured*	*afternoon*	
reparar	*to repair*	**a esa hora**	*at that time*
goma (f)	*tyre* (Arg)		

Notas explicativas

Usage

Most Latin Americans use the word **la llanta** for *tyre*, while

Argentinians use the word **la goma**. Other countries use **el neumático**, which is the term used in Spain, where the word **llanta** refers to the rim of a car wheel.

Tener una rueda pinchada (*to have a puncture*) should be understood in most countries. Mexicans use the phrase **tener una llanta ponchada**.

In Spanish **el garage** or **el garaje** is used for *garage*, both pronounced in the same way. In some countries, for example in Argentina and Chile, the word is pronounced **garash** or **garall** (**ll** sounding similar to **j** in *John*).

Use of para to refer to time

¿Para cuándo lo quiere?	*When do you want it for?*
Para esta misma tarde.	*For this (very) afternoon.*

5 Una llamada telefónica

On Sunday, Gonzalo returns the car to the agency and returns to the hotel with his family. Gonzalo needs to make an international telephone call and he rings the hotel switchboard from his room.

Telefonista	¿Hola?
Gonzalo	Hola, telefonista. Llamo desde la habitación trescientos diez. ¿Sería posible hacer una llamada internacional desde mi habitación? Quiero llamar a Londres.
Telefonista	Sí, sí se puede. ¿A qué número de Londres desea llamar?
Gonzalo	Al 81-601 1326.
Telefonista	81-601 1326.
Gonzalo	Es una llamada de persona a persona.
Telefonista	¿Su nombre, por favor?
Gonzalo	Gonzalo Lira.
Telefonista	¿Y el nombre de la persona con quien desea hablar?
Gonzalo	Robert Major. M-a-j-o-r, Major. ¿Hay mucha demora?
Telefonista	No, en este momento no. Cuelgue por favor. Yo lo llamaré.
Gonzalo	Gracias.

llamo desde (llamar) *I am calling from (to call, to telephone)*	**número** (m) *number*
¿sería posible . . .? *would it be possible . . .?*	**llamada de persona a persona** (f) *person-to-person call*
llamada (f) *telephone call*	**demora** (f) *delay*
se puede . . . *it is possible . . .*	**cuelgue (colgar)** *hang up (to hang up)*

Responda en inglés

(*a*) What city does Gonzalo want to call?
(*b*) What sort of telephone call does he need to make?

—— Notas explicativas ——

Using public telephones

In many Latin American countries, public telephones work with tokens, **fichas** (f) (usually sold in newspaper kiosks) instead of coins, **monedas** (f), and you cannot normally make international phone calls from them, except in a few countries which have modernised their telephone system. In more isolated places in Latin America, international phone calls, and even calls within the same country, have to be made through the operator.

Expressing possibility

¿Sería posible hacer una llamada internacional desde mi habitación?
Sí, sí se puede.

Would it be possible to make an international phone call from my room?
Yes, it is possible.
(Lit. *Yes, one can.*)

Sería (*it would be*) is a conditional form of **ser** (*to be*).

In the present tense, you can express possibility by saying:

(No) es posible.
Es imposible.

It is (not) possible.
It is impossible.

⚙ – Frases y expresiones importantes –

- Saying what you would like to do

Me gustaría alquilar un coche / un carro.	*I would like to hire a car.*
Quisiera alquilar un coche / un carro.	*I would like to hire a car.*

- Hiring a car

Quisiera / me gustaría alquilar un coche / un carro.	*I would like to hire a car.*
¿Quiere un coche / carro chico?	*Do you want a small car?*
No demasiado chico.	*Not too small.*
¿Cuánto cuesta el alquiler?	*How much is the rental?*
Cuesta noventa dólares diarios.	*It costs US $90 per day.*
Por semana vale cuatrocientos dólares.	*Per week it costs US $400.*

- Other words and phrases used in the context of car hire

¿Está incluido el IVA / el seguro?	*Is VAT / insurance included?*
¿Incluye el IVA / el seguro?	*Does it include VAT / insurance?*
Un coche / carro mediano / grande / automático.	*A medium-sized / large / automatic car.*
¿Cuánto cuesta / vale el alquiler por día / por semana?	*How much is the rental per day / per week?*
¿Cuánto cobran por kilómetro?	*How much do you charge per km?*
¿Aceptan tarjetas de crédito?	*Do you accept credit cards?*
¿Tiene su licencia (de conducir)?	*Have you got your driving licence?*

All the above phrases related to cars and car hire are standard and should be understood in all Latin American countries, even when some of these countries do in fact use other terms. See the Glossary of Latin American terms on page 281.

- Buying petrol and getting your car serviced

Llénelo.	*Fill it up.*
Me revisa la presión de las ruedas.	*Will you check the air pressure for me?*

- Other words and phrases used in the context of car servicing

¿Hay una estación de servicio por aquí?	*Is there a petrol station nearby?*
¿Dónde puedo encontrar un garaje?	*Where can I find a garage?*
Quiero (veinte) litros.	*I want (twenty) litres.*
. . . de gasolina.	*. . . of petrol.*
. . . de super / normal	*. . . of super (premium) / regular.*
. . . de gasolina sin plomo.	*. . . of unleaded petrol.*
¿Podría revisar el agua / el aceite / el líquido de frenos / la batería . . .?	*Could you check the water / oil / brake fluid / battery . . .?*
¿Podría limpiar el parabrisas?	*Could you clean the windscreen?*

- Getting something repaired

¿Podrían repararme esta goma / llanta?	*Could you repair this tyre for me?*
¿Para cuándo la quiere?	*When do you want it for?*
Para esta misma tarde.	*For this very afternoon.*

- Making a telephone call through the operator

Quiero llamar a Londres.	*I want to call London.*
¿A qué número de Londres desea llamar?	*What number do you want to call in London?*
Es una llamada de persona a persona / personal.	*It is a person-to-person call.*
¿Hay mucha demora?	*Is there a long delay?*
Cuelgue, por favor.	*Hang up, please.*

- Other words and phrases used on the telephone

Habla . . .	*. . . speaking.*
Quiero la extensión . . .	*I want extension . . .*
Quiero hacer una llamada con cobro revertido.	*I want to reverse the charges.*
No le oigo bien.	*I can't hear you well.*
No se oye bien.	*I can't hear well. (Lit. one can't hear well.)*
¿Podría hablar más fuerte, por favor?	*Could you speak louder, please?*
No entiendo muy bien el español.	*I don't understand Spanish very well.*
¿Podría hablar más despacio?	*Could you speak more slowly?*

🔊 —————— **Notas gramaticales** ——————

1 The conditional tense

To say what you would like, as in *I would like to hire a car*, and to ask whether something is possible, e.g. *Could you repair this tyre?* or *Would it be possible to make an international phone call from my room?*, you can use the conditional tense.

Formation of the conditional tense

Like the future tense (see Unit 8), the conditional is formed with the infinitive, to which the appropriate ending is added. The endings are the same for -**ar**, -**er** and -**ir** verbs. Here is the conditional tense of a regular verb:

ser	to be	
sería	*I would be*
serías	*you would be* (fam, sing)
sería	*you would be* (pol, sing)
	he, she, it would be
seríamos	*we would be*
serían	*you would be* (pl)
	they would be

Notice that the first and third person singular are the same and that all forms carry an accent. Note also that the plural familiar, **vosotros seríais**, has been omitted, as this is not normally used in Latin America.

Here are some further examples of the use of the conditional tense with regular verbs:

Me gustaría ir a la Argentina.	*I would like to go to Argentina.*
¿Qué te gustaría hacer?	*What would you like to do?*
Preferiría un coche chico.	*I would prefer a small car.*
¿Cuándo irían a Sudamérica?	*When would you / they go to South America?*

Nota: Remember that with **gustar** (*to like*) you need to use the third person of the verb: **me gustaría**, **te gustaría**, **le gustaría**, **nos gustaría**, **les gustaría**. For revision of **gustar**, see Unit 6.

Irregular conditional forms

Verbs with irregular stems in the future tense (see Unit 8) also have them in the conditional. The endings are the same as those of regular verbs. Here are some of the most common:

decir	(*to say, to tell*)	diría, dirías, diría, diríamos, dirían
hacer	(*to do, to make*)	haría, harías, haría, haríamos, harían
poder	(*can, to be able*)	podría, podrías, podría, podríamos, podrían
salir	(*to go out, to leave*)	saldría, saldrías, saldría, saldríamos, saldrían
tener	(*to have*)	tendría, tendrías, tendría, tendríamos, tendrían
venir	(*to come*)	vendría, vendrías, vendría, vendríamos, vendrían

Examples:

¿Qué diría él?	*What would he say?*
Yo no lo haría.	*I wouldn't do it.*
¿Podrían repararlo?	*Could you repair it?*

For other irregular conditional forms, see the table starting on page 276.

2 Conmigo, contigo . . . (*with me, with you . . .*)

With me translates into Spanish as **conmigo**. *With you* (fam) becomes **contigo**.

¿Quieres venir conmigo?	*Do you want to come with me?*
No puedo ir contigo.	*I can't go with you.* (fam)

With other persons, use **usted** (pol), **él, ella, nosotros, ustedes, ellos**.

Iré con usted.	*I will go with you.* (pol)
Iremos con él.	*We will go with him.*

Remember that, in the first and second person singular, other prepositions (words like *for, without, to*) are followed by **mí** and **ti**.

Para mí un café.	*Coffee for me.*
¿Y para ti?	*And for you?*

For a revision of this, see **Notas gramaticales**, Unit 5.

☑ ———— **Actividades** ————

1 You are in a Latin American city, staying at a hotel in **calle Mac Iver** (marked on the map). You would like to hire a car and you ask the hotel receptionist to recommend a car rental firm. He recommends **agencia Lys**, which is on **calle Agustinas**, opposite **cerro** (*hill*) **Santa Lucía**, two blocks down **calle Moneda**, then left at **Santa Lucía** and left again at **calle Agustinas**, as shown on the map. Use dialogue 1 as a model to write the conversation between you and the hotel receptionist. You can then compare your own version of the dialogue with the one in the **Key to the exercises**.

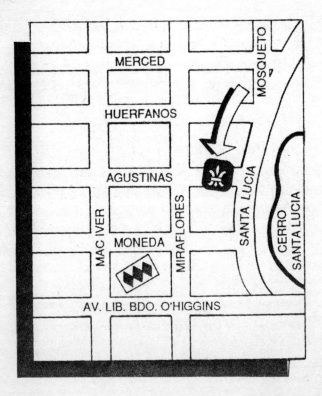

(Lys Rent a Car, Agustinas 535, Santiago, Chile)

2 At Lys Rent a Car you speak to the person in charge.

T A R I F A S

MODELO	DIA	SEMANA
CHEVROLET CHEVETTE	**$15.900**	**$104.300**
NISSAN SENTRA LX	**$18.500**	**$122.500**
SENTRA LX AT/AA	**$19.500**	**$129.500**
NISSAN PICK UP	**$18.500**	**$122.500**
PICK UP DOBLE CAB.	**$22.500**	**$147.000**

Empleado Buenos días. ¿Qué desea?
Ud. *Say you would like to hire a car. Ask him what he recommends.*
Empleado Bueno, tenemos tres modelos de coches y dos de camionetas.

Ud.	*You want a small car, not too expensive.*
Empleado	El más económico que tenemos es el Chevrolet Chevette. Es un coche mediano.
Ud.	*Ask what the rental is per day.*
Empleado	Por día cuesta quince mil novecientos pesos.
Ud.	*And per week?*
Empleado	Ciento cuatro mil trescientos pesos.
Ud.	*Ask if that is with unlimited mileage.*
Empleado	Sí, no hay recargo por kilómetro.
Ud.	*Ask if VAT and insurance are included.*
Empleado	Sí, están incluidos.
Ud.	*Say that is fine. You'll take the Chevette.*
Empleado	¿Tiene su licencia de conducir al día?
Ud.	*Yes, here it is.*
Empleado	Gracias.
Ud.	*Ask if it would be possible to leave the car in another city. You want to travel south and leave the car there. You prefer to come back by train.*
Empleado	No, no se puede. Tendría que devolver el coche aquí mismo.

camioneta (f)	*van*	**al día**	*up to date, valid*
recargo (m)	*surcharge*	**devolver**	*to return (something)*

3   You may have difficulties with your car, so be prepared! What would you say in Spanish in these situations?

Before you do this exercise, revise, if necessary, dialogue 3 and the relevant vocabulary under **Frases y expresiones importantes**.

(a) Your car is running out of petrol. You stop a passer-by and ask if there is a service station nearby.

(b) At the service station you ask the attendant for 20 litres of unleaded petrol.

(c) You need the oil and the tyre pressure checked.

(d) The windscreen is dirty, so you ask the attendant to clean it for you.

(e) Fifty miles down the road you have a puncture. You change the wheel, then stop at a garage where you ask the mechanic to mend the tyre for you.

(f) Before continuing your journey, you ask the mechanic if Santa Isabel is a long way off.

4   You have reached the town of Santa Isabel where you will be spending a couple of days. As there were some problems in your office back home before you left the country, you decide to telephone your manager, Andrew Bronson, from your hotel room. It is company business, so you decide to reverse the charges. Use dialogue 5 as a model to write the conversation between you and the operator (**la telefonista**). Check the relevant vocabulary under **Frases y expresiones importantes**. You can then compare your own version of the dialogue with the one in the **Key to the exercises**.

5   Carlos García, from Buenos Aires, Argentina, was asked where he would like to spend his next holiday. Listen to what he says, or read the transcript on page 273, then answer the questions below. First, look at these key words:

pasar *to spend*	**solo o acompañado** *alone or*
próximo/a *next*	*accompanied*
imagen (f) *image*	**recorrería** *I would visit / tour*
quedó profundamente grabada	**naturaleza** (f) *nature*
remained deeply imprinted	**vida frívola** (f) *frivolous life*

Responda en inglés

(a) Why would Carlos like to spend his next holiday in Bariloche?

(b) Who would he go with and for how long?

6   Carlos García was then asked what sort of car he would like to have. Listen to his reply or read the transcript on page 273, then answer the questions below. First, look at these key words:

marca (f) *make*	**donde abunde la naturaleza**
auto (m) *car*	*where I can be in contact with*
coche deportivo (m) *sports car*	*nature* (lit. *where there is plenty*
salir a pasear *to go for a ride*	*of nature*)
lugares cercanos (m, pl) *nearby*	
places	

Complete estas frases

(a) Carlos preferiría un coche _____ . (*size*)
(b) Él preferiría un coche _____ . (*type*)
(c) Él compraría un coche _____ . (*colour*)
(d) Él usaría el coche para _____ y _____ . (*use*).

— Imágenes de Hispanoamérica —

Driving in Latin America

Probably the best way to see Latin America is by car, and many countries now have good roads linking the main cities. Mexico, Venezuela, Argentina and Chile have an extensive road network, but in the smaller countries and in the more isolated areas of the continent, especially in mountainous terrain, roads are generally bad.

Whether you are driving your own vehicle or a hired car, bear in mind that, in the more remote areas, you may have to travel long distances before you are able to refuel so it is advisable to find out how far you will have to drive before you reach the next petrol station, as you may need to take some spare fuel. In more populated areas and on roads leading to large towns, service stations are plentiful, and you will have no such problem. However, it may be difficult to find spare parts, particularly if your vehicle is one not commonly found in the country. This is less likely to occur now that many Latin American countries are importing thousands of cars of all makes, from Europe, Japan and the United States.

If you decide to bring your own car to Latin America, make sure you comply with all regulations regarding entry into different countries, as this will save you a lot of trouble. Once you have all the necessary documentation you should have no difficulty in crossing the borders, provided your car returns to the country of origin. Find out about car insurance too, as regulations differ from country to country. You will need to be insured in each country in order to make a claim locally in case of an accident. International insurers in your own country should be able to help you.

Some useful tips for drivers

To make the most of driving in Latin America and really enjoy your journey, bear in the mind the following tips:

● Try not to leave your car unattended. In towns, find a car park, **un aparcamiento** (called **un parqueadero** in some countries, **un estacionamiento** in others), or, if you have to leave your car in the street, leave it with a car attendant if possible. In many Latin American cities there are people who, officially or unofficially, look after people's cars in exchange for a small tip.

● Theft is common in large cities, so never leave documents, money or valuables in your car. If you have no alternative but to leave your luggage in the vehicle, make sure it is out of sight.

● Speed limits vary from country to country, so if you want to avoid trouble with the police, find out what these are. In many Latin American countries now, speed is controlled by radar or by police helicopters near big cities.

● As a general rule, try to avoid contact with the local police! In some Latin American countries they are renowned for their dishonesty, and they may demand a bribe for even a minor traffic offence. In Mexico this is known as **una mordida**.

● If you are unfamiliar with the country, avoid driving at night. Road signs are poor or non-existent in some places, and animals may sometimes wander onto the road.

Un día sin auto

To reduce air pollution in the capital, Mexican transport authorities have introduced a system by which cars whose plates end in a certain number are restricted from travelling on certain days. This restriction, which has been named **Un día sin auto**, applies to two digits each day, from Monday to Friday, with a rotation system which avoids always restricting vehicles on the same day. Transport authorities in Santiago de Chile, where air pollution is also a big problem, have introduced a similar system. The passage overleaf, taken from a leaflet produced by the Mexican immigration authorities for foreign tourists and Mexicans living abroad, gives information about this programme. Study the key words before you read the text.

recuerda *remember*	contaminación ambiental (f)
municipio (m) *district*	*environmental pollution*
circunvecino *neighbouring*	terminación (f) *ending*
aplicar *to apply*	placa (f) *car licence plate*
auto (m) (short for automóvil) *car*	circular *to drive*
disminuir *to reduce*	

RECUERDA

● En el Distrito Federal y municipios circunvecinos que forman la zona metropolitana se aplica el programa "Un día sin auto", para disminuir la contaminación ambiental. Con base en la terminación del último número de tu placa, no circulan los números:

HOY

5 y 6 Lunes
7 y 8 Martes
3 y 4 Miércoles
1 y 2 Jueves
9 y 0 Viernes

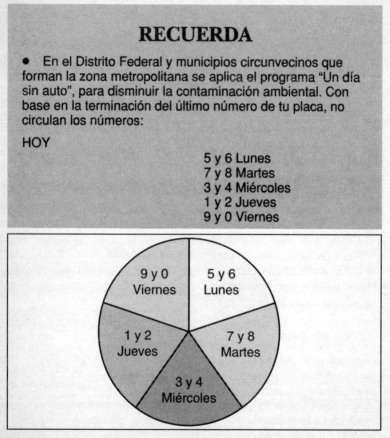

(Asesoría de Comunicación del Programa Nacional de Solidaridad)

Responda en español

(a) ¿Cómo se llama el programa de restricción vehicular en México?
(b) ¿Cuál es el objetivo de este programa?
(c) ¿Qué número determina la restricción?

12

¿HA ESTADO EN EL CUZCO?

Have you been to Cuzco?

In this unit you will learn how to

- talk about what you and others have done
- express obligation and need
- ask people to do something and give suggestions

Diálogos

1 Tengo que estar a las siete en el aeropuerto

Roberto Bernaola, from Argentina, is in Lima, Peru. At a party, Roberto talks to Pilar, a Peruvian.

Pilar ¿Es la primera vez que viene a Lima?

Roberto No, he estado aquí varias veces. Vengo aquí por negocios y, además, el Perú me gusta mucho. ¿Usted es de Lima?

Pilar No, yo soy de Arequipa, pero vengo mucho a Lima. Tengo parientes aquí. ¿Ha ido alguna vez a Arequipa?

Roberto No, no he estado nunca allá. No he tenido tiempo. Me han dicho que es una ciudad muy linda. Me gustaría mucho ir.

Pilar	Sí, no deje de ir. Le va a gustar. Es muy diferente a Lima. Si va a Arequipa, llámeme. Le daré mi número de teléfono. Yo misma le enseñaré la ciudad.
Roberto	Muchas gracias.
Pilar	¿Se sirve otro pisco sour?
Roberto	No, gracias. Ya he tomado demasiado y tengo que irme pronto. Mañana tengo que estar a las siete en el aeropuerto.

---

primera vez (f)   *first time*
he estado   *I have been*
varias veces   *several times*
por negocios   *on business*
además   *besides*
parientes (m, pl)   *relatives*
¿Ha ido alguna vez a ...?   *Have you ever been to ...?* (Lit. *gone*)
No he estado nunca allá   *I have never been there.*
no he tenido   *I haven't had*

me han dicho   *I have been told*
no deje de ir   *don't fail to go*
llámeme   *call me*
yo misma (f)   *I myself*
le enseñaré (enseñar)   *I will show you (to show)*
¿Se sirve ...?   *Will you have ...? (food or drink)*
he tomado   *I have drunk, I have had (drink)*

¿Verdadero o falso?

(*a*)   Roberto no ha estado en Lima antes.
(*b*)   Pilar no es de Lima, pero tiene parientes allí.

Notas explicativas

Peruvian pronunciation

Unlike what happens in neighbouring Chile or in Argentina, Peruvians, in common with people in Bolivia and Ecuador, pronounce the **s** fully at the end of a word or before a consonant. Therefore, a foreigner who is not very familiar with Spanish may find it easier to understand a sentence such as **Buenos días, ¿cómo está usted?** when pronounced by a Peruvian than by someone from Chile or Argentina. As you listen to the dialogues, pay special attention to pronunciation and intonation and compare Peruvian speech with that of the Argentinian speaker in the same dialogues. Note also that in formal address Argentinians use standard verb forms.

Talking about what you have done

He estado (*I have been*), **ha ido** (*you have gone, he / she has gone*), **no he ido** (*I haven't gone*), **no he tenido** (*I haven't had*), **me han dicho** (*I have been told*), **he tomado** (*I have drunk / had*) are all examples of the perfect tense. For an explanation of its use and formations, see **Notas gramaticales**.

Making suggestions

No deje (*don't fail*) and **llámeme** (*call me*), are imperative or command forms, used here to make suggestions. The second is followed by a pronoun: **llame** + **me**. In the dialogues which follow, you will find other similar forms. For more information on the imperative or command form, see **Notas gramaticales**.

Enseñar, mostrar (*to show*)

Both are used in Latin America, but different countries seem to have preference for one or the other. In Spain, **enseñar** is more common.

El pisco

El pisco is a kind of brandy which is very popular in Peru and Chile, as popular as **el tequila** in Mexico. Un **pisco sour** is **pisco** mixed with lemon juice and sugar.

2 Lléveme al Hotel Continental

Roberto takes a taxi to his hotel.

Roberto   ¡Taxi!
           (*The taxi stops and Roberto gets in.*)
Taxista   Buenas noches, señor.
Roberto   Buenas noches, lléveme al Hotel Continental en la calle Puno, por favor.
Taxista   Muy bien, señor.

lléveme	*take me*

Nota explicativa

In some Latin American countries, especially away from big cities, taxis do not use meters, and taxi drivers charge according to distance. If you are not familiar with the town, ask the driver how much it is going to cost you before you get in.

3 Deme la cuenta

Roberto asks the hotel receptionist to prepare the bill for him and to wake him up in the morning.

Roberto	Buenas noches.
Recepcionista	Buenos noches, señor.
Roberto	Por favor, deme la cuenta de la habitación doscientos treinta. Me voy mañana temprano.
Recepcionista	Sí, señor. Se la daré enseguida.
Roberto	Ah, y me despierta a las seis de la mañana, por favor. Tengo que salir del hotel a las seis y media.
Recepcionista	¿Quiere tomar el desayuno en la habitación o prefiere bajar al comedor?
Roberto	Envíemelo a la habitación, por favor.
Recepcionista	Muy bien, señor.
Roberto	Gracias.

---

deme *give me*
me voy (irse) *I am leaving (to leave)*
temprano *early*
se la daré *I will give it to you*
enseguida / en seguida *right away*

me despierta (despertar) *will you wake me up (to wake up)*
bajar *to go down*
envíemelo (enviar) *send it to me (to send)*

Responda en inglés

(*a*) What times does Roberto need to be woken up?
(*b*) What time does he need to leave the hotel?

Nota explicativa

The present tense in instructions

Notice the use of the present tense in the following:

Me despierta a las seis.   *Will you wake me up at six?*

The present tense here is an alternative to the imperative form: **despiérteme** (*wake me up*). More on this under **Notas gramaticales**.

4   En el aeropuerto

At the airport, Roberto goes to the Aerolatina desk and hands in his ticket.

Empleada	Me da su pasaporte, por favor. (*Roberto hands in his passport.*) Gracias. ¿Cuál es su equipaje?
Roberto	Tengo esta valija solamente.
Empleada	¿Tiene equipaje de mano?
Roberto	Este bolso.
Empleada	Bien. ¿Fumador o no fumador?
Roberto	No fumador. Y prefiero un asiento junto al pasillo, por favor.

Empleada   Sí, cómo no . . . Aquí está su pasaje, su pasaporte y su tarjeta de embarque. Primero tiene que pagar su impuesto de aeropuerto y después pase por policía internacional. Tiene que embarcar a las nueve y media por la puerta número seis.

Roberto   ¿Está retrasado el vuelo?

Empleada   Sí, hay media hora de retraso.

Me da . . .? *Will you give me . . .?*	**tiene que pagar** *you have to pay*
equipaje de mano (m) *hand luggage*	**impuesto de aeropuerto** (f) *airport tax*
valija (f) *suitcase* (Arg)	**pase por (pasar)** *go through (to go through)*
bolso (m) *bag*	
¿fumador / no fumador? *smoker / non smoker?*	**policía internacional** (f) *international police*
un asiento junto al pasillo (m) *an aisle seat*	**tiene que embarcar** *you have to board*
pasaje (m) *ticket* (Latin Am.)	**puerta** (f) *gate*
tarjeta de embarque (f) *boarding card*	**retrasado** *delayed*
	retraso (m) *delay*

¿Verdadero o falso?

(*a*)   Roberto tiene dos maletas (valijas).

(*b*)   Roberto prefiere un asiento en la sección de no fumadores.

——— Nota explicativa ———

Impuesto (*tax*). In some countries you will hear the word **la tasa**.

— Frases y expresiones importantes –

- Talking about what you and others have done

He estado aquí varias veces.	*I have been here several times.*
¿Ha ido alguna vez a Arequipa?	*Have you ever been to Arequipa?*

No he estado nunca allá.	*I have never been there.*
No he tenido tiempo.	*I haven't had time.*
He tomado demasiado.	*I have drunk too much.*

- Expressing obligation and need

Tengo que estar a las siete en el aeropuerto.	*I have to be at the airport at seven.*
Tiene que embarcar a las nueve y media.	*You have to embark at half past nine.*

- Other ways of expressing obligation and need with **deber** (*to have to, must*)

Debo estar allí a las dos.	*I must be there at two.*
(No) debería hacerlo.	*You should (not) do it.*

- With **hay que** (*one has to*)

Hay que estar allí dos horas antes.	*You have / one has to be there two hours earlier.*

- Asking people to do something and making suggestions

Deme la cuenta.	*Give me the bill.*
Me despierta a las seis.	*Will you wake me up at six?*
Si va a Arequipa, llámeme.	*If you go to Arequipa, call me.*
No deje de ir.	*Don't fail to go.*

Notas gramaticales

1 The perfect tense

The perfect tense is used to say what you or others have done. It is much less frequent in Latin America than in Spain. To refer to recent past events, e.g. *I have worked too much today*, Latin Americans will normally use the preterite tense, **Hoy trabajé demasiado**, while most Spaniards will use the perfect tense, **Hoy he trabajado demasiado**. However, with certain phrases, such as **alguna vez** (*ever*), **una vez / dos veces** (*once / twice*), **varias veces** (*several times*), **nunca** (*never*) and **todavía** (*still*), which bear some relationship with the present tense (the idea of *so far, up till now*), the perfect tense is fairly frequently used in Latin America. Look at the following examples.

He estado aquí varias veces.	*I have been here several times.*
¿Ha ido alguna vez a Arequipa?	*Have you ever been to Arequipa?*
No he ido nunca.	*I have never been.*

Formation of the perfect tense

To form the perfect tense, you need to use the present tense of **haber** (auxiliary verb *to have*) followed by a past participle (the Spanish equivalent of forms like *drunk*, *gone*), which is invariable. To form the past participle of **-ar** verbs, add **-ado** to the stem, e.g. **estar** (*to be*) – **estado** (*been*); to form the past participle of **-er** and **-ir** verbs, add **-ido** to the stem: **tener** (*to have*) – **tenido** (*had*), **ir** (*to go*) – **ido** (*gone*). Here are two examples, one showing an **-ar** verb, the other showing an **-er** verb.

estar	*to be*
he estado	*I have been*
has estado	*you have been* (fam, sing)
ha estado	*you have been* (pol, sing)
	he, she, it has been
hemos estado	*we have been*
han estado	*you have been* (pl)
	they have been

tener	*to have*
he tenido	*I have had*
has tenido	*you have had* (fam, sing)
ha tenido	*you have had* (pol, sing)
	he, she, it has had
hemos tenido	*we have had*
han tenido	*you have had* (pl)
	they have had

Notice that the plural familiar forms **habéis estado** (*you have been*) and **habéis tenido** (*you have had*), have been omitted, as these are not normally used in Latin America.

Here are some further examples of the use of the perfect tense:

Todavía / Aún no hemos terminado.	*We haven't finished yet.*
Nunca he viajado a Sudamérica.	*I have never travelled to South America.*
He ido muchas veces al Perú.	*I have been to Peru many times.*

Irregular past participles

Some verbs form the past participle in an irregular way. Here are the most common:

abrir (*to open*)	**abierto** (*opened*)
decir (*to say, to tell*)	**dicho** (*said, told*)
escribir (*to write*)	**escrito** (*written*)
hacer (*to do, to make*)	**hecho** (*done, made*)
ver (*to see*)	**visto** (*seen*)
volver (*to come back*)	**vuelto** (*come back*)

Me han dicho que es una ciudad muy bonita.	*I have been told it's a very nice city.*
Aún / Todavía no le he escrito.	*I still haven't written to him / her.*
Los he visto varias veces.	*I have seem them several times.*

For other irregular past participles, see the table starting on page 276.

2 The imperative or command form

To ask people to do something and to make suggestions, e.g. *call me, please take me to the hotel*, you can use the imperative form, which is normally followed or preceded by the phrase **por favor** to soften the command:

Si va a Arequipa, llámeme.	*If you go to Arequipa, call me.*
Lléveme al hotel Continental, por favor.	*Please take me to the hotel Continental.*

Formation of the imperative

In Spanish there are different imperative forms depending on who you are talking to (polite or familiar) and whether you are speaking to one or more than one person (singular or plural). To form the imperative you need the stem of the first person singular of the present tense followed by the appropriate ending, one for **-ar** verbs, another for **-er** and **-ir** verbs. Here are two examples:

Infinitive	Present (1st person)	Imperative
llev**ar** (*to take*)	llev**o**	llev**e(n)** (sing/pl)
sub**ir** (*to go up, to take up*)	sub**o**	sub**a(n)** (sing/pl)

Notice that the imperative is formed by adding **-e** to the stem of **-ar** verbs and **-a** to the stem of **-er** and **-ir** verbs. The negative imperative is formed by placing **no** before the verb: **no lleve** (*don't take*), **no suba** (*don't go up / take up*).

Examples:

Lleve esta maleta a la habitación   *Please take this suitcase*
   número veinte, por favor.   *to room twenty.*
Suba mi equipaje a la   *Take my luggage to my*
   habitación, por favor.   *room please.*

Nota: Familiar imperatives have different positive and negative forms, and are not given here. If you wish to learn their forms, consult your grammar book.

Irregular imperatives

As the imperative is formed from the first person singular of the present tense, verbs which are irregular or stem-changing in the first person singular of the present tense are also irregular (though not always in the same way) or stem-changing in the imperative. Here are some examples:

Infinitive	Present (1st person)	Imperative
dar (*to give*)	doy	dé/den
decir (*to say*)	digo	diga(n)
hacer (*to do, to make*)	hago	haga(n)
oír (*to hear, to listen*)	oigo	oiga(n)
traer (*to bring*)	traigo	traiga(n)
venir (*to come*)	vengo	venga(n)

Haga el favor de venir.   *Please come.*
¿Diga?   *Can I help you?* (Lit. *Say?*)
Traiga un café, por favor.   *Bring a coffee, please.*

For other irregular imperatives, see the table starting on page 276.

Pronouns with imperatives

Pronouns go at the end of a positive form but before a negative one. Positive imperatives which carry a pronoun may need an accent. Here are some examples:

Lláme**me**.	*Call me.*
No **me** llame.	*Don't call me.*
Envíe**melo** a la habitación.	*Send it to my room.*
	(Lit. *Send it to me.*)
No **me lo** envíe a la habitación.	*Don't send it to my room.*

3 The present tense as a substitute for the imperative

The present tense is often used instead of the imperative, to soften the command. Compare these sentences:

Por favor, me **lleva** al aeropuerto.	*Will you take me to the airport, please?*
Lléveme al aeropuerto, por favor.	*Take me to the airport, please.*
Me **llama** a las seis, por favor.	*Will you call me at six, please?*
Llámeme a las seis, por favor.	*Call me at six, please.*

Actividades

1   You are visiting Perú, and at a party given by some Peruvian friends you meet someone. Use the guidelines in English to complete the conversation.

Conocido/a	¿Es la primera vez que viene al Perú?
Ud.	*Yes, it is the first time. You like it very much. It is a nice country, although you haven't seen very much yet.*
Conocido/a	¿Ha estado en el Cuzco?
Ud.	*No, you haven't been to Cuzco yet, but you hope to*

	go next week. You are going to visit Machu Picchu too. You've been told it is very interesting. Now, ask if he / she has ever been to Europe.
Conocido/a	No, no he estado nunca en Europa, pero me encantaría ir. Tengo parientes en España y me han invitado. ¿Usted conoce España?
Ud.	*Yes, you have been there several times. You like Spain a lot, especially the south.*
Conocido/a	Usted habla muy bien español. ¿Dónde lo aprendió?
Ud.	*Thank him / her and say you studied Spanish at school. Ask if he / she speaks English.*
Conocido/a	He estudiado inglés varios años, pero todavía no lo hablo muy bien. Lo encuentro muy difícil. Prefiero que hablemos español.
Ud.	*Say that's all right.*
Conocido/a	¿Se sirve otro pisco sour?
Ud.	*Say no, thank you. You've already had two. It is enough. And, besides, tomorrow you have to get up early so you must go back to your hotel soon.*
Conocido/a	No se preocupe usted, yo lo / la llevaré en mi carro.

aunque	*although*	**suficiente**	*enough*
Europa	*Europe*	**además**	*besides*
me encantaría	*I would love*	**así que ...**	*so ...*
aprender	*to learn*	**carro** (m)	*car* (Peru)
estudiar	*to study*		

2 Your Peruvian acquaintances do not seem to realise you have only been in the country a few days. They keep asking you what places you have visited. Look at the examples, then answer their questions below.

- ¿Ha visto la catedral?
- Sí, ya la ví.
- ¿Ha ido al Museo Nacional de Arte?
- No, todavía no he ido.

(*a*) ¿Ha estado en el Museo de Cultura Peruana? (sí)
(*b*) ¿Ha visitado el Palacio de Gobierno? (no)

(*c*) ¿Ha visto el Palacio de Torre Tagle? (sí)
(*d*) ¿Ha conocido el barrio de Miraflores? (no)

3 Karina Tomas from Peru was asked whether she had ever been to Cuzco. Listen to her answer and to what she says about travelling to this old Inca city and the ancient Inca ruins of Machu Picchu. The key words which follow will help you to understand and the questions that follow will help you to check your comprehension. If you do not have the cassette, look at the transcript on page 274 before you answer the questions.

conserva *it retains*	**no sé a cuánto tiempo está**
cultura incaica (f) *Inca culture*	*I don't know how long it takes*
mediante *by*	**la única forma** *the only way*

Responda en inglés

(*a*) When was Karina in Cuzco?
(*b*) What does she say about the city?
(*c*) How can you travel from Lima to Cuzco?
(*d*) How can you travel from Cuzco to Machu Picchu?

4 You are flying from Lima to Cuzco early in the morning. Here are some key phrases you will need to use. How would you say them in Spanish?

(*a*) Give me the bill, please.
(*b*) Please wake me up at 6.30.
(*c*) Could you send breakfast to my room, please?
(*d*) Take me to the airport, please.

5 Match each question on the left with the corresponding answer on the right.

(*a*)	¿Dónde está el mostrador de Aerolatina?	(i)	Esta mochila y una maleta.
(*b*)	¿Fumador o no fumador?	(ii)	No, hay una hora y media de retraso.
(*c*)	¿Cuál es su equipaje?	(iii)	Fumador.
(*d*)	¿Tiene equipaje de mano?	(iv)	Número doce.
(*e*)	¿Va a salir a la hora el avión?	(v)	Este bolso solamente.
(*f*)	¿Cuál es la puerta de embarque?	(vi)	Al fondo del pasillo, frente al mostrador de Aeroperú.

mostrador (m) *desk*	**mochila** (f) *rucksack*
a la hora *on time*	

6 At a tourist office in a Latin American country you are given a leaflet giving advice on what to do and what not to do whilst visiting the country. Read it through and see how much you can understand, then translate the leaflet for a travelling companion who does not understand Spanish.

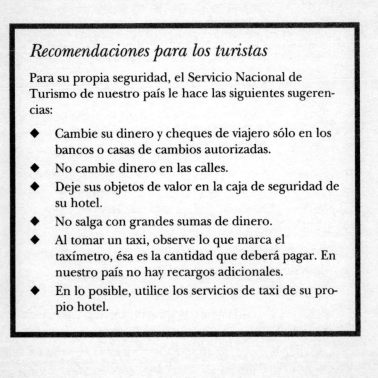

Recomendaciones para los turistas

Para su propia seguridad, el Servicio Nacional de Turismo de nuestro país le hace las siguientes sugerencias:

◆ Cambie su dinero y cheques de viajero sólo en los bancos o casas de cambios autorizadas.

◆ No cambie dinero en las calles.

◆ Deje sus objetos de valor en la caja de seguridad de su hotel.

◆ No salga con grandes sumas de dinero.

◆ Al tomar un taxi, observe lo que marca el taxímetro, ésa es la cantidad que deberá pagar. En nuestro país no hay recargos adicionales.

◆ En lo posible, utilice los servicios de taxi de su propio hotel.

autorizados/as *authorised*	**suma** (f) *sum*
objetos de valor (m, pl)	**marcar** *to indicate, to show*
valuables	**taxímetro** (m) *taxi meter*
caja de seguridad (f)	**cantidad** (f) *amount*
safe deposit box	**recargo** (m) *surcharge*

— Imágenes de Hispanoamérica —

Ancient civilisations

When the Spanish **conquistadores** arrived in America in 1492, the continent was inhabited by millions of Indians, with some highly developed civilisations. The **Mayas**, who established themselves in southern Mexico and part of Central America, built several cities, with some magnificent pyramids and palaces, such as those of Chichén Itzá, founded in the 9th century A.D., in Yucatán, Mexico. The **Aztecs**, who occupied the valley of Mexico, founded Tenochtitlán (1325), the greatest pre-Columbian city, which was destroyed by the Spaniards two hundred years later. On the same site they founded **la Ciudad de México**, which later became the capital of **la Nueva España**. In South America, the most important indigenous civilisation was that of the **Incas**, who founded the city of Cuzco in the year 1100. Their civilisation extended from present-day Peru to Bolivia, Ecuador and part of Chile and Argentina.

Pirámide del Sol, Teotihuacán, México

Religion

Religion played an important role in ancient pre-Columbian civilisations, and it had a bearing on their political and social structure as well as on their daily life. Religion was one of the things the **conquistadores** brought with them. Their domain on the continent was soon established; cities and churches were founded, and the native population, whose numbers soon began to diminish due to hard labour, diseases and killings, were to embrace the new religious order brought to them by the Catholic church. However, the old religion and culture were never completely forgotten, and some religious practices and customs of the indigenous people of the Americas today still bear the sign of the ancient civilisations.

Quinientos años después de la Conquista

It is 500 years since the Spanish **conquistadores** arrived in America, and the continent is now inhabited by about 30 million Indians. At the time of the Conquest, the estimated indigenous population was around 60 million. The following lines from a Mexican newspaper relate the way in which the surviving Indians of the American continent presently live. Study these key words before you read the text.

siglo (m) *century*	**pobreza** (f) *poverty*
albores (m, pl) *beginning*	**marginación** (f) *on the fringe of*
descendiente (m) *descendant*	*society*
pobladores (m, pl) *settlers*	**falta** (f) *lack*
sumergidos *submerged*	**desnutrición** (f) *malnutrition*

En los finales del siglo XX y albores del XXI, los 30 millones de indios descendientes de los primeros pobladores del continente americano viven sumergidos en la extrema pobreza, marginación, discriminación, falta de educación y desnutrición.

(Diario Novedades, México D.F.)

Líder indígena ganó Premio Nobel de la Paz

In 1992, Rigoberta Menchú, an Indian woman from Guatemala, won the Nobel Peace Prize for her defence of the Indians and their rights. This extract from an article published by a Chilean newspaper reproduces firstly the words expressed by a member of the Norwegian Nobel committee and then Rigoberta Menchú's comments when she heard about the prize. Study the key words before you read the text, then answer the questions which follow.

paz (f) *peace*	**ayudar** *to help*
a pesar de *in spite of*	**pueblos** (m, pl) *peoples*
mundo (m) *world*	**para siempre** *for ever*
declaró *declared*	**dijo** *said*
noruego *Norwegian*	**periodista** (m/f) *journalist*
esperanza (f) *hope*	**población** (f) *town*
premio (m) *prize*	**guatemalteca** *from Guatemala*
sea *is, will be*	**galardonada** (f) *prize-winner*

RIGOBERTA MENCHU, DE GUATEMALA:

Líder Indígena Ganó Premio Nobel de la Paz

● La galardonada anunció que con el dinero del premio creará una fundación, en memoria de su padre.

"RIGOBERTA MENCHÚ es un vívido símbolo de paz y reconciliación, a pesar de las divisiones étnicas, culturales y sociales de su país, del continente americano y del mundo", declaró el noruego Comité del Nobel.

"Tengo muchas esperanzas de que (el premio) sea una contribución para ayudar a los pueblos indígenas de América a vivir para siempre", dijo Menchú a los periodistas en la población de San Marcos, 150 kilómetros al noroeste de la capital guatemalteca.

(Diario El Mercurio, Santiago de Chile)

Responda en inglés

(a) What was said about Rigoberta Menchú by one of the members of the Nobel committee?

(b) What did Rigoberta Menchú say when she heard about the prize?

13

SIGA DERECHO

Go straight on

In this unit you will learn how to

- express hope
- express certainty and doubt
- make complaints
- ask and give directions
- describe minor ailments

Diálogos

1 Mi maleta no ha llegado

Diana Ray has just arrived in Peru on a two week holiday. Unfortunately her suitcase is missing, so Diana goes to the airline desk to report the loss.

Diana	Buenos días.
Empleada	Buenos días. ¿Qué desea?
Diana	Acabo de llegar en el vuelo 435 de Aerolatina que venía de Londres, pero mi maleta no ha llegado.
Empleada	Perdone, ¿en qué vuelo dice que venía?
Diana	En el vuelo 435 de Aerolatina.
Empleada	Y usted tomó el avión en Londres, ¿verdad?
Diana	Sí, en Londres.

Empleada	¿Cuál es su nombre?
Diana	Diana Ray, r-a-y, Ray.
Empleada	¿Tiene usted el ticket de su equipaje?
Diana	Sí, aquí está.
Empleada	Este vuelo hizo escala en París, y posiblemente, por error, su maleta fue enviada a París. No se preocupe usted. Estoy segura de que aparecerá.
Diana	Espero que la encuentren. Tengo toda mi ropa en la maleta. Es una maleta grande, de color verde oscuro. Tiene una etiqueta con mi nombre.
Empleada	Deme la dirección y el teléfono del hotel donde se quedará para llamarla cuando aparezca. Mañana hay otro vuelo de Aerolatina que viene de París. Es muy posible que llegue en ese vuelo. Yo misma me encargaré de buscarla.
Diana	Muchas gracias.

acabo de llegar	*I have just arrived*	**esperar**	*to hope*
hizo escala	*it stopped over*	**verde oscuro**	*dark green*
por error	*by mistake*	**etiqueta** (f)	*label*
fue enviada	*it was sent*	**encargarse**	*to be responsible, to be in charge*
estoy segura	*I am sure*		
aparecer	*to appear*	**buscar**	*to look for*

Responda en inglés

(a) What explanation does the airline employee offer Diana for the loss of her suitcase?

(b) How does Diana describe the suitcase?

——— Notas explicativas ———

Tomar un avión, un autobús, un tren (*to take a plane, bus, train*)

Note that, in this context, Latin Americans use **tomar** instead of **coger**, which is normally heard in Spain. Avoid the use of **coger**, as this is a taboo word in some Latin American countries.

El ticket

The Spanish word for *luggage receipt* is **el talón**, but in many places you will hear the English word **el ticket**. In some countries you will hear the word **el ticket** used instead of **el boleto** (*a bus or train ticket*).

The present subjunctive

In this unit you will also learn another tense, the present subjunctive, which is frequently used in both Spain and Latin America. The following examples from the dialogue use this tense.

Espero que la **encuentren**.	*I hope you find it.*
Es muy posible que **llegue** en ese vuelo.	*It is very likely that it will come on that flight.*
Deme el teléfono del hotel para llamarla cuando **aparezca**.	*Give me the telephone number of the hotel so I can call you when it appears.*

See **Notas gramaticales** for an explanation of how to form and use the present subjunctive.

2 Una habitación ruidosa

Diana Ray is staying at the hotel Riviera on avenida Inca Garcilaso de la Vega, a main road in the centre of Lima. The traffic noise on her first night was too much for Diana, and the following morning she complains to the receptionist about it.

Diana	Buenos días.
Recepcionista	Buenos días. ¿En qué puedo servirle?
Diana	Yo estoy en la habitación número 315 y anoche no pude dormir debido a la bulla del tráfico. La habitación es demasiado ruidosa. ¿No tendría una más tranquila?
Recepcionista	Un momentito, por favor. Veré qué habitación puedo darle.
	(*The receptionist comes back to the desk.*)
	Sí, puedo darle una habitación interior si no le importa. Es un poco oscura, pero muy tranquila.
Diana	No me importa. Prefiero cambiarme ahora mismo.
Recepcionista	Muy bien, señora. La habitación 420, en el cuarto piso, estará lista dentro de un momento. Acaba de irse la persona que estaba allí.
Diana	Muchas gracias.

anoche	*last night*	**ruidoso/a**	*noisy*
no pude (poder)	*I couldn't (to be able, can)*	**interior**	*at the back*
		importar	*to matter*
dormir (o → ue)	*to sleep*	**oscuro/a**	*dark*
debido a	*due to*	**dentro de un momento**	*in a moment*
bulla (f)	*noise*		

Responda en español

(*a*) ¿Cómo es la habitación que la recepcionista le dará a Diana?

(*b*) ¿Está lista la habitación?

Notas explicativas

Bulla (*noise*)

This is frequently used in Latin America. The standard term is **el ruido**.

Asking people whether they mind

Si no le importa.

If you don't mind. (Lit. If it doesn't matter to you.)

No me importa.

It doesn't matter to me. / I don't mind.

Notice that, in this construction, the verb **importar** (*to matter*) is used in the third person singular and is preceded by a pronoun. This construction is similar to that with **gustar**, **le / te gusta** (*you like (it)*, pol/fam), **no me gusta** (*I don't like (it)*) (see Unit 6).

3 Doble a la izquierda

Luckily for Diana, her suitcase has appeared and now she is ready to tour the city with her travelling companions. On the first day, she goes to the Museo Nacional de Arte, from the Hotel Riviera. She asks the receptionist how to get there.

Diana   Perdone, ¿podría decirme si está muy lejos el Museo Nacional de Arte?

Recepcionista   No, no está lejos. Está a unas siete u ocho cuadras de aquí, en el Paseo Colón. Al salir del hotel doble a la izquierda y siga derecho por la avenida Garcilaso de la Vega hasta el Paseo Colón. Allí tuerza a la izquierda otra vez y continúe por esa calle. El museo está en la segunda cuadra, a la derecha.

Diana   Muchas gracias.

Recepcionista   De nada.

---

u *or* (before a word beginning with o)	**siga derecho** *go straight on*
tuerza a la izquierda (torcer) *turn left (to turn)*	**hasta** *as far as*

Responda en español

(*a*) ¿En qué calle está el Museo Nacional de Arte?
(*b*) ¿A qué distancia del hotel está?

Notas explicativas

Al salir del hotel . . . (*When you leave the hotel . . .*)

This construction of **al** followed by an infinitive is fairly frequent in Spanish and may be translated into English in more than one way. Here are some further examples:

Al llegar vi a Luisa.	*On arriving / When I arrived I saw Luisa.*
Al volver entramos en un café.	*On our way back / When we were coming back we went into a cafe.*

Giving directions

Directions can be given by using the imperative (see Unit 12), e.g. **doble** (*turn*), **siga** (*go on*) **continúe** (*continue*), from **doblar**, **seguir** and **continuar** respectively. They can also be given using the present tense, e.g. (**usted**) **dobla** (*you turn*), (**usted**) **sigue** (*you go on*), (**usted**) **continúa** (*you continue*).

Both forms are equally frequent in this context, and it may be easier to use the present tense, although you will need to understand the imperative form when native speakers use it.

4 Un dolor de estómago

Problems again for Diana. She has been having some stomach trouble, so she decides to go to a chemist's to buy something.

Empleada	Buenas tardes. ¿Qué desea?
Diana	Quisiera algo para el dolor de estómago. Anoche comí algo que me cayó mal. No dormí en toda la noche.
Empleada	¿Tiene fiebre?
Diana	No, fiebre no tengo, pero no me siento bien. Todavía me duele un poco el estómago y tengo náuseas.
Empleada	No creo que sea nada serio. Posiblemente se trata de una infección muy leve. Le daré estas pastillas que son muy buenas. Tome una cada cuatro horas con un poco de agua hasta que se sienta mejor. Y trate de comer sólo comidas livianas. Nada de frituras.
Diana	Muchas gracias. ¿Cuánto es?

Empleada   Son cuatro soles.

dolor de estómago (m) *stomach ache*	**no creo que . . .** *I don't think that . . .*
me cayó mal *it didn't agree with me* (food)	**se trata de (tratarse de)** *it is (to be, to have to do with)*
¿Tiene fiebre? *Have you got a fever?*	**leve** *slight*
	pastilla (f) *tablet, pill*
No me siento bien. (sentirse) *I don't feel well. (to feel)*	**cada cuatro horas** *every four hours*
todavía *still*	**hasta que se sienta mejor** *until you feel better*
me duele el estómago (doler) (o → ue) *I have a stomach ache (to ache)*	**trate de (tratar de)** *try to (to try to)*
	comidas livianas (f, pl) *light meals*
tener náuseas *to feel sick*	**fritura** (f) *fried food*

Responda en inglés

(*a*)   Has Diana got a fever?
(*b*)   How many tablets does she have to take and how often?

Notas explicativas

Medicines over the counter

Regulations regarding the sale of medicines over the counter in Latin America are fairly loose in comparison with those in Europe or the United States, and you can often obtain medicines for which you would need a prescription in developed countries. Although standards and rules vary from country to country, it is not unusual for Latin Americans to seek the advice of a chemist for minor ailments or even more serious complaints, instead of going to the doctor. Self-medication is very common among Latin Americans, in spite of the risk involved. Most people have to pay the full price for the medicines, which can be very expensive.

Imperative forms to give instructions and advice

Tome una cada cuatro horas.   *Take one every four hours.*
Trate de comer sólo comidas   *Try to have only light meals.*
  livianas.

La pastilla (*tablet*)

In other Latin American countries you are more likely to hear the word **la tableta** or **la píldora**.

El sol

El sol is the currency used in Peru. The plural is **soles**, e.g. **son cien soles** (*it is a hundred soles*).

🔑— Frases y expresiones importantes —

- Expressing hope
Espero que la encuentren.	*I hope you find it.*
Espero que sí / no.	*I hope so / not.*

- Expressing certainty and doubt
Estoy segura de que aparecerá.	*I am sure it will appear.*
No creo que sea nada serio.	*I don't think it is anything serious.*

- Other ways of expressing certainty and doubt
Estoy seguro/a.	*I am sure.*
No estoy seguro/a.	*I am not sure.*
Seguramente.	*For certain, surely.*
Creo que sí / no.	*I think so. / I don't think so.*
Parece que sí / no.	*It seems so. / It doesn't seem so.*

- Making complaints about a noisy room
La habitación es demasiado ruidosa.	*The room is too noisy.*
Anoche no pude dormir debido al ruido del tráfico.	*I couldn't sleep last night due to the traffic noise.*

- Other common complaints
No funciona.	*It doesn't work.*
El aire acondicionado no funciona.	*The air conditioning doesn't work.*
El ventilador ...	*The fan ...*
La calefacción ...	*The central heating ...*
La llave del agua caliente ...	*The hot water tap ...*

No hay suficientes . . .	There are not enough . . .
cobijas / frazadas (f, pl)	blankets /
toallas (f, pl)	towels
No hay . . .	There is no . . .
. . . agua caliente.	. . .hot water.
. . . jabón.	. . .soap.
El lavamanos / lavatorio	The washbasin is blocked.
está tapado.	

- Lost and stolen property

Perdí / he perdido mi . . .	I lost / have lost my . . .
Me robaron / han robado mi . . .	My . . . was / has been stolen.
dinero / cheques de viajero /	money / travellers cheques /
pasaporte	passport

For other words, see the Glossary of Latin American terms starting on page 281.

- Asking for and giving directions

¿Podría decirme si está muy	Could you tell me if the
lejos el museo?	museum is very far?
Siga derecho.	Go straight on.
Doble a la izquierda.	Turn left.
Continúe por esa calle.	Continue along that street.

- Describing minor ailments

No me siento bien.	I don't feel well.
Me duele el estómago.	I have a stomach ache.
Tengo fiebre.	I have a fever.
Tengo náuseas.	I feel sick.
He vomitado.	I have vomited.

- Describing other minor ailments

Me duele la cabeza /	I have a headache / backache /
la espalda / una muela /	toothache / sore throat.
la garganta.	
Me duelen los pies.	My feet ache.
Tengo dolor de cabeza /	I have a headache /
estómago / oídos.	stomach ache / ear ache.
Tengo diarrea / indigestión.	I have diarrhoea / indigestion.
Estoy resfriado/a.	I have a cold.
Tengo gripe.	I have a cold.
Estoy enfermo/a.	I am ill.

Estoy mareado/a.	*I feel dizzy* or *seasick.*
Me siento mal.	*I feel unwell.*

Notas gramaticales

1 The subjunctive

Alongside ordinary tenses, like those you have learned in this book, Spanish also uses a small range of other tenses which correspond to what is known as the subjunctive. The subjunctive is little used in English, but you will find it in sentences like *If I were you . . .* and *Wish you were here!*

In Spanish, however, the subjunctive is quite common, but it is not normally used on its own as it is usually dependent on other verbs.

Using the subjunctive

(a) Look at this sentence: *I hope (that) you find it.*

It has two clauses: a main clause, *I hope*, and a subordinate clause, *(that) you find it.* The verb in the main clause and the one in the subordinate clause are both in the same tense: the present tense. In Spanish, however, certain verbs such as those expressing hope, doubt and possibility, require the use of the subjunctive. Look at these examples from the dialogues:

Espero que la **encuentren**.	*I hope you find it.* (hope)
Es muy posible que **llegue** en ese vuelo.	*It is very likely that it will come on that flight.* (possibility)
No creo que **sea** nada serio.	*I don't think it is anything serious.* (doubt)

Notice that all these sentences carry a clause introduced by **que** (*that*), which cannot be omitted. The verbs which follow the clause introduced by **que** are all in the present subjunctive.

However, if there is certainty, e.g. *I am sure*, the subjunctive is not used:

Estoy segura de que aparecerá.	*I am sure it will appear.*

(b) The idea of something which has not yet taken place also requires the subjunctive in Spanish. Look at these two sentences from the dialogue:

Deme el teléfono del hotel para llamarla **cuando aparezca**.
Give me the telephone number of the hotel so I can call you when it appears.

Tome una cada cuatro horas **hasta que se sienta** mejor.
Take one every four hours until you feel better.

The present subjunctive is the most frequently used subjunctive tense, and is the only one covered by this book. If you wish to study other subjunctive tenses and uses of the subjunctive, refer to your grammar book.

2 The present subjunctive

The present subjunctive normally occurs in sentences which carry a main clause in the ordinary present tense, as in the examples under (a) above, but it may also occur after a verb in the future tense or the imperative, for example:

Le **diré** que **venga**.
I will tell him / her to come.

Dile que **venga**.
Tell him / her to come.

Formation of the present subjunctive

Like the imperative, which you learned in Unit 12, the present subjunctive is formed from the first person singular of the present tense, e.g. **viajo** (*I travel*), **como** (*I eat*), **subo** (*I go up*). Drop the -**o** and add the appropriate ending: there is one set of endings for -**ar** verbs and another for -**er** and -**ir** verbs. The first and third person singular of the present subjunctive have the same form as the polite imperative that you learned in Unit 12. Here are three examples:

viajar (*to travel*)   viaj**e**, viaj**es**, viaj**e**, viaj**emos**, viaj**en**
comer (*to eat*)   com**a**, com**as**, com**a**, com**amos**, com**an**
subir (*to go up*)   sub**a**, sub**as**, sub**a**, sub**amos**, sub**an**

Note that the plural familiar forms **vosotros viajéis**, **vosotros comáis** and **vosotros subáis**, which are used in Spain, have been omitted, as these are not normally used in Latin America.

Here are some further examples demonstrating the use of the present subjunctive:

Es probable que ellos **escriban**.	*They may write.* (possibility)
Espero que él **viaje** a Venezuela.	*I hope he travels to Venezuela.* (hope)
No creo que él **llame**.	*I don't think he will call.* (doubt)

Notas:

(i)   In sentences where there is only one subject (words like **yo**, **tú**, **Carlos**) you must use the infinitive as you would in English:

Espero viajar a Venezuela.	*I hope to travel to Venezuela.*

(ii)   In an affirmative sentence with **creer**, the verb in the second clause does not require the subjunctive.

Creo que él llamará.	*I think he will call.*

Irregular forms of the present subjunctive

As with imperatives, verbs which are irregular or stem-changing in the first person of the present tense, e.g. **tener** (*to have*), and **encontrar** (*to find*), are also irregular or stem-changing in the present subjunctive. Here is an example:

Present tense: **tengo** (*I have*)
Present subjunctive: tenga, tengas, tenga, tengamos, tengan

No creo que él **tenga** dinero.	*I don't think he has money.*
Espero que **tengamos** tiempo.	*I hope we have time.*

For other examples of irregular forms look at irregular imperatives in Unit 12.

Some verbs are irregular in a different way:

dar	(*to give*)	dé, des, dé, demos, den
estar	(*to be*)	esté, estés, esté, estemos, estén
haber	(*to have*)	haya, hayas, haya, hayamos, hayan
ir	(*to go*)	vaya, vayas, vaya, vayamos, vayan
ser	(*to be*)	sea, seas, sea, seamos, sean

Espero que esta habitación **sea** mejor.	*I hope this room is better.*
No creo que él **esté** allí.	*I don't think he is there.*
Cuando **vayas** a Lima llámalo.	*When you go to Lima, call him.*

For other irregular present subjunctive forms, see the table of irregular verbs starting on page 276.

☑———————— **Actividades** ————————

1 You have just arrived in a Latin American country. Unfortunately, your luggage is missing, so you decide to go to the airline desk to complain.

Empleada	¿Qué desea?
Ud.	*Say you have just arrived on flight 310 of Hispanair which was coming from . . ., but unfortunately your luggage has not arrived.*
Empleada	¿Qué equipaje traía usted?
Ud.	*You had two suitcases, one large one and one small one. Say you have the luggage receipts. Both suitcases have labels with your name (say your name).*
Empleada	Lo siento mucho. Estas situaciones ocurren a veces, pero normalmente el equipaje aparece uno o dos días después. Seguramente no lo enviaron, o lo enviaron a otra ciudad. El vuelo hizo escala en Amsterdam y Madrid.
Ud.	*Say you hope they find them. You have all your clothes in them and also some presents you brought for friends.*
Empleada	No se preocupe usted. Seguramente van a aparecer. Yo misma me encargaré de buscarlas y lo/la llamaré por teléfono cuando aparezcan. Por favor, deme su nombre completo, su teléfono y su dirección.

---

ambos/as *both*	**traer** *to bring*
lo siento mucho *I am very sorry*	**nombre completo** (m) *full name*
ocurrir *to happen*	

---

2 As in other countries, authorities in Peru have decided to increase airport security to prevent terrorism and theft. The following passage from a Venezuelan newspaper reports this.

Look at the key vocabulary first, then check your comprehension by answering the questions that follow.

poner coto *to put a stop*	**reforzar** *to strengthen*
peligroso *dangerous*	**empresa de seguridad** (f)
hurto (m) *theft*	*security company*
inversión (f) *investment*	**vigilar** *to guard*
donar *to give*	**robo** (m) *theft*
bastón (m) *baton*	**se encontraba sin freno** *it was*
de fabricación canadiense	*uncontrolled*
manufactured in Canada	**inseguro** *insecure*
redoblar *to intensify*	**debido a** *due to*
medidas de seguridad (f, pl)	
security measures	

Con 10 detectores de armas

Perú pone coto
a inseguridad aérea

El aeropuerto de Lima era considerado hace pocas semanas como el más peligroso del mundo por el terrorismo y el hurto

Inversión en seguridad

La Organización de Aviación Civil Internacional donó 10 bastones detectores de armas de fabricación canadiense al Aeropuerto Internacional de Lima, Perú.

Estos aparatos permitirán redoblar las medidas de seguridad, además se reforzará con empresas privadas de seguridad, que vigilarán el terminal para combatir el robo de equipajes que se encontraba sin freno. Hasta hace pocas semanas este aeropuerto era considerado como el más inseguro del mundo debido a los hurtos y al terrorismo.

(El Diario de Caracas, Venezuela)

Responda en inglés

(a) What was Lima airport like a few weeks ago?
(b) How will the new arms detectors help security at Lima airport?
(c) How will security be strengthened?

3 Your first night at a hotel was a nightmare (**una pesadilla**). Several things went wrong, so you want to complain to the hotel management. Here is what you want to say. How would you express it in Spanish?

(a) The air conditioning didn't work.
(b) There was no hot water.
(c) The washbasin was blocked.
(d) There were no towels in the bathroom.
(e) The room is too noisy. You couldn't sleep last night.
(f) You want to move into a quieter room.

 4

| **No había . . .** | *There was no . . .* |

Some people are never happy! Listen to these complaints, or read the transcripts on page 274, then say in English what each person is complaining about. The first complaint takes place in an airplane and both speakers are Chilean. The second and third take place in a restaurant and the people complaining are first a Venezuelan and then a Chilean. First, look at these new words:

asiento (m) *seat*	**pedí** *I ordered*
¡Lo siento tanto! *I am so sorry!*	**sopa de mariscos** (f) *seafood*
No es culpa nuestra. *It is not*	*soup*
our fault.	**pasar** *to happen*
cambiar *to change*	**tan ocupados** *so busy*
¡Epa muchacho! Lit. *Come one*	**hoy día** *today*
boy! (Venezuela, very informal)	**tantos clientes** *so many*
¿vale? *OK?* (very frequent in	*customers*
Venezuela)	

5   Your hotel is at the corner of **avenida Abancay** and **calle Miró Quesada**, number 2 on the map. Today you want to visit the Cathedral, number 1 on the map. How would you get there from your hotel? Choose the correct directions, (*a*), (*b*) or (*c*).

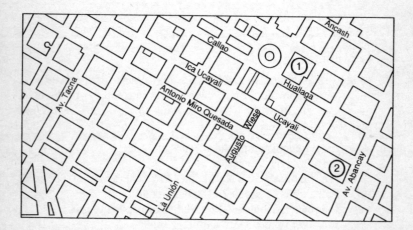

(*a*)   Siga derecho por Miró Quesada hasta la calle Augusto Wiese. Allí doble a la izquierda y camine tres cuadras hasta llegar a la Catedral.

(*b*)   Al salir del hotel, doble a la derecha y camine tres cuadras hasta la calle Augusto Wiese. En Augusto Wiese doble a la derecha. La Catedral está a dos cuadras de allí, a la derecha, en la esquina de la calle Huallaga.

(c) Cuando salga del hotel, siga por la calle Miró Quesada y continúe hasta la calle La Unión que está pasado Augusto Wiese. Doble a la derecha y siga por esa calle hasta que encuentre la Catedral, que está en la esquina de las calles Callao y La Unión.

6 While you are waiting to ask for information in the tourist office in Lima, you hear another tourist asking for directions. Listen to the conversation and complete the transcript below with the missing words. If you do not have the cassette, try guessing what those words are. The complete transcript is on page 275.

Turista	Buenas tardes. Para _____ al Teatro Segura, por favor.
Recepcionista	Sí, cómo no. Al _____ de aquí, _____ por la calle Ucayali, camine de frente hacia Abancay. Ahí _____ a la _____ izquierda, camine dos _____ y media, y ahí está el Teatro Segura.
Turista	Gracias.
Recepcionista	_____.

| **camine de frente** | *walk straight on* | **hacia** | *towards* |
| **ahí** | *there* |

7 You are not feeling very well and decide to see a doctor. It probably has something to do with some food you had last night. Use the guidelines to complete this conversation with the doctor.

Doctor	¿Qué le pasa?
Ud.	*Say you are feeling unwell. You have a stomach ache and diarrhoea.*
Doctor	¿Desde cuándo se siente así?
Ud.	*It started last night. You went out for a meal with some friends and you had fish and fried potatoes. Surely that was it. Later when you got back to your hotel you started to feel unwell.*
Doctor	¿Ha tenido vómitos?
Ud.	*Yes, you have vomited and you seem to have a fever too.*
	(*The doctor examines you and gives you a prescription* (**una receta**).)

Doctor	No creo que sea nada grave. Se trata simplemente de una infección estomacal. Con esta receta vaya a la farmacia y compre estas pastillas que son muy buenas. Tome dos cada seis horas. Estoy seguro de que se sentirá mejor.
Ud.	*Say you hope so.*

¿Qué le pasa? *What's wrong with you?*	grave *serious*
empezar *to start*	infección estomacal (f) *stomach infection*

8 You might not like the idea of visiting a doctor who needs to advertise on the radio to get patients, but if you had to, here is one from Veracruz, in Mexico! Listen to the advertisement, or read the transcript on page 275, then answer the questions that follow. First, look at these key words:

fractura (f) *fracture*	ortopedia (f) *orthopaedics*
luxación (f) *dislocation*	consultas (f, pl) *surgery hours*
cirugía (f) *surgery*	
traumatología (f) *orthopaedic surgery*	

Complete estas frases

(a) Las horas de consulta del doctor Manuel Loyo de Valdés son de _____ a _____ y de _____ a _____ .

(b) El doctor atiende en González Pajés número _____ .

(c) El número de teléfono del doctor es el _____ .

9 A patient arrives at a doctor's surgery in Peru. Listen to his conversation with the receptionist and note down the days and times when the surgery is open. If you do not have the casette, use the transcript on page 275 for reading comprehension. First look at these key words:

pedir hora *to ask for an appointment* (with doctor or dentist)	atender *to be available*

—— Imágenes de Hispanoamérica ——

Fiestas

Latin Americans love **fiestas** and almost any event, whether a public holiday or a religious festival, is an occasion for celebration. Some festivities remember old Indian traditions, while others, mostly religious in nature, are a legacy of Spanish colonisation. In places where black people are more predominant, especially around the Caribbean, the African element is evident in many celebrations. All these traditions merge to give Latin American festivals a unique character.

Christmas, Easter and **El Día de los Muertos** (lit. *the day of the dead*), on 1st November, are celebrated throughout Latin America, although the latter is not a public holiday in all countries. Many places have their own religious celebrations, such as those in honour of patron saints. Some public holidays commemorate historical events, like independence day for instance, which is a big occasion for celebration, in some countries lasting more than one day.

This love of **fiestas** is expressed in simple words by Octavio Paz, a well-known Mexican writer who won the Nobel Prize for Literature in 1990. Although Paz refers specifically to Mexicans, what he says is also true of other Latin American people:

"El solitario mexicano ama las fiestas y las reuniones públicas. Todo es ocasión para reunirse. Cualquier pretexto es bueno para interrumpir la marcha del tiempo y celebrar con festejos y ceremonias hombres y acontecimientos. Somos un pueblo ritual."

(*El laberinto de la soledad*, Octavio Paz, Fondo de Cultura Económica, page 42, 1959, México.)

amar *to love*	**festejo** (m) *feast*
reunirse *to meet*	**hombres** (m, pl) *men*
cualquier *any*	**acontecimiento** (m) *event*
interrumpir *to interrupt*	**pueblo** (m) *people*

Long weekends

Public holidays may sometimes fall near a weekend, e.g. on Tuesday or Thursday, in which case workers, public officials and students are sometimes given the Monday or Friday off too. This is called **un puente** (*a bridge*) in most countries. In Chile, this practice is known as **hacer sandwich** (*to make a sandwich*). Beware, as banks sometimes remain closed for up to three days. And if you are travelling within the country, bear in mind that on these long weekends you may have difficulty with transport and in finding a hotel room.

Música y baile

Most Latin Americans love music and dance, and this is especially true in Mexico and the Caribbean. Each region has its own form of folk and popular music. The **mariachis** of Mexico, in their colourful outfits and big **sombreros**, playing **rancheras** to the sound of trumpets, guitars and violins, are probably the best known. Along the Gulf coast, you can enjoy the romantic sound of the **marimbas** (a kind of xylophone), while sitting in an open-air cafe or bar.

Along the Caribbean, in countries like Cuba, the Dominican Republic and Colombia, you will find different forms of music and dance, in which the African influence is clearly evident. The **cumbia** of Colombia and the **salsa**, made popular by the Cuban singer Celia

Cruz, have gone far beyond the borders of this region. In the Andean countries, notably Peru and Bolivia, people sing and dance to the sound of old Indian instruments such as the **charango** (a small guitar) or the **zampoña** (panpipe). Argentina is the land that gave the world the **tango**, less popular now but nevertheless still enjoyed by many. Young Latin Americans, as in other parts of the world, prefer the sound and rhythm of pop music while adults tend to stick to their traditional favourites, like the old **bolero**, which has made a comeback.

—— PRONUNCIATION ——

The aim of this brief pronunciation guide is to offer hints which will enable you to produce sounds recognisable to a speaker from any part of the Spanish-speaking world. It cannot by itself teach you to pronounce Spanish accurately. The best way to acquire a reasonably good accent is to listen to and try to imitate native speakers.

This guide gives hints on individual sounds only and does not take into account differences in accent which may occur within Latin America. Information on pronunciation related to specific countries is given in the following units: Mexico, Unit 1; Colombia, Unit 5; Chile, Unit 7; Venezuela, Unit 8 (dialogue 3); Argentina, Unit 10 and Peru, Unit 12.

—————— Vowels ——————

Spanish vowels are generally shorter, clearer and more precise than English vowels. Unstressed vowels are not weakened as in English but are given much the same value in pronunciation as those which are stressed. For example, in the English word *comfortable*, the vowels which follow the syllable *com* are weak, while in Spanish every vowel in the word **confortable** has the same quality.

There are only five vowel sounds in Spanish:

a	like the **u** in *butter*, as in standard south of England pronunciation	**gracias**
e	like the **e** in *end*	**él**
i	like the **i** in *marine*	**inglés**

o	like the **o** in *God*	**so**l
u	like the **oo** in *moon*	**u**no

Note:

When **i** occurs before another vowel, it is pronounced like the **y** in *yes*.	**ti**ene
When **u** occurs before another vowel, it is pronounced like the **w** in *wind*.	b**ue**no
After **q**, **u** is not pronounced at all.	q**u**e
u is also silent in **gui** and **gue**.	g**u**ía, g**u**erra
u is pronounced in **güi** and **güe**,	ling**ü**ística
a very infrequent sound combination in Spanish.	verg**ü**enza

Consonants

The pronunciation of Spanish consonants is generally similar to that of English consonants. But note the following features:

b and **v**	in initial position and after **n**, like the **b** in *bar*.	**b**ien, in**v**ierno
	in other positions, more like the **v** in *very*.	Cari**b**e, El Sal**v**ador
c	before **a**, **o**, **u**, like the **c** in *coast*.	**c**astellano
	before **e**, **i**, like the **s** in *sea*.	ha**c**er, gra**c**ias
ch	like the **ch** in *chair*.	**Ch**ile
d	like the **d** in *day*.	**d**ía
	between vowels and after **r**, more like the **th** in *those*.	na**d**a, tar**d**e
g	before **a**, **o**, **u**, like the **g** in *government*.	ha**g**o, **G**uatemala
	before **e**, **i**, like the **h** in *hand* in Central America and the Caribbean, but more like the Scottish **ch** in *loch* in other countries.	Ar**g**entina, Ser**g**io
j	like the **h** in *hand* in Central America and the Caribbean, but more like the Scottish **ch** in *loch* in other countries.	**J**uan
h	is silent.	a**h**ora
ll	like the **y** of *yawn*.	**ll**amar
ñ	like the **ni** in *onion*.	ma**ñ**ana

q(u) like the **c** in *cake*.	**que**
r in initial position is strongly rolled.	**río**
rr strongly rolled.	**carro**
y like the **y** in *yes*.	**mayo**
z like the **s** in *sale*.	**Venezuela**

Nota: In Mexico, there are many place names derived from indigenous languages which carry an **x**. The pronunciation of **x** varies, as can be seen from these examples:

Taxco	pronounced as **ks**
Xochimilco	pronounced as **s**
Oaxaca	pronounced as **h**
Ixtapa	pronounced as **sh**

—— Stress and accentuation ——

Words which end in a vowel, **n** or **s** stress the last syllable but one.

bueno, a**mi**gos

Words which end in a consonant other than **n** or **s**, stress the last syllable.

ho**tel**, se**ñor**

Words which do not follow the above rules, carry a written accent over the stressed syllable.

A**mé**rica, auto**bús**

Differences in meaning between certain similar words are shown through the use of an accent.

sí (*yes*) **si** (*if*)
él (*he*) **el** (*the*, m)
sé (*I know*) **se** (*pronoun*)
dé (*give*) **de** (*of, from*)
mí (*me*) **mi** (*my*)
sólo (*only*) **solo** (*alone*)

Question words carry an accent, and are preceded by an inverted question mark.

¿dónde? (*where?*)
¿cuándo? (*when?*)
¿qué? (*what?*)
¿cuál? (*which?*)
¿cómo? (*how?*)

In exclamations, **que** carries an accent. Notice also the inverted exclamation mark at the beginning.

¡Qué lindo! (*How beautiful!*)
¡Qué difícil! (*How difficult!*)

Spelling

Note the following changes in spelling.

Verbs may change their spelling in certain forms in order to keep the sound of the infinitive. For example:

lle**gar** (*to arrive*)   but lle**gué** (*I arrived*)
pa**gar** (*to pay*)   but pa**gué** (*I paid*)
bus**car** (*to look for*)   but bus**qué** (*I looked for*)

Liaison

If a word ends in a vowel and is followed by a word beginning with a vowel, the two vowels are normally pronounced as though both were part of the same word. When the two vowels are the same, these are usually pronounced as one, for example:

¿Cómo está usted?
No está aquí.
¿Habla español?

Pronouncing the alphabet

a	**a**	n	**ene**
b	**be**	ñ	**eñe**
c	**c**	o	**o**
ch	**che***	p	**pe**
d	**de**	q	**cu**
e	**e**	r	**ere**
f	**efe**	s	**ese**
g	**ge**	t	**te**
h	**ache**	u	**u**
i	**i**	v	**uve***
j	**jota**	w	**doble u***
k	**ka**	x	**equis**
l	**ele**	y	**i griega**
ll	**elle**	z	**zeta**
m	**eme**		

Notas:

* When spelling a word with **ch**, **ch** is split into **ce** and **ache**, for example *Chile*: **ce**, **ache**, **i**, **ele**, **e**.

* As Spanish does not make a distinction in pronunciation between **b** and **v**, when spelling a word, **v** is normally qualified as **ve pequeña**, **ve chica** or **ve corta**, depending on the country, or else, examples are given: **be** de bonito, **ve** de Venezuela.

* **w** is called **doble uve** in some countries and **doble ve** in others.

KEY TO THE EXERCISES

Unit 1

Diálogos 4 (*a*) Señor Molina is from Monterrey. (*b*) Señora Lagos is from Puebla. **5** (*a*) Mark is English. (*b*) He is from London. (*c*) Nora is Mexican. (*d*) She is from Jalapa.
Actividades 1 Buenos días. / Tengo una reservación. / Mi nombre es . . . *or* Me llamo . . . (*name*). / Gracias. **2** Buenas tardes. / No, no soy Emilio/a Zapata. Soy . . . (*your name*). / No se preocupe. **3** Mi nombre es . . . *or* Me llamo . . . (*name*), soy de . . . (*place where you come from*). / Mucho gusto *or* Encantado/a. / Siéntese, por favor. **4** No, no soy americano/a. Soy inglés / inglesa (*or* Sí, soy americano/a). / Soy de (*city*). / Me llamo . . . (*name*). ¿Y tú? / Mucho gusto *or* Encantado/a. **5** (*a*) Buenas tardes. (*b*) ¿Cuál es su nombre? *or* ¿Cómo se llama Ud.? (*c*) ¿De dónde es (usted)? (*d*) ¿Es usted mexicano/a? (*e*) ¿De qué parte de México es? **7** Pablo Miranda Frías es venezolano. Pablo es de Caracas. **8** (*a*) Initia is from Córdoba in Veracruz. (*b*) ¿De qué país es Ud.? (*c*) Clotilde is from Veracruz. (*d*) ¿De dónde es Ud.? (*e*) Elizabeth is from Panama City. (*f*) Hola, me llamo Elizabeth.
Imágenes de Hispanoamérica
(*a*) There are 19 countries (including Puerto Rico). (*b*) They are in the Caribbean. (*c*) Spanish.

Unit 2

Diálogos 1 (*a*) Room fifty. (*b*) Fifth floor. **5** (*a*) It is two blocks from the hotel, near the monument to Cuauhtemoc. (*b*) It is on the right.
Actividades 1 habitación doscientos veinte, en el segundo piso; habitación cuatrocientos treinta, en el cuarto piso; habitación quinientos cincuenta, en el quinto piso (*follow the model to complete the dialogues*). **2** Hola, ¿cómo estás? *or* ¿cómo te va? / Estoy muy bien. Siéntate. Me alegro mucho de verte. / ¿Cómo están tus papás? **3** Buenos días, ¿cómo está usted? *or* ¿Cómo le va? / Bien, gracias. Siéntese, por favor. Me alegro mucho de verla. **5** (*a*) He is looking for a bureau de change. (*b*) There is one in the calle Amazonas. (*c*) Five blocks away. (*d*) He is in his office. (*e*) 240 (*f*) On the second floor. (*g*) At the end of the corridor, on the right. **6** ¿Hay una (*or* alguna) estación (de metro) por aquí? (*b*) ¿Dónde está? *or* ¿Está lejos? (*c*) ¿Hay un (*or* algún) hotel por aquí? (*d*) ¿Está lejos? (*e*) ¿Dónde está el Banco Nacional, por favor? (*f*) ¿Dónde está la calle Panuco? *or* ¿Está cerca / lejos la calle Panuco? **7** (*a*) F. (*b*) F. (*c*) V. **8** (*a*) It is half a block from the main street. (*b*) It is one and a half blocks from the main park.

Imágenes de Hispanoamérica (*a*) It is in a valley, at an altitude of 2,240 m. (*b*) It has a rich cultural and artistic life, and is the intellectual centre of Latin America. (*c*) It is a mixture of old and new. It is a modern city, with wide avenues and lively squares, elegant districts, popular markets, futuristic buildings, colonial buildings and baroque churches.

Unit 3

Diálogo 6 (*a*) Rosa has breakfast at 8.30 a.m. (*b*) Raúl has breakfast at 7.00 a.m. (*c*) Raúl has lunch between 12.30 and 1.00 p.m. (*d*) Rosa has lunch at 2.00 p.m. **Actividades 1** (*a*) Es la una y media. (*b*) Son las seis veinticinco. (*c*) Son las siete y cuarto. (*d*) Son veinte para las nueve. *or* Son las nueve menos veinte. (*e*) Es un cuarto para las diez. *or* Son las diez menos cuarto. (*f*) Son las once. **2** (*a*) Son las diez. (*b*) Son las cinco. (*c*) Es la una. (*d*) Son las seis. **3** (*a*) Está detrás del Auditorio Nacional. (*b*) El viernes quince hay una función. (*c*) Es a las ocho de la noche. (*d*) Es a las doce. **4** (*a*) ¿A qué hora abren las tiendas? (*b*) ¿A qué hora abre(n) el supermercado? (*c*) ¿A qué hora cierra(n) el correo? (*d*) ¿A qué hora cierran los museos? **5** (*a*) F. (*b*) V. (*c*) F. **6** Disculpe, ¿Qué hora tiene? / Son las dos y media. / ¿A qué hora abren las casas de cambio? / Abren a las cuatro. / ¿Hay una casa de cambio por aquí? / Sí, La Internacional está a dos cuadras de aquí . . . **7** (*a*) Tomo el desayuno (*or* Desayuno) a las . . . (*time*). (*b*) Almuerzo a las . . . (*time*). (*c*) Almuerzo en (casa / la oficina / una cafetería / un restaurante / un bar). (*d*) No, no muy tarde. *or* Sí, bastante / muy tarde. Ceno a las . . . (*time*). **8** (*a*) Breakfast between 8.00 and 9.00 a.m., lunch between 1.30 and 3.30 p.m. and dinner between 8.30 and 9.00 p.m. (*b*) It is at 11.30 p.m. (*c*) mediodía. (*d*) 1.00 y 2.00. (*e*) de las 7.00 en adelante.

Unit 4

Diálogos 1 (*a*) Luisa lives in Cancún. (*b*) She works in a travel agency. (*c*) Juan is an architect. **2** (*a*) Because it is a beautiful place and it has a good climate. (*b*) She starts at nine in the morning and finishes at seven. **3** (*a*) Sometimes he goes out of Santiago, to the beach or the countryside. When he stays in Santiago he goes to the cinema or out with friends. (*b*) She normally watches television, reads or listens to music. **4** (*a*) She has two children. (*b*) They are aged twelve and ten.

Actividades 1 *The only changes are*: Te presento a mi mamá. Éste es Raúl. / Encantada. **2** *Ud.*: Buenas tardes, señor Molina. ¿Cómo está Ud.? *Sr. Molina*: Muy bien, gracias. ¿Y Ud.? *Ud.*: Bien, gracias. Le presento a mi colega John Evans. Éste es el señor Molina. *Sr. Molina*: Encantado. *J. Evans*: Mucho gusto. *Sr. Molina*: Siéntense, por favor. **3** (*a*) ¿Dónde vives? / Vivo en . . . (*place*). ¿En qué trabajas? / Soy . . . (*occupation or profession*) *or* Trabajo en . . . (*place of work*). (*b*) ¿De dónde son ustedes? / Soy de . . . (*country*). ¿Dónde viven (ustedes)? / ¿Y en qué trabajan? / Yo soy . . . (*occupation or profession*) *or* Trabajo en . . . (*place of work*). **4** (*a*) F. (*b*) V. (*c*) F. **5** *Key phrases*: Soy . . . (*occupation*) *or* Trabajo en . . . (*place of work*) *or* Estudio en . . . (*place where you are studying*). Trabajo de lunes a viernes *or* Voy a la universidad / al colegio de lunes a viernes. Empiezo a las . . . (*time*) y termino a las . . . (*time*). Generalmente almuerzo en . . . (*place*). Cuando salgo del trabajo / de la universidad / del colegio, generalmente (veo la televisión / leo el periódico / escucho música / estudio / visito a mis amigos/as / riego el jardín / cocino, etc.). Los fines de semana (me levanto tarde / trabajo en casa / salgo de compras / juego al tenis / voy al cine / salgo a caminar / salgo a correr, etc.). **6** (*a*) She visits her nephews in Tijuana. (*b*) Because she very rarely sees her family. **8** *Name*: Clotilde Montalvo Rodríguez *Age*: 44 *Marital status*: Married *Profession*: Secretary *Husband's profession*: Coach or lorry driver *N^O of children*: 2 *Ages*: 23, 6$^1/_2$ **9** (*a*) Soy casado/a *or* Soy soltero/a. (*b*) Tengo (dos) hijos. / No tengo hijos. (*c*) Tengo (tres) hermanos. / No tengo hermanos. (*d*) John tiene (doce) años, Anne tiene (siete). (*e*) Vivo en . . . (*city or town*).

Imágenes de Hispanoamérica (*a*) She reads the newspaper *The News* and listens to the news in English on CBS. (*b*) She buys an eau de cologne for her husband. (*c*) She buys Aunt Jemina flour to make hot cakes and some Miller Light beer. (*d*) She thinks it is a guarantee of quality.

Unit 5

Diálogos 1 (*a*) He orders fillet steak. (*b*) He drinks red wine and then coffee. **3** (*a*) Vegetable soup. (*b*) Roast chicken with rice and a mixed salad. **4** (*a*) James orders a fruit salad. (*b*) Señor Donoso orders chocolate ice-cream.

Actividades 1 Buenos días, quisiera reservar una mesa para dos (personas). / Sí, para hoy. / Para la una y media. / A nombre de . . . (*your name*). **2** Buenas tardes, tengo (*or* tenemos) una reservación para la una y media. / Mi nombre es . . . *or* Me llamo . . . (*your name*). **3** *Mesera*: ¿Qué desean comer? *Ud*: Yo quiero un cocktail de camarones para empezar y después quiero pescado. *M*: El pescado, ¿cómo lo quiere? *Ud*: Lo quiero a la plancha. *M*: ¿Y con qué lo quiere? *Ud*: (Lo quiero) con puré. *M*: ¿Algo más? *Ud*: Nada más, gracias. *M*: ¿Y para Ud., señor? *Colega*: Para mí, crema de zapallo. *M*: ¿Y qué más? *Colega*: Quiero chuletas de ternera. *M*: ¿Con qué las quiere? *Colega*: (Las quiero) con arroz. Y tráigame una ensalada de tomate y lechuga también. *M*: Muy bien, señor. ¿Y qué van a tomar? *Ud*: Una botella de vino tinto. *M*: ¿Qué desean de postre? *Ud*: Yo quiero mangos en almíbar.

Colega: Yo prefiero fresas con crema. *M*: ¿Van a tomar café? *Ud*: Sí, yo sí. *Colega*: Para mí no, gracias. **4** (*a*) Sopa de pollo. (*b*) Soufflé de calabaza. (*c*) Una cerveza. **5** (*a*) Because the food tastes good, the service is good, the prices are low and it's a nice place. (*b*) They serve fish, seafood and meat.

Imágenes de Hispanoamérica (*a*) The two main products which came to Europe from the Americas are potates and tomatoes. (*b*) It is difficult to imagine European cuisine without these products. (*c*) The most typical food in Mexico are tortillas, a maize bread used in many Mexican dishes. Another basic ingredient in Mexican food is chilli. (*d*) the staple food in Central America is maize. (*e*) A typical dish in many Caribbean and South American countries is chicken with rice. (*f*) Argentinians and Uruguayans prefer to eat beef.

Unit 6

Diálogos 1 (*a*) F. (*b*) F. **2** (*a*) verde (*b*) efectivo **3** (*a*) 250 pesos a pound. (*b*) She buys two lettuces. (*c*) She pays 1,185 pesos in total. **4** (*a*) She buys two 1,200 peso stamps and five 600 peso stamps. (*b*) It is outside.

Actividades 1 Quisiera ver ese bolso que está en la vitrina. / Ése, el café (*or* marrón). / Es muy bonito. ¿Es de cuero? / ¿Cuánto cuesta? / ¿(No) tiene otro más barato? / Me gusta mucho. / Lo voy a llevar. ¿Puedo pagar con tarjeta de crédito? / Sí, es para regalo. **2** Quisiera ver (una chaqueta), por favor. / Talla . . . (*your size*). / ¿Qué colores tiene? / La prefiero en blanco. / No me gusta mucho el modelo. ¿Tiene otras? / Sí, ésas me gustan más. / ¿Me la puedo probar? / Me queda muy bien. ¿Cuánto cuesta (*or* vale)? / Sí, la voy a llevar. / Voy a pagar en efectivo. **3** *Precio sin descuento*: 32,000 pesos. *Precio con descuento*: 28,800 pesos. *Color*: negro. *Número*: 42. **4** (*a*) Long and short sleeved sport shirts are on offer. (*b*) Men's trousers have a 30, 40 and 50% discount. (*c*) Todos los pantalones para caballeros. No incluye promociones. **5** (*a*) ¿Cuánto valen (*or* cuestan) los aguacates? (*b*) ¿Tiene mangos? (*c*) ¿Qué precio tienen los duraznos? (*d*) Quiero un kilo de zanahorias. (*e*) Deme una lechuga. (*f*) Quiero dos repollos. (*g*) Eso es todo. (*h*) ¿Cuánto es? **6** mandar *or* enviar; a; pesos; estampilla; de; Eso; es; tres mil cuatrocientos; buzón; a. **7** A bedroom suite, a double sofabed, a 10-foot refrigerator, a washing machine, a TV table, a stereo system, a 14" TV. The total is 1,050,000 pesos.

Unit 7

Diálogos 1 (*a*) V. (*b*) F. **2** (*a*) No, not at this time of the year. (*b*) She proposes to take something for the rain.
Actividades 1 Pienso ir a México y Quito. / No, voy a estar allí doce días en total. / Sí, es un tour y no es muy caro. Cuesta novecientos cuarenta y nueve dólares. / Sí, incluye el pasaje aéreo (*or* el vuelo), hoteles de cuatro estrellas, excursiones y traslados. / No, voy a viajar con un colega. ¿Y tú, qué vas a hacer este verano? **2** (*a*) Coyoacán is a typical district, with good restaurants and some important monuments. (*b*) You will be able to visit the Frida Khalo Museum. (*c*) Cuernavaca and Taxco. (*d*) No. **3** (*a*) It is quite pleasant. (*b*) It is a little cold. (*c*) It does not rain much. (*d*) A sweater for the mornings and evenings. **4** está; tiene; hay; tiene. **5** Facilities include air conditioning in the rooms, water bed, jacuzzi, suites with a pool, satellite TV and piped music. **6** (*a*) It has 216 rooms. (*b*) It has two restaurants. (*c*) It has a swimming pool, conference rooms, a casino and a disco. **7** (*a*) Voy a ir (*or* Iré) al banco a comprar cheques de viajero. (*b*) Voy a tener (*or* Tendré *or* Tengo) una reunión con el director de producción. (*c*) Voy a almorzar con el gerente. (*d*) Voy a estar (*or* Estaré *or* Estoy) libre entre

las dos y media y las tres. **8** (*a*) F. (*b*) V. (*c*) V. (*d*) She says Lima is a nice, big and modern city, which retains some of the characteristics of colonial culture. (*e*) Lima has nice beaches, museums and zoos. (*f*) The weather is warm and there is almost no rain. **9** (*a*) Es una ciudad grande / mediana / pequeña / moderna / antigua / industrial / agrícola. (*b*) Tiene . . . habitantes. (*c*) (No) hace mucho frío. *or* (No) llueve mucho. *or* En verano (generalmente) hace calor (*or* sol). **10** (*a*) No, en México está nublado. (*b*) En Londres está despejado. (*c*) No, en París está despejado. (*d*) En Madrid está lloviendo (*or* lluvioso).

Unit 8

Diálogos 1 (*a*) 18.30 (6.30 p.m.) (*b*) 14.00 (2.00 p.m.) **2** (*a*) A double room costs 18,000 pesos. (*b*) No, breakfast is not included. **3** (*a*) Ella quiere una habitación individual. (*b*) Ella prefiere una habitación con baño. **4** (*a*) He is there on holiday with his wife and children. (*b*) They have been there for a week.
Actividades 1 *Ud*: ¿A qué hora hay tren a Concepción? *Empleado / a*: Hay uno a las veintidós treinta (10.30 p.m.). *Ud*: ¿A qué hora llega a Concepción? *E*: Llega a las siete y media de la mañana. *Ud*: ¿Tiene (*or* Lleva) coche dormitorio? *E*: Sí, sí tiene (*or* lleva). *Ud*: ¿Cuánto cuesta la cama? *E*: La cama baja vale trece mil quinientos pesos y la alta nueve mil novecientos. *Ud*: ¿De ida o de ida y vuelta? *E*: De ida y vuelta. *Ud*: Muy bien. Deme un boleto de ida y vuelta para el lunes veinte de julio. Prefiero una cama baja. **2** Voy a viajar a Concepción. / Me voy el veinte de julio. / No, voy a viajar en tren. / Demora nueve horas. / No, para en San Rosendo. **3** *Ud*: Buenos días. ¿Tiene una habitación? *Recepcionista*: Sí, sí tenemos. ¿Quiere una habitación doble o sencilla? *Ud*: Sencilla. ¿Cuánto vale? *R*: Veinticinco mil pesos. *Ud*: ¿Está incluido el desayuno? *R*: No, el desayuno es

aparte. ¿Cuánto tiempo va a quedarse? *Ud*: Cinco días solamente. *R*: Bien, me da su nombre, por favor. *Ud*: (*Say your name.*) *R*: ¿Cómo se escribe? *Ud*: (*Spell your name.*) *R*: ¿Y la dirección? *Ud*: (*Give your address.*) *R*: Gracias. Su habitación es la 320, en el tercer piso. Aquí tiene la llave. El ascensor está al fondo. **4** (*a*) It lasts three days. (*b*) It leaves early on Friday morning. (*c*) It returns on Sunday night. (*d*) It includes return air ticket from Santiago, land transport, food, accommodation in tents, equipment and professional guides. (*e*) There are discounts for groups of over eight people. **5** (*a*) Llega en el vuelo 173. (*b*) Viaja en LAN Chile. (*c*) Llega a las veintiuna cincuenta y cinco (9.55 p.m.). **6** (*a*) F. (*b*) F. (*c*) V. (*d*) F.

Imágenes de Hispanoamérica
(*a*) Most people in Latin America travel by bus. (*b*) In Mexico, there is a first-class bus service with air conditioning and toilet. Seats can be booked in advance, and the service is much more comfortable than the second-class service. (*c*) During holiday time you have to book in advance because many people travel by bus.

Unit 9

Diálogos 1 (*a*) She booked it about a week ago. (*b*) No, she booked it over the telephone. **2** (*a*) She has gone out to lunch with a client. (*b*) He asks the secretary to tell señora Miranda that Dennis Clerk, from London, phoned to inform her that he arrived in Santiago yesterday and is staying at the Plaza Hotel. He will phone again at 4.30. **4** (*a*) He arrived on Wednesday night. (*b*) No, he was in Santiago five years ago.

Actividades 1 *Ud*: Buenas tardes. Mi nombre es . . . (*name*). Tengo una habitación reservada. *Recepcionista*: Perdone, ¿puede repetir su nombre, por favor? *Ud*: (*Say your name again and spell it.*) *R*: ¿Cuándo hizo la reserva (*or* reservación)? *Ud*: No la hice yo, mi

secretaria reservó la habitación por teléfono desde (*town*) hace cinco días más o menos. *R*: Ah sí, aquí está. Es la habitación número cincuenta en el quinto piso. ¿Podría llenar esta ficha, si es tan amable? **2** (*a*) ¿Aló? (*b*) Quiero el anexo dos, cinco, cinco, dos (*or* veinticinco cincuenta y dos), por favor. (*c*) Quisiera hablar con el señor Juan Miguel García, por favor. *or* ¿Está el señor . . . ? (*d*) ¿De parte de quién? – De parte de (*your name*). (*e*) Encantado de conocerlo, señor García. (*f*) Por favor, dígale que llamó . . . (*your name*). Llegué a Santiago hace dos días y estoy en el hotel Plaza, en la habitación número cincuenta. **3** (*a*) Carmen Puig, from Caracas, needs to speak to señor Solís urgently. She wants him to phone her at the Sheraton Hotel, room 500, where she is staying. But it has to be now, as she is leaving for Caracas tomorrow.
(*b*) Marilú Pérez came to see señor Solís. She is staying at the Gala Hotel, in room 324. The telephone number is 687951. **5** (*a*) ¿Cuándo llegó (usted)? (*b*) ¿Qué tal el viaje? (*c*) ¿Volvió (ya) la señorita Alonso? (*d*) ¿Es la primera vez que viene (usted) a Santiago? (*e*) ¿Le gustó Chile? (*f*) ¿Cenó (usted) ya? 5 fue; fui; estuvimos; entramos; gustó; levanté; tomé; senté. **6** (*a*) She went to the coast with her family. (*b*) They stayed in a hotel opposite the beach. (*c*) She says the place is pleasant, quiet, has wonderful beaches and that the air is very clean. (*d*) Salimos mucho, tomamos el sol, nadamos, hicimos deportes. **7** (*a*) Fui a . . . (*place*). (*b*) Fui solo/a / acompañado/a. (*c*) Me quedé en . . . (*place*). (*d*) Estuve . . . (*length of time*) allí. (*e*) *Possible replies*: nadé, tomé el sol, salí a pasear, fui a bailar, comí mucho, bebí mucho, etc.

Imágenes de Hispanoamérica (*a*) The war ended on Tuesday, 15th December. (*b*) More than 75,000 people died. (*c*) More than half a million people escaped abroad.

Unit 10

Diálogos 1 (*a*) He was there two years ago. (*b*) She is a psychologist and she worked with an Argentinian colleague. **2** (*a*) She used to travel by train. (*b*) She was quite young and very nice.

Actividades 1 vivía; trabajaba; viajaba; pasaba; compartía; se llamaba; vivían; era; tenía; estaba... gustaba; había. **2** (*a*) Ella vivía en Bariloche. (*b*) Trabajaba como guía en una agencia de turismo. (*c*) Era muy agradable. (*d*) Estaba frente al lago. (*e*) La vida era muy tranquila y a veces un poco monótona. (*f*) Porque ella extrañaba a su familia. **3** (*a*) Tenía dos dormitorios. (*b*) Tenía dos baños. (*c*) La cocina estaba entre el dormitorio dos y el estar-comedor. (*d*) Había una cama. **4** (*a*) V. (*b*) F. (*c*) F. (*d*) V. (*e*) F. **5** (*a*) Hace cinco/diez años yo vivía en . . . (*town or old address*). (*b*) Estaba soltero/a / casado/a. (*c*) Vivía con . . . (mis padres / mi novio/a / mi marido / mujer / mis hijos, etc.). (d) Estudiaba / Trabajaba. (*e*) Estudiaba / Trabajaba en . . . (*place*). *or* Trabajaba en una empresa / compañía / con un colegio que se llamaba . . . (*name*). (*f*) (No) me gustaba (mucho). (*g*) Mi casa / departamento / apartamento era grande / chico / agradable / cómodo, etc. **6** (*a*) ¿Dónde vivías antes? (*b*) ¿En qué parte de Ecuador vivías? (*c*) ¿Qué hacías allá? (*d*) ¿Y qué estás haciendo acá? **7** (*a*) He describes Buenos Aires as a very large city, with many different corners, but with a unity. A city with a cultural life, a city which has 'a soul'. (*b*) He likes its nightlife, and the possibility it gives its people for expressing themselves. He likes its cultural life. (*c*) He does not like the tendency the 'porteños' have towards sadness and melancholy. **8** Él era guapo. / Ella era bonita / linda. Era trigueño/a (moreno/a *in certain countries*), alto/a y delgado/a. Tenía pelo negro y ojos verdes. Tenía unos veinticinco años y era muy simpático/a.

Imágenes de Hispanoamérica (*a*) F. (*b*) F. (*c*) V. (*d*) mexicana (*e*) un millón (*f*) ochenta por ciento

Unit 11

Diálogos 1 (*a*) It is half a block away. (*b*) It is two blocks further down, on the right. **2** (*a*) A car with room for four people, comfortable and economical. (*b*) He wants it for two days only, Saturday and Sunday. **3** (*a*) He asks the attendant to fill the petrol tank and to check the tyre pressure. (*b*) It is about twenty kilometres **5** (*a*) He wants to phone London. (*b*) He wants to make a person-to-person call.

Actividades 1 *Ud*: Buenos días. Quisiera alquilar un coche. ¿Me podría recomendar una agencia? *Recepcionista*: Sí, en la calle Agustinas, frente al cerro Santa Lucía, está la agencia Lys. *Ud*: ¿Frente al cerro Santa Lucía me dijo? *R*: Sí, dos cuadras más abajo por calle Moneda, después a la izquierda en Santa Lucía y a la izquierda otra vez en calle Agustinas. *Ud*: Gracias. **2** Quisiera alquilar un coche. ¿Qué me recomienda? / Quiero un coche chico, no demasiado caro. / ¿Cuánto cuesta el alquiler por día? / ¿Y por semana? / ¿Es con kilometraje ilimitado? / ¿El IVA y el seguro están incluidos? / Está bien. Llevaré el Chevette. / Sí, aquí está. / ¿Sería posible dejar el coche en otra ciudad? Me gustaría viajar al sur y dejar el coche allí. Quiero volver en tren. **3** (*a*) ¿Hay una estación de servicio por aquí? (*b*) Quiero veinte litros de gasolina sin plomo. (*c*) ¿Podría revisar el aceite y la presión de las ruedas, por favor? *or* Me revisa . . . (*d*) ¿Podría limpiar el parabrisas, por favor? *or* Me limpia . . . (*e*) ¿Me podría reparar esta llanta (*or* este neumático), por favor? *or* Me repara . . . (*f*) ¿Falta mucho para llegar a Santa Isabel? **4** *Telefonista*: ¿Dígame? *or* ¿Aló? *or* ¿Hola? *or* ¿Bueno? *Ud*: ¿Sería posible hacer una llamada internacional con cobro revertido desde mi habitación? *T*:

Sí, cómo no. ¿Adónde quiere llamar? *Ud*: A . . . (*place*). *T*: ¿Y a qué número? *Ud*: (*telephone number*). *T*: ¿Y con quién desea hablar? *Ud*: Con . . . (*name*). *T*: ¿Su nombre, por favor? *Ud*: Me llamo or Mi nombre es . . . (*name*). *Y*: Un momento, por favor. Cuelgue y yo lo vuelvo a llamar. **5** (*a*) Because he went there many years ago and its image is deeply engraved in him. (*b*) He would go with his family or friends, for fifteen or twenty days. **6** (*a*) grande (*b*) tradicional (*c*) gris o azul (*d*) ir al trabajo y salir a pasear. **Imágenes de Hispanoamérica** (*a*) El programa se llama 'Un día sin auto'. (*b*) El objetivo es disminuir la contaminación ambiental. (*c*) El último número de la placa determina la restricción.

Unit 12

Diálogos 1 (*a*) F. (*b*) V. **3** (*a*) At 6.00 a.m. (*b*) At 6.30 a.m. **4** (*a*) F. (*b*) V. **Actividades 1** Sí, es la primera vez. Me gusta mucho. Es un país bonito, aunque todavía no he visto mucho. / No, todavía no he ido al Cuzco (*or* Todavía no he estado en ...), pero espero ir la próxima semana. Voy a visitar Machu Picchu también. Me han dicho que es muy interesante. ¿Usted ha estado en Europa alguna vez? / Sí, he estado allí varias veces. Me gusta mucho España, especialmente el sur. / Gracias. Estudié español en el colegio. ¿Usted habla inglés? / Está bien. / No, gracias. Ya he tomado dos. Es suficiente. Y, además, mañana tengo que levantarme temprano, así que debo volver pronto al hotel. **2** (*a*) Sí, ya estuve allí. (*b*) No, todavía no lo he visitado. (*c*) Sí, ya lo vi. (*d*) No, todavía no lo he conocido. **3** (*a*) She was there when she was 11 years old. (*b*) She says the city is very beautiful. It is a traditional city, as it still retains the characteristics of Inca culture. (*c*) From Lima, you can travel to Cuzco by bus, train or plane. (*d*) The only way of getting to Machu Picchu is by train.

4 (*a*) Deme (*or* Me da) la cuenta, por favor. (*b*) Por favor, me despierta (*or* Despiérteme) a las seis y media. (*c*) ¿Me podría enviar (*or* ¿Podría enviarme) el desayuno a la habitación, por favor? (*d*) Lléveme (*or* Me lleva) al aeropuerto, por favor. **5** (*a*) (vi) (*b*) (iii) (*c*) (i) (*d*) (v) (*e*) (ii) (*f*) (iv) **6** Recommendations for tourists. For your own security, the National Tourist Service in our country makes the following suggestions: Change your money and travellers cheques only in banks or at authorised bureaux de change. Do not change money in the street. Leave your valuables in the safe deposit box at your hotel. Do not go out carrying large sums of money. When you take a taxi, see what the meter shows, as that is the amount that you will have to pay. In our country, there are no additional surcharges. If possible, use the taxi services of your own hotel. **Imágenes de Hispanoamérica** (*a*) He said that Rigoberta Menchú is a vivid symbol of peace and reconciliation, in spite of ethnic, cultural and social divisions in her country, in the American continent and in the world. (*b*) She said she had great hopes that the prize might contribute towards helping the indigenous peoples of the Americas to live forever.

Unit 13

Diálogos 1 (*a*) She says the flight stopped over in Paris, and the suitcase was probably sent to Paris by mistake. (*b*) It is big, dark green and it has a label with her name on it. **2** (*a*) La habitación es un poco oscura, pero muy tranquila. (*b*) Estará lista dentro de un momento. **3** (*a*) Está en el Paseo Colón. (*b*) Está a siete u ocho cuadras del hotel. **4** (*a*) No, she hasn't got a fever. (*b*) She has to take one tablet every four hours. **Actividades 1** Recién llegué en el vuelo trescientos diez de Hispanair que venía de . . . (*city or country*), pero desgraciadamente mi equipaje no ha llegado (*or* no llegó). / Traía dos maletas, una grande y una chica. Aquí tengo los tickets (*or* talones) del equipaje. Las dos maletas tenían etiquetas con mi nombre (*say your name*). / Espero que las encuentren. Tengo toda mi ropa en ellas y también unos regalos que traía para unos amigos. **2** (*a*) It was considered to be the most dangerous airport in the world due to terrorism and theft. (*b*) They will help by intensifying security measures. (*c*) Security will be strengthened by private security firms, which will guard the airport against luggage theft. **3** (*a*) El aire acondicionado no funcionó. (*b*) No había agua caliente. (*c*) El lavatorio estaba tapado. (*d*) En el baño no había toallas. (*e*) La habitación es muy ruidosa. No pude dormir anoche. (*f*) Quiero cambiarme a una habitación más tranquila. **4** (*a*) The man had asked for a seat in the non-smoking section of

the plane. (*b*) The Venezuelan lady in the restaurant had ordered fish with mashed potatoes and the waiter brought her fish with fried potatoes instead. (*c*) The young Chilean lady ordered a seafood soup 15 minutes ago and it still hasn't arrived. **5** (*b*) **6** ir; salir; doble; doble; mano; cuadras; de nada. **7** No me siento bien. Tengo dolor de estómago (*or* Me duele el estómago) y tengo diarrea. / Empezó anoche. Salí a comer (*or* cenar) con unos amigos y comí pescado y papas fritas. Seguramente fue eso. Más tarde, cuando volví al hotel empecé a sentirme mal. / Sí, he vomitado y parece que tengo fiebre también. / Espero que sí. **8** (*a*) 11.00 a 13.00; 18.00 a 21.00. (*b*) 1016 (*c*) 325228 **9** Surgery days and hours are Mondays from 4.00 to 6.00 p.m. and Wednesdays and Fridays from 11.00 a.m. to 1.00 p.m.

TRANSCRIPTS

Unit 1

8

(a)

Entrevistador	Buenas tardes. ¿Cómo se llama usted?
Initia	Buenas tardes. Mi nombre es Initia Muñoz García.
Entrevistador	Initia, ¿de qué país es usted?
Initia	Soy de aquí de México. Soy mexicana.
Entrevistador	¿De qué parte de México?
Initia	De la ciudad de Córdoba. Veracruz.

(b)

Entrevistador	Buenas tardes.
Clotilde	Buenas tardes.
Entrevistador	¿Cómo se llama usted?
Clotilde	Me llamo Clotilde Montalvo Rodríguez, para servirle.
Entrevistador	Clotilde, ¿de dónde es usted?
Clotilde	Soy de aquí de Veracruz.
Entrevistador	Veracruz. ¿Es usted mexicana?
Clotilde	Sí, soy mexciana.

(c)

Elizabeth	Me llamo Elizabeth. Soy de Panamá, de la Ciudad de Panamá.

Unit 2

5

(a)

Señor	Disculpe, señorita.
Señorita	A sus órdenes.
Señor	¿Hay una casa de cambio por aquí?
Señorita	Sí, hay una en la calle Amazonas.
Señor	¿Dónde está la calle Amazonas?
Señorita	Está a cinco cuadras de aquí, a la izquierda.
Señor	Muchas gracias. Muy amable.
Señorita	Para servirle.

(b)

Sr. Ramos	Buenos días.
Recepcionista	Buenos días. ¿Qué desea?
Sr. Ramos	¿Está el señor Silva?
Recepcionista	Sí, sí está. Está en su oficina.
Sr. Ramos	¿Cuál es el número de la oficina?
Recepcionista	La oficina del señor Silva es la doscientos cuarenta. Está en el segundo piso, al final del pasillo, a la derecha.
Sr. Ramos	¿Dónde está el elevador?
Recepcionista	Está allá.

7

Turista	Por favor, ¿dónde está la estación?
Colombiana	Está en la carrera diecisiete, al final de la calle dieciséis.
Turista	¿Está lejos de aquí?
Colombiana	¿A pie?
Turista	Sí, a pie.
Colombiana	Está a quince minutos más o menos.
Turista	Muchas gracias.
Colombiana	De nada.

8

Jorge	Soy director de un centro de lenguas modernas.
Entrevistador	¿Dónde . . .dónde está el centro?

Jorge	El Centro de Lenguas Modernas está localizado en la ciudad de Veracruz, a media cuadra de la calle principal, es decir, a una y media cuadra del parque principal de la ciudad.

Unit 3

5

En la mañana abren a las nueve de la mañana y, entonces, trabajan de nueve a una, nueve de la mañana a una de la tarde, cierran de una a cuatro, abren a las cuatro, para trabajar hasta las ocho de la noche.

8

(*a*)

Entrevistador	Dime, ¿cuáles son las comidas principales en México, y cuál es el horario de cada comida?
Jorge	O.K. Las comidas principales en México son el desayuno entre las ocho y las nueve; el almuerzo entre la una y media y las tres y media; la cena, entre ocho y media y nueve; y, opcionalmente, hay una . . . podríamos llamarle poscena, que puede ser a las once y media de la noche, si nos acostamos tarde.

(*b*)

Entrevistador	Coty, buenas tardes. Coty, ¿cuáles son las comidas principales en México y cuáles son los horarios de las comidas?
Coty	Las comidas . . . la comida principal es la de mediodía, que varía entre una y dos de la tarde, en que se toma. El desayuno . . ., pues, bueno, tenemos tres en el día: desayuno, almuerzo y cena. El desayuno es temprano, a las ocho de la mañana, almuerzo entre una y dos, y cena, pues, de las siete en adelante.

Unit 4

4

Entrevistador	Coty, ¿en qué trabaja usted?

Coty   Yo soy secretaria, eh . . . mi horario de trabajo es . . ., por la mañana entro a las diez de la mañana, salgo a almorzar a la una de la tarde, regreso a las cuatro de la tarde a seguir laborando y salgo a las nueve de la noche.

6

En las vacaciones normalmente aprovecho para visitar a mis sobrinos. Tengo tres sobrinos que viven en Tijuana, Baja California. En la frontera con Estados Unidos. Es un viaje largo, porque de Veracruz hasta allá son varios días, pero lo disfruto, porque veo a la familia muy de vez en cuando.

8

Entrevistador	¿Cómo se llama usted?
Clotilde	Mi nombre es Clotilde Montalvo Rodríguez.
Entrevistador	Clotilde, ¿cuántos años tiene usted?
Clotilde	Tengo cuarenta y cuatro años.
Entrevistador	¿Está casada o soltera?
Clotilde	Estoy casada.
Entrevistador	¿Cuántos hijos tiene?
Clotilde	Tengo dos hijas, una de veintitrés años y una pequeña de seis años y medio.
Entrevistador	¿En qué trabaja usted?
Clotilde	Soy secretaria y trabajo en el Centro Cultural de Lenguas Modernas.
Entrevistador	¿Y su esposo, qué hace?
Clotilde	Mi esposo, pues . . . maneja, es chofer de carretera.

Unit 5

4

Mesero	¿Qué le traigo, señorita?
Señorita	¿Qué tiene de almuerzo?
Mesero	Tenemos sopa de pollo, sopa de verduras, crema de espárragos, de champiñones, . . .
Señorita	Tráigame una crema de espárragos. No, no, no, mire, prefiero tomar una sopa de pollo.
Mesero	¿Y qué otra cosa? Tenemos arroz con pollo, pollo

en salsa de mostaza, soufflé de calabaza, carne guisada . . .

Señorita	¿Pescado no tiene?
Mesero	No, no queda. Le recomiendo el soufflé de calabaza. Está muy bueno.
Señorita	Sí, tráigame eso.
Mesero	¿Y para tomar? ¿Una cerveza, vino, un jugo . . .?
Señorita	Una cerveza.
Mesero	Muy bien, señorita.

Unit 6

3

Clienta	Buenos días.
Vendedor	Buenos días. ¿A la orden?
Clienta	¿Podría decirme cuánto valen esos zapatos?
Vendedor	¿Cuáles?
Clienta	Ésos, los negros.
Vendedor	Ésos valen treinta y dos mil pesos, pero hay un descuento del diez por ciento. Con descuento son veintiocho mil ochocientos pesos.
Clienta	Sí, está bien. Quisiera probármelos.
Vendedor	¿Qué número?
Clienta	Cuarenta y dos.
Vendedor	Sí, un momento, por favor.

4

Almacenes García, calidad y economía. García. Por fin de temporada todas las camisas sport manga larga y manga corta para caballeros, cuarenta por ciento de descuento. Todos los pantalones para caballero, treinta, cuarenta y cincuenta por ciento de descuento. No incluye promociones. García.

7

Cliente	¿Cuánto es todo?
Vendedora	Bueno, tenemos ciento cuarenta y siete mil . . . ochenta y ocho mil . . . ciento sesenta y cinco mil . . . doscientos ochenta y seis mil . . . quince mil . . . ciento noventa y ocho mil . . . ciento cincuenta y un mil. El total es . . . un millón cincuenta mil pesos.

Unit 7

5

Entre la gloria y el paraíso está Motel Miraflores, con todos los servicios para que usted disfrute cómodamente de su estancia. Habitaciones con aire acondicionado, cama de agua, jacuzzi, suites con alberca, antena parabólica y música ambiental. Motel Miraflores, el lugar al que siempre deseará volver. Carretera Boticaria-Mocambo s/n (sin número), Veracruz.

6

El hotel tiene doscientas dieciséis habitaciones, una piscina en la parte trasera con un gran espacio verde, patios bien grandes, dos restaurantes, uno de primera categoría, que es el Techo del Mundo, la otra la cafetería y muchos . . . y varios salones donde se hacen muchas convenciones. Es de cinco estrellas. Aparte, tiene casino y la discoteca.

8

(a)

Entrevistador	¿Cómo es el clima en Panamá?
Elizabeth	Hace calor. Es de una temperatura promedio de veintiocho grados centígrados todo . . ., durante todo el año. Es un país netamente tropical; tiene dos estaciones, la de invierno, que es lluviosa, y la de verano, que es seca.

(b)

Lima, la capital del Perú, es una ciudad bonita, grande, moderna, y donde en algunos lugares se conservan las características de la época colonial. También tiene bonitas playas, museos, zoológicos y, en cuanto al clima, es cálido y casi no existen las lluvias.

Unit 8

6

Guillermo	Me gustaría ir a Mendoza. No sé en qué ir, si en bus o en avión. ¿Qué me recomiendas?
Carlos	Bueno, mira, yo te recomiendo el bus, porque el viaje es mucho más interesante. El bus demora aproximadamente cinco o seis horas. El avión demora

treinta minutos, pero en bus vas a ver muchísimo más. Hay buses dos o tres veces por día y el pasaje no te va a costar mucho. Ahora, si tú quieres que te recomiende algún hotel en Mendoza, te puedo recomendar un hotel bastante bueno y económico, el hotel Plaza que está a dos cuadras de la calle principal de Mendoza. Tengo la dirección y el teléfono y te los puedo dar.

Unit 9

3

(a)

Sra. Puig	Buenas tardes. ¿Está el señor Solís, por favor?
Recepcionista	El señor Solís está ocupado. Está en una reunión. ¿Quiere dejarle algún mensaje?
Sra. Puig	Dígale, por favor, que vino Carmen Puig, de Caracas, que yo necesito hablar urgentemente con él. Dígale que me llame al hotel, al hotel Sheraton. Yo estoy en la habitación 500. Pero tiene que ser ahora, porque yo me voy a Caracas mañana.
Recepcionista	Muy bien, señora.

(b)

Srta. Pérez	Buenas tardes. ¿Está el señor Solís?
Recepcionista	No, el señor Solís no está. Está en una reunión en este momento.
Srta. Pérez	¿A qué hora llega?
Recepcionista	Va a llegar a las 2.00.
Srta. Pérez	Por favor, dígale que vino Marilú Pérez. Estoy en el hotel Gala, en la habitación 324. Aquí tengo el teléfono. Es el 687951.
Recepcionista	Muy bien, señorita. Yo le daré su recado.
Srta. Pérez	Gracias.
Recepcionista	De nada.

6

Marilú	En las vacaciones fui con mi familia a la costa y estuvimos dos semanas en un hotel frente a la playa. Disfrutamos mucho, ya que el lugar donde fuimos es

agradable, tranquilo y tiene unas playas maravillosas, y el aire es tan puro. Salimos mucho, harto, tomamos el sol, nadamos, hicimos deportes. Y volvimos, pero llenos de energía a la ciudad.

Nota: pero (*but*) in the last sentence is emphatic.

Unit 10

4

Entrevistador	Carlos, ¿siempre has vivido en Buenos Aires?
Carlos	No, no siempre, también viví en San Pablo, Brasil.
Entrevistador	¿Y qué hacías en San Pablo?
Carlos	En San Pablo daba clases de pintura.
Entrevistador	¿Y en qué parte de San Pablo vivías?
Carlos	Vivía en el barrio de Vila Mariana.
Entrevistador	¿Y qué tal era el barrio?
Carlos	Era excelente. Uno de los más arborizados y con más vegetación de San Pablo.
Entrevistador	¿Vivías en una casa o un departamento?
Carlos	Vivía en un departamento.
Entrevistador	¿Un buen departamento tenías allí?
Carlos	Sí, pequeño, pero agradable.
Entrevistador	Y tus vecinos, ¿qué tal eran?
Carlos	Muy buenos vecinos, como todos los brasileros.
Entrevistador	¿Tenías muchos amigos en San Pablo?
Carlos	Muchos, muchos que todavía tengo.
Entrevistador	¿Y por qué volviste a Buenos Aires?
Carlos	Bueno, porque extrañaba mucho la ciudad.

7

Entrevistador	Carlos, ¿cómo describirías Buenos Aires?
Carlos	Buenos Aires es una ciudad muy grande, con muchos rincones diferentes, pero con una unidad común. Es una ciudad con mucho movimiento cultural y la expresión que más . . . este . . . la respresenta, para mí, es que es una ciudad que tiene alma.
Entrevistador	¿Y qué es lo que más te gusta de Buenos Aires?
Carlos	Me gusta su vida nocturna, me gusta la posibilidad de expresarse que le da a la gente que vive en ella. Me gusta su movimiento cultural.

Entrevistador	¿Hay algo que no te guste de Buenos Aires?
Carlos	Sí, hay algo que no me gusta, que es la tendencia que tenemos los porteños a entristecer y a la melancolía extrema.

Unit 11

5

Entrevistador	Carlos. ¿dónde te gustaría pasar tus próximas vacaciones?
Carlos	Me gustaría pasarlas en Bariloche.
Entrevistador	¿Y por qué en Bariloche?
Carlos	Porque fui hace muchos años y su imagen quedó profundamente grabada en mí.
Entrevistador	¿Irías solo o acompañado?
Carlos	No, iría con mi familia o con amigos.
Entrevistador	¿Y por cuánto tiempo irías?
Carlos	Bueno, iría por quince días o veinte.
Entrevistador	¿Y qué harías allí?
Carlos	Recorrería todo lo que de naturaleza se pueda visitar. No me gusta demasiado la vida . . . frívola del lugar.

6

Entrevistador	¿Tienes coche?
Carlos	No tengo.
Entrevistador	¿Te gustaría tener uno?
Carlos	Sí, me gustaría mucho.
Entrevistador	¿Y qué marca de coche preferirías?
Carlos	Preferiría un Ford.
Entrevistador	Un Ford . . . ¿Y comprarías uno grande o uno chico?
Carlos	Me gustan más los autos grandes.
Entrevistador	¿Preferirías un coche deportivo o tradicional?
Carlos	Preferiría un coche tradicional.
Entrevistador	¿Y qué color comprarías?
Carlos	Un color gris o azul.
Entrevistador	¿Lo usarías para ir al trabajo o para salir a pasear?
Carlos	Por supuesto, para las dos cosas.
Entrevistador	¿Y adónde irías, por ejemplo, a pasear el fin de semana o en las vacaciones?

Carlos   Iría a lugares cercanos, pero donde abunde la naturaleza.

Unit 12

3

Entrevistador   Karina, ¿has estado en el Cuzco alguna vez?
Karina   Sí, estuve cuando yo tenía once años de edad.
Entrevistador   ¿Y qué tal es la ciudad?
Karina   Es muy bonita. Es muy tradicional, pues (que) conserva las características de la cultura incaica.
Entrevistador   ¿Y está . . .? ¿Cómo se puede ir desde Lima al Cuzco?
Karina   Bueno, se puede viajar mediante bus, avión o tren.
Entrevistador   ¿Y el avión cuánto demora?
Karina   Aproximadamente dos horas.
Entrevistador   Dos horas. Y para ir a Machu Picchu desde el Cuzco, ¿está muy lejos?
Karina   Exactamente, no sé a cuánto tiempo está. Está lejos de Machu Picchu y la única forma de llegar es mediante el tren.

Unit 13

4

(*a*)

Señor   Señorita, mire, yo pedí un asiento en la sección de *no* fumadores.
Azafata   Lo siento, tanto, señor, pero no es culpa nuestra. Inmediatamente voy a ver qué puedo hacer para cambiarlo.
Señor   Gracias.

(*b*)

Señora   ¡Epa, muchacho!
Mesero   Sí, señora.
Señora   Mire, yo le pedí pescado con puré y usted . . . usted me trajo pescado con papas fritas, ¿vale?
Mesero   Disculpe, se lo cambio ahorita.

(c)

Señorita	¡Mozo!
Mozo	Señorita, ¿sí?
Señorita	Mire por favor, hace quince minutos que pedí una sopa de mariscos y todavía no me la traen. ¿Qué pasa?
Mozo	Perdone, señorita, pero estamos tan ocupados hoy día. Hay tantos clientes. Mire, voy a ver lo que pasó. Se la traigo enseguida.

6

Turista	Buenas tardes. Para ir al Teatro Segura, por favor.
Recepcionista	Sí, cómo no. Al salir de aquí, doble por la calle Ucayali, camine de frente hacia Abancay. Ahí doble a la mano izquierda, camine dos cuadras y media, y ahí está el Teatro Segura.
Turista	Gracias.
Recepcionista	De nada.

8

Doctor Manuel Loyo de Valdés, fracturas, luxaciones, cirugía, traumatología y ortopedia. Doctor Manuel Loyo de Valdés. Consultas, de 11.00 a 13.00 horas y de 18.00 a 21.00 horas, en González Pajés 1016, entre Iturbide y Mina. Teléfono 325228, en Veracruz.

9

Paciente	Quisiera pedir hora con el doctor Martínez, por favor. ¿Qué días atiende?
Recepcionista	Atiende los lunes, miércoles y viernes. Los lunes atiende de cuatro a seis y los miércoles y viernes de once de la mañana a una de la tarde.

—— IRREGULAR VERBS ——

The following list includes only the most common irregular verbs.
Only irregular forms are given (verbs marked with an asterisk are
also stem-changing). The plural familiar form which is used in Spain
is also included here (e.g. **anduvisteis** *you walked*).

abrir
  (*to open*)
                 past participle: abierto

andar
  (*to walk*)
                 preterite: anduve, anduviste, anduvo, anduvimos,
                     anduvisteis, anduvieron
                 imperfect subjunctive: anduviese, anduvieses,
                     anduviese, anduviésemos, anduvieseis,
                     anduviesen; anduviera, anduvieras, *etc.*

caer
  (*to fall*)
                 present tense: (yo) caigo
                 present subjunctive: caiga, caigas, caiga, caigamos,
                     caigáis, caigan
                 present participle: cayendo
                 preterite: (él, ella, Vd.) cayó, (ellos, ellas, Vds.)
                     cayeron

conducir
  (*to drive*)
                 present tense: (yo) conduzco
                 present subjunctive: conduzca, conduzcas,
                     conduzca, conduzcamos, conduzcáis,
                     conduzcan
                 preterite: conduje, condujiste, condujo,
                     condujimos, condujisteis, condujeron

cubrir
  (*to cover*)
                 past participle: cubierto

dar (*to give*)	*present tense*: (yo) doy *preterite*: di, diste, dio, dimos, disteis, dieron *present subjunctive*: dé, des, dé, demos, deis, dieron
decir* (*to say*)	*present tense*: (yo) digo *present subjunctive*: diga, digas, diga, digamos, digáis, digan *preterite*: dije, dijiste, dijo, dijimos, dijisteis, dijeron *future*: diré, dirás, dirá, diremos, diréis, dirán *conditional*: diría, dirías, diría, diríamos, diríais, dirían *imperative*: (tú) di *present participle*: diciendo *past participle*: dicho
escribir (*to write*)	*past participle*: escrito
estar (*to be*)	*present tense*: estoy, estás, está, estamos, estáis, están *present subjunctive*: esté, estés, esté, estemos, estéis, estén *preterite*: estuve, estuviste, estuvo, estuvimos, estuvisteis, estuvieron *imperative* (*fam, sing*): está
hacer (*to do, make*)	*present tense*: (yo) hago *present subjunctive*: haga, hagas, haga, hagamos, hagáis, hagan *preterite*: hice, hiciste, hizo, hicimos, hicisteis, hicieron *future*: haré, harás, hará, haremos, haréis, harán *conditional*: haría, harías, haría, haríamos, haríais, harían *imperative*: (Vd.) haga, (tú) haz *past participle*: hecho
ir (*to go*)	*present tense*: voy, vas, va, vamos, vais, van *present subjunctive*: vaya, vayas, vaya, vayamos, vayáis, vayan *imperfect*: iba, ibas, iba, íbamos, íbais, iba *preterite*: fui, fuiste, fue, fuimos, fuisteis, fueron *imperative*: (Vd.) vaya, (tú) ve

	present participle: yendo
leer	*preterite*: (él, ella, Vd.) leyó, (ellos, ellas, Vds.)
(*to read*)	leyeron
	present participle: leyendo
morir*	*past participle*: muerto
(*to die*)	
oír	*present tense*: oigo, oyes, oye, oímos, oís,
(*to hear*)	oyen
	present subjunctive: oiga, oigas, oiga, oigamos,
	oigáis, oigan
	preterite: (él, ella, Vd.) oyó, (ellos, ellas, Vds.)
	oyeron
	imperative: (Vd.) oiga, (tú) oye
	present participle: oyendo
poder*	*preterite*: pude, pudiste, pudo, pudimos, pudisteis,
(*to be able*	pudieron
to, can)	*future*: podré, podrás, podrá, podremos, podréis,
	podrán
	conditional: podría, podrías, podría, podríamos,
	podríais, podrían
	present participle: pudiendo
poner	*present tense*: (yo) pongo
(*to put*)	*present subjunctive*: ponga, pongas, ponga,
	pongamos, pongáis, pongan
	preterite: puse, pusiste, puso, pusimos, pusisteis,
	pusieron
	future: pondré, pondrás, pondrá, pondremos,
	pondréis, pondrán
	conditional: pondría, pondrías, pondría,
	pondríamos, pondríais, pondrían
	imperative: (Vd.) ponga, (tú) pon
	past participle: puesto
querer*	*preterite*: quise, quisiste, quiso, quisimos,
(*to want*)	quisisteis, quisieron
	future: querré, querrás, querrá, querremos,
	querréis, querrán
	conditional: querría, querrías, querría,
	querríamos, querríais, querrían
romper	*past participle*: roto
(*to break*)	

saber	*present tense*: (yo) sé
(*to know*)	*present subjunctive*: sepa, sepas, sepa, sepamos, sepáis, sepan
	preterite: supe, supiste, supe, supimos, supisteis, supieron
	future: sabré, sabrás, sabrá, sabremos, sabréis, sabrán
	conditional: sabría, sabrías, sabría, sabríamos, sabríais, sabrían
	imperative: (Vd.) sepa
salir	*present tense*: (yo) salgo
(*to go out*)	*present subjunctive*: salga, salgas, salga, salgamos, salgáis, salgan
	future: saldré, saldrás, saldrá, saldremos, saldréis, saldrán
	conditional: saldría, saldrías, saldría, saldríamos, saldríais, saldrían
	imperative: (Vd.) salga, (tú) sal
ser	*present tense*: soy, eres, es, somos, sois, son
(*to be*)	*present subjunctive*: sea, seas, sea, seamos, seais, sean
	preterite: fui, fuiste, fue, fuimos, fuisteis, fueron
	imperfect: era, eras, era, éramos, erais, eran
	imperative: (Vd.) sea, (tú) sé
soltar	*past participle*: suelto
(*to loosen*)	
tener*	*present tense*: (yo) tengo
(*to have*)	*present subjunctive*: tenga, tengas, tenga, tengamos, tengáis, tengan
	preterite: tuve, tuviste, tuvo, tuvimos, tuvisteis, tuvieron
	future: tendré, tendrás, tendrá, tendremos, tendréis, tendrán
	conditional: tendría, tendrías, tendría, tendríamos, tendríais, tendrían
	imperative: (Vd.) tenga, (tú) ten
traer	*present tense*: (yo) traigo
(*to bring*)	*present subjunctive*: traiga, traigas, traiga, traigamos, traigáis, traigan

	preterite: traje, trajiste, trajo, trajimos, trajisteis, trajeron
	imperative: (Vd.) traiga
	present participle: trayendo
venir*	*present tense*: (yo) vengo
(*to come*)	*present subjunctive*: venga, vengas, venga, vengamos, vengáis, vengan
	preterite: vine, viniste, vino, vinimos, vinisteis, vinieron
	future: vendré, vendrás, vendrá, vendremos, vendréis, vendrán
	conditional: vendría, vendrías, vendría vendríamos, vendríais, vendrían
	imperative: (Vd.) venga, (tú) ven
	present participle: viniendo
ver	*present tense*: (yo) veo
(*to see*)	*present subjunctive*: vea, veas, vea, veamos, veais, vean
	imperfect: veía, veías, veía, veíamos, veíais, veían
	imperative: (Vd.) vea
	past participle: visto
volver* (*to come back*)	*past participle*: vuelto

GLOSSARY OF
—— LATIN AMERICAN ——
TERMS

This glossary is intended as a reference section and includes essential words which vary within major Latin American countries or in relation to Spain. Words which are the same in all countries have not been included.

The words in bold in each group, after their English equivalent, are those normally used in Spain. Most of these words are not exclusive to Spain, as they are also used, unless specified, in some Latin American countries. And even in places where they are not normally used they will be understood. Thus, the word **el autobús** (*bus*), which many countries do not use, will probably be understood everywhere. Therefore, with a few exceptions, you will be able to get along with the words used in Spain, but you will need to understand what different native speakers mean when they use other terms. Words which do not indicate a specific country in brackets are used in several places. Other, more restricted terms show the country where they are used. For a general list of word groups in Spanish, consult a phrase book.

—————— Transport and travel ——————

bus
el autobús
el bus
el camión (Mex)

el pesero e el colectivo (Mex, minibus in which fare depends on distance you travel)

el colectivo (a shared taxi with a fixed route; in Argentina, the word refers to a city bus)

la guagua (Caribbean) (in Chile, Peru and Bolivia, **la guagua** is *a baby*)

el ómnibus

el micro (from **el microbús**)

to take (a bus, train, etc.)
coger (a taboo word in some Latin American countries)
tomar

underground, subway
el metro
el subte (Arg)

car
el coche
el carro
el auto

car park
el aparcamiento
el estacionamiento

to park
aparcar
estacionar

ticket (bus, train, etc.)
el billete
el boleto
el pasaje

to hire, rent
alquilar (un coche, etc.)
rentar
arrendar

ticket office
la taquilla
la boletería

petrol
la gasolina

la bencina (Chile)
la nafta (Arg)

service station
la estación de servicio
la bomba
el grifo (Perú)

tyre
el neumático
la llanta (in Spain and some other countries, **la llanta** is the metal
  rim of a car wheel)
la goma (Arg)

to drive
conducir
manejar

driving licence
el carnet (or **carné**)/**el permiso de conducir**
la licencia de conducir / manejar
el pase (Col)
el registro (de conductor) (Arg)
el brevete (Perú)

——————— **House and hotel** ———————

reservation
la reserva
la reservación

room
la habitación
el cuarto
la pieza

single room
una habitación individual
una habitación sencilla
una habitación simple
una single

bedroom
el dormitorio
el cuarto
la pieza (Arg, Chile)
la recámara (Mex)
la alcoba

blanket
la manta
la cobija
el cobertor
la frazada

washbasin
el lavabo
el lavatorio
el lavamanos
la pileta (Arg)

water tap
el grifo
la llave (del agua)
la canilla (Arg)
la pluma (Col)
el caño (Peru)

shower
la ducha
la regadera (Mex)

bath tub
la bañera
la tina

light bulb
la bombilla
el bombillo (Col)
la ampolleta (Chile)
el foco (Mex)

swimming pool
la piscina
la alberca (Mex)
la pileta (Arg)

flat, apartment
el apartamento (also **el piso**)
el departamento

lift
el ascensor
el elevador

———— Restaurants and food ————

Words for different dishes are not given, as in this area there are many more variations within Latin America and between Latin America and Spain. With a few exceptions, most basic food and farm produce carry the same names everywhere. However, as you travel in Latin America, you will encounter many names for products which are typical of certain countries or of certain regions, and which you may not hear anywhere else.

waiter, waitress
el camarero, la camarera
el mesero, la mesera
el mozo, la señorita (Arg, Chile, Peru)
el mesonero, la mesonera (Ven)

to have breakfast
desayunar
tomar el desayuno

dinner
la cena
la comida (Col, Chile)

set-price meal
el menú (del día)
el plato del día
la comida corrida (Mex)

potatoes
las patatas
las papas

beans
las judías
los frijoles / frejoles
los porotos
las caraotas (Ven)

peas
los guisantes
los chícharos (Mex)
las arvejas

chilli
el chile
el ají (Arg, Chile, Peru)

avocado
el aguacate
la palta (Arg, Chile, Peru)

peach
el melocotón
durazno

apricot
el albaricoque
damasco
melocotón (Col)

strawberry
la fresa
la frutilla (Arg, Chile)

black coffee
un café solo
un café
un tinto (Col)

to drink
beber
tomar

toilets
el lavabo
el servicio / los servicios
el baño / los baños

— Telephone and postal services —

Hello?
¿Díga(me)?
¿Sí?
¿Aló?
¿Bueno? (Mex)
¿Hola? (Arg)

extension
la extensión
el anexo (Chile, Peru)
el interno (Arg)

call
una llamada
un llamado

a reverse-charge call
un(a) llamado/a a / con cobro revertido
un(a) llamado/a a cobrar/pagar (allá)

it is engaged
está comunicando
está ocupado

stamp
el sello
la estampilla

post office
correos
el correo

post box
el apartado (de correos)
el apartado (postal)
la casilla (de correos) (Chile, Arg)
el buzón

SPANISH–ENGLISH VOCABULARY

Abbreviations: **adj** = adjective; **m** = masculine; **f** = feminine; **pl** = plural; **pol** = polite; **fam** = familiar

a   *to, at, on*
abajo: más abajo   *further down*
abrir   *to open*
abuelos (m, pl)   *grandparents*
acabar de   *to have just*
aceite (m)   *oil*
acerca de   *about*
acompañado/a   *accompanied*
acostarse   *to go to bed*
activar   *to activate*
adelante   *see:* en adelante
además   *besides*
adentro   *inside*
adicional   *additional*
adiós   *goodbye*
aeropuerto (m)   *airport*
afuera   *outside*
agencia (f)   *agency*
agencia de viajes (f)   *travel agency*
agradable   *pleasant*
agua (f)   *water*
ahora   *now*
ahora mismo   *right now*
ahorita   *right now* (diminutive)
aire (m)   *air*
aire acondicionado (m)   *air conditioning*

al (a + el)   *to the, on the, at the*
a la derecha   *on the right*
a la izquierda   *on the left*
alberca (f)   *swimming pool* (Mexico)
alegrarse   *to be glad*
al final de   *at the end of*
al fondo de   *at the end of*
algo   *something*
algún (m)   *some, any*
alguna (f)   *some, any*
alguna vez   *ever*
alimento (m)   *food*
allá   *there*
al lado de   *next to*
allí   *there*
alma (f)   *soul*
almacenes (m, pl)   *department store*
almorzar   *to have lunch*
almuerzo (m)   *lunch*
aló   *hello* (on the phone)
alojamiento (m)   *accommodation*
alquilar   *to rent*
alquiler (m)   *rent*
alto/a   *tall; top*
amable   *kind*
amarillo/a   *yellow*

americano/a *American*
amigo/a (m/f) *friend*
amplio/a *wide*
anexo (m) *extension* (Chile)
animado/a *animated*
año (m) *year*
año pasado (m) *last year*
anoche *last night*
antena (f) *aerial, antenna*
antes *before*
antiquísimo/a *very ancient*
anunciar *to announce*
aparecer *to appear*
aparte *separate*
a partir de *starting in / on*
apellido (m) *surname*
a pesar de *although, despite, in spite of*
aprender *to learn*
aprovechar *to take up the opportunity*
aquí *here*
arquitecto (m) *architect*
arquitectónica *architectural*
arquitectura (f) *architecture*
arroz (m) *rice*
artículo (m) *article*
asado/a *roast*
así *thus*
asiento (m) *seat*
asistir *to attend*
a sus órdenes *at your service*
aunque *although, even though*
autorización (f) *permission*
a veces *sometimes*
avenida (f) *avenue*
aventura (f) *adventure*
avión (m) *plane*
ayer *yesterday*
azafata (f) *stewardess*
azteca (m/f) *Aztec*
azul *blue*

bajar *to go down*
bajo/a *low, lower*
balsa (f) *raft*
bañarse *to take a bath*
banco (m) *bank*
baño (m) *toilet, bathroom*
bar (m) *bar*
barato/a *cheap*

barrio (m) *district, area*
barroco/a *baroque*
bastante *quite*
beber *to drink*
bebida gaseosa (f) *fizzy drink*
bien *well*
bienvenido/a *welcome*
blanco/a *white*
boleto (m) *ticket*
bonito/a *pretty*
botella (f) *bottle*
brasilero/a *Brazilian*
brevedad: a la brevedad *as soon as possible*
bueno/a *good*
bueno *well*
bus (m) *bus*
buscar *to look for*
buzón (m) *post box*

caballero (m) *gentleman*
cada *each, every*
caer mal *to be ill* (from food)
café (m) *coffee, cafe*
calabaza (f) *pumpkin*
calidad (f) *quality*
cálido/a *warm*
calle (f) *street*
calor (m) *heat;* (adj) *warm, hot*
cama de agua (f) *water bed*
cambiar *to change*
cambiarse *to move*
caminar *to walk*
camino (m) *road*
camión (m) *bus* (Mex)
camioneta (f) *van*
camisa (f) *shirt*
campo (m) *countryside*
cansado/a *tired*
capacidad (f) *room*
carne (f) *meat*
carnet de conducir (m) *driving licence*
caro/a *expensive*
carrera (f) *street* (Colombia)
carretera (f) *highway*
carro (m) *car*
carta (f) *menu, letter*
casa (f) *house, home*
casa de cambio (f) *bureau de change*

casado/a *married*
caso (m) *case*
castellano (m) *Castilian*
catedral (f) *cathedral*
categoría (f) *category*
cena (f) *dinner*
cenar *to have dinner*
centro (m) *centre*
Centroamérica *Central America*
cerca *near*
cerrar *to close*
cerveza (f) *beer*
cine (m) *cinema*
ciudad (f) *city*
cliente (m/f) *client*
clima (m) *climate*
coche dormitorio (m) *sleeping car*
colega (m/f) *colleague*
colgar *to hang up*
colombiano/a *Colombian*
color (m) *colour*
comedor (m) *dining room*
comer *to eat*
comida (f) *meal, food, dinner*
como también *as well as*
cómo *how, what*
como *such as, like, as*
cómodo/a *comfortable*
compañía (f) *company*
comparación (f) *comparison*
compartir *to share*
completo/a *complete, full*
comprar *to buy*
computerizado/a *computerised*
con *with*
concluyendo *finishing*
conectar *to connect*
conocer *to know*
conseguir *to get*
contar *to tell*
contar con *to have, depend on*
contento/a *happy*
continuar *to continue*
copa (f) *glass*
correo (m) *post office*
corto/a *short*
costa (f) *coast*
costar *to cost*
costoso/a *expensive*

creer *to believe, think*
crema (f) *soup*
crema de espárragos (f) *asparagus soup*
crema del día (f) *soup of the day*
creo que sí *I think so*
cuadra (f) *block*
cuál *what?, which?*
cuándo *when?*
cuando *when*
cuanto: en cuanto a *as regards*
cuánto *how much?*
cuántos *how many?*
cuarto (m) *quarter, room*
cuarto/a *fourth*
cuenta (f) *bill*
cuero (m) *leather*
culpa (f) *fault*
cultura (f) *culture*
curso (m) *course*
cuyo/a *whose*

chao *goodbye*
chico/a *boy, girl*
chileno/a *Chilean*
chofer (m) *driver*

dar *to give*
dar paseos *to walk*
de *of, from, on*
debido a *due to*
decidir *to decide*
decir *to say*
dejar *to leave*
del *of the*
demasiado/a *too, too much*
deme *give me*
demora (f) *delay*
demorar *to take* (time)
de nada *don't mention it, not at all*
dentro de *within*
departamento (m) *flat, apartment*
dependiente/a *shop assistant*
derecha (f) *right*
desayunar *to have breakfast*
desayuno (m) *breakfast*
descansar *to rest*
describir *to describe*
descuento (m) *discount*
desde *from*

desear *to wish, to want*
despejado/a *clear*
despertar *to wake up*
después *after, afterwards*
destino (m) *destination*
devolver *to return* (something)
día (m) *day*
día siguiente (m) *following day*
día: al día *valid*
diario *per day*
diarrea (f) *diarrhoea*
diciembre *December*
diferente *different*
difícil *difficult*
dígale *tell him/her*
dígame *Hello* (on the phone), *Can I help you?*
digamos *let's say*
dinero (m) *money*
dirección (f) *address*
discoteca (f) *disco*
disculpe/a *I am sorry, excuse me*
disfrutar *to enjoy*
Distrito Federal (m) *Federal District* (Mexico City)
doblar *to turn*
dolor (m) *pain*
dolor de estómago (m) *stomach ache*
domingo (m) *Sunday*
dónde *where?*
donde *where*
dormir *to sleep*
dormitorio (m) *bedroom*
durante *during*
durazno (m) *peach*

e *and* (before i)
edificio (m) *building*
efectivo *see:* en efectivo
ejecutivo/a *executive*
el (m) *the*
elevador (m) *lift*
ello *this, that*
embarcar *to board*
empezar *to begin*
empleado/a *employee, clerk*
empresa (f) *company*
en todo caso *in any case*
en efectivo *in cash*

en adelante *onwards*
en *in, on, at*
encantado/a *pleased to meet you*
encantar *to love, like*
encargarse *to be responsible*
encontrar *to find*
energía (f) *energy*
enero *January*
enorme *huge*
ensalada (f) *salad*
ensalada de fruta (f) *fruit salad*
enseguida *right away*
entonces *then*
entrar *to begin, start*
entre *between, among*
entrevista (f) *interview*
enviar *to send*
época (f) *time*
equipaje (m) *luggage*
equipaje de mano (m) *hand luggage*
equipo (m) *equipment*
es decir *that is to say*
escalera (f) *stairs*
escribir *to write, spell*
escritorio (m) *desk*
escuchar *to listen*
ese/a (m/f) *that*
esos/as (m/f, pl) *those*
espárragos (f, pl) *asparagus*
esperar *to hope, wait, expect*
esposo/a *husband, wife*
esquina (f) *corner*
establecimiento (m) *establishment*
estación (f) *station, season*
estación de metro (f) *underground station*
estación de servicio (f) *petrol station*
estadía (f) *stay*
Estados Unidos (m, pl) *United States*
estancia (f) *stay*
estar *to be*
estar seguro/a *to be sure*
este/a (m/f) *this*
estomacal *stomach* (adj)
estos/as (m/f, pl) *these*
estrella (f) *star*
estudiante (m/f) *student*
estudiar *to study*
estudios (m, pl) *studies*

estupendo/a   *very good, fantastic*
etiqueta (f)   *label*
excitante   *exciting*
experimentado/a   *experienced*
explicadas   *explained*
extrañar   *to miss*

faltar   *to be lacking*
familia (f)   *family*
famoso/a   *famous*
febrero   *February*
felicitar   *to congratulate*
ficha (f)   *registration form*
fiebre (f)   *fever*
filete de pescado (m)   *fillet of fish*
fin (m)   *end*
final (m)   *end*
finalmente   *finally*
fin de semana (m)   *weekend*
fino/a   *good, of good quality*
flan (m)   *caramel*
fondo   *see: al fondo de*
frente a   *opposite*
fresa (f)   *strawberry*
frío (m)   *cold*
frito/a   *fried*
fritura (f)   *fried dish*
frontera (f)   *border*
fruta (f)   *fruit*
fuera   *outside*
fumador   *smoker*
fumar   *to smoke*

ganar   *to earn*
generalmente   *generally, usually*
gerente (m/f)   *manager*
gesticular   *to gesticulate*
gloria (f)   *glory*
gracias   *thank you*
grado (m)   *degree*
gran   *big*
grande   *big*
gris   *grey*
guía (m/f)   *guide* (person)
guisado/a   *stewed*
gustar   *to like*

habitación (f)   *room*
habitante (m)   *inhabitant*

hablar   *to speak*
hace   *for, ago*
hace sol   *it is sunny*
hacer   *to do, make*
hacer deportes   *to practise sports*
hacer escala   *to stop over*
hacer frío / calor   *to be cold / warm*
harto   *a lot*
hasta   *until, as far as*
hay   *there is, there are*
helado (m)   *ice-cream*
hermano/a (m/f)   *brother, sister*
hermanos (m, pl)   *brothers and sisters*
hijo/a (m)   *son, daughter*
hijos (m, pl)   *children*
Hispanoamérica   *Spanish-speaking*
   countries in the Americas
hispanoamericano/a   *Spanish American*
historia (f)   *history*
hola   *hello*
hora (f)   *time*
hora: a la hora   *on time*
horario (m)   *times, timetable*
horario de trabajo (m)   *working hours*
hoy   *today*
huésped (m/f)   *guest*

ida (f)   *single* (ticket)
ida y vuelta (f)   *return* (ticket)
idioma (m)   *language*
iglesia (f)   *church*
ilimitado/a   *unlimited*
importar: si no le importa   *if you don't mind*
   no me importa   *I don't mind*
impuesto (m)   *tax*
incluido/a   *included*
incluir   *to include*
independiente   *independent*
infección (f)   *infection*
informe (m)   *report*
ingeniería (f)   *engineering*
ingeniero/a (m/f)   *engineer*
Inglaterra   *England*
inglés (m)   *English*
inglesa (f)   *English*
inmediatamente   *immediately*
inmediato: de inmediato   *immediately*
instituto de idiomas (m)   *school of*
   languages

interesante *interesting*
interesar *to be interested*
interior *at the back*
interrupción (f) *interruption*
invierno (m) *winter*
ir *to go*
ir de compras *to go shopping*
irse *to leave*
izquierda (f) *left*

jefe (m) *boss, manager*
jugo (m) *juice*
junto a *next to*
juntos *together*

kilometraje (m) *mileage*
kilometraje ilimitado (m) *unlimited mileage*

la (f) *the, it, her*
laborar *to work*
lado *see:* al lado de
lago (m) *lake*
largo/a *long*
las (f, pl) *the, them*
lástima (f) *pity, shame*
le *to him, to her, to you* (pol)
lechuga (f) *lettuce*
leer *to read*
lejos *far*
lengua (f) *language*
levantarse *to get up*
leve *slight*
libre *free*
licencia de conducir (m) *driving licence*
lindo/a *pretty, beautiful*
listo/a *ready*
liviano/a *light*
lo *you* (pol), *him, it*
localizar *to trace, look for*
los (m, pl) *the*
lo siento *I am sorry*
lugar (m) *place*
luna (f) *moon*
lunes (m) *Monday*
llamada (f) *telephone call*
llamar *to call*
llamarse *to be called*
llave (f) *key; water tap*

llegada (f) *arrival*
llegar *to arrive, get to*
llenar *to fill in*
llevar *to take*
llover *to rain*
lluvia (f) *rain*
lluvioso/a *rainy*

maestro/a *teacher*
mal *bad*
maleta (f) *suitcase*
maletín (m) *briefcase*
mamá (f) *mother*
mañana (f) *morning*
mañana *tomorrow*
mandar *to send*
manejar *to drive*
mantequilla (f) *butter*
maravilla (f) *marvel*
maravilloso/a *marvellous*
marido (m) *husband*
mariscos (m, pl) *seafood*
marrón *brown*
más *more, else*
más o menos *more or less*
materno/a *maternal*
mayor *elder, eldest, bigger*
mayoría (f) *majority*
me *me, to me, myself*
mediano/a *medium sized*
médico/a *doctor*
medio/a *half*
mediodía (m) *midday*
mejor *better*
menor *younger, youngest*
mensaje (m) *message*
mercado (m) *market*
mes (m) *month*
mesa (f) *table*
mexicano/a *Mexican*
mí *me*
mi *my*
millón (m) *million*
minuto (m) *minute*
mira *look* (fam)
mire *look* (pol)
mismo/a *same, itself*
mitad (f) *half*
mochila (f) *rucksack*

modelo (m)   *model*
momentito (m)   *moment* (diminutive)
monótono/a   *monotonous*
mostaza (f)   *mustard*
mostrador (m)   *desk*
mostrar   *to show*
mozo (m)   *waiter*
muchas gracias   *thank you very much*
mucho/a   *much, a lot*
mucho gusto   *pleased to meet you*
muchos/as   *many*
mundo (m)   *world*
museo (m)   *museum*
música ambiental (f)   *piped music*
muy   *very*
muy bien   *very well*

nacionalidad (f)   *nationality*
nada   *nothing*
nadar   *to swim*
naranja   *orange* (colour)
negocio (m)   *business*
neumático (m)   *tyre*
nevar   *to snow*
ni   *nor*
niño/a (m/f)   *boy / girl, child*
niños (m, pl)   *children*
nocturno/a   *night* (adj)
no dejar de   *not to fail to*
no me digas   *you don't say*
noche (f)   *night*
nombre (m)   *name*
normalmente   *normally*
norte (m)   *north*
Norteamérica   *North America*
nos   *us, to us*
nublado/a   *cloudy*
nuestro/a   *our*
número (m)   *number*
número de teléfono (m)   *telephone number*
nunca   *never*

o   *or*
ocupado/a   *occupied, engaged*
ocurrir   *to happen, occur*
oficial   *official*
oficina (f)   *office*
ofrecer   *to offer*

ómnibus (m)   *bus*
opcionalmente   *optionally*
oportunidad (f)   *opportunity, chance*
oscuro/a   *dark*
otra vez   *again*
otro/a   *other, another*
otros/as   *others*

padres (m, pl)   *parents*
pagar   *to pay*
país (m)   *country*
paisaje (m)   *landscape*
palacio (m)   *palace*
pantalones (m, pl)   *trousers*
papa (f)   *potato*
papá (m)   *father*
par (m)   *pair*
para   *for, to, in order to*
paralela   *parallel*
para que   *so that*
para servirle   *at your service*
parecer   *to seem*
pariente (m/f)   *relative*
parque (m)   *park*
parte (f): ¿de parte de quién?   *who is speaking?*
pasado   *past*
pasado mañana   *the day after tomorrow*
pasaje (m)   *ticket*
pasaje aéreo (m)   *air fare*
pasaporte (m)   *passport*
pasar   *to come in, spend* (time)
pasar: ¿qué le pasa?   *what's the matter with you?*
pasarlo bien   *to have a good time*
pasear   *to go for a walk*
pasillo (m)   *corridor*
paso (m)   *step*
pedir   *to ask for*
pensar   *to think*
pensión (f)   *boarding house*
pequeño/a   *small*
pero   *but*
persona (f)   *person*
persona a persona   *personal* (telephone call)
pescado (m)   *fish*
peso (m)   *Latin American currency*
pinchazo (m)   *puncture*

pintura (f)   *painting*
pirámide (f)   *pyramid*
piscina (f)   *swimming pool*
piso (m)   *floor*
playa (f)   *beach*
plaza (f)   *square*
plazoleta (f)   *small square*
poco   *little*
poder   *to be able, can*
podríamos   *we could*
policía (f)   *police*
pollo (m)   *chicken*
por   *for, by, along, per*
por aquí   *near here, nearby*
por ciento   *per cent*
por ejemplo   *for example*
por error   *by mistake*
por favor   *please*
por la noche   *in the evening, at night*
por lo general   *usually, generally*
porque   *because*
por qué   *why?*
por semana   *per week*
por si acaso   *just in case*
por supuesto   *of course, certainly*
porteño/a (m/f)   *inhabitant of Buenos Aires*
posgrado   *postgraduate*
posible   *possible*
posiblemente   *possibly*
postre (m)   *dessert*
precio (m)   *price*
precioso/a   *very beautiful*
preferir   *to prefer*
preocuparse   *to worry*
presentar   *to introduce*
presente (m)   *present*
presión (f)   *pressure*
primero/a   *first*
privado/a   *private*
probar   *to try on*
procedencia (f)   *place of origin*
programa (m)   *programme*
promedio (m)   *average*
prometer   *to promise*
pronto   *soon*
propio   *itself*
proporcionar   *to provide*
próximo/a   *next*

psicólogo/a   *psychologist*
puerta (f)   *gate, door*
pues   *well*
puré (m)   *mashed potatoes*
puro/a   *pure*

que   *than, that*
qué   *what?, which?, who?, how?*
quedar bien   *to fit well*
quedarse   *to stay*
querer   *to want*
querido/a   *dear*
quién   *who?*
quien   *who*
quinto/a   *fifth*
quisiera   *I would like*
quizá(s)   *perhaps*

rápidos (m, pl)   *rapids*
realizar   *to carry out*
recado (m)   *message*
recargo (m)   *surcharge*
recepción (f)   *reception*
recepcionista (m/f)   *receptionist*
receta (f)   *prescription*
recomendar   *to recommend*
reconfirmar   *to reconfirm*
recorrido (m)   *tour*
recuerdos (m, pl)   *memories*
regalo (m)   *gift, present*
regresar   *to come back*
reparar   *to repair*
repetir   *to repeat*
reservación (f)   *reservation, booking*
reservado/a   *booked, reserved*
reservar   *to book, reserve*
residencia (f)   *house, residence*
retrasado/a   *delayed*
retraso (m)   *delay*
reunión (f)   *meeting*
revisar   *to check*
rincón (m)   *corner*
rojo/a   *red*
ropa (f)   *clothing*
rueda (f)   *wheel*
ruido (m)   *noise*
ruidoso/a   *noisy*

sábado (m)   *Saturday*

sala de conferencia (f)   *conference room*
salir   *to go out*
salir a   *to cost*
salón (m)   *railway carriage with wider and more comfortable seats* (Chile)
salsa (f)   *sauce*
se   *to you*
se   *yourself* (pol), *himself, herself, one*
sección (f)   *area, section*
secretario/a   *secretary*
seguir   *to continue, follow, go on*
seguir derecho   *to go straight on*
segundo/a   *second*
seguramente   *surely*
seguridad (f)   *security*
seguro (m)   *insurance*
seleccionado/a   *chosen, of your choice*
semana (f)   *week*
señora (f)   *lady, Mrs, wife*
sentarse   *to sit*
sentirse   *to feel*
ser   *to be*
serio/a   *serious*
servicio (m)   *service*
servir   *to serve*
servirse   *to help oneself*
si   *if*
sí   *yes*
siempre   *always*
siéntate   *sit down* (fam)
siéntense   *sit down* (pl)
siguiente   *following*
sin   *without*
situado/a   *situated*
sobrino/a (m/f)   *nephew, niece*
sol (m)   *sun; Peruvian currency*
solamente   *only*
solo/a   *alone*
sólo   *only*
soltero/a   *single*
sopa (f)   *soup*
sopa de pollo (f)   *chicken soup*
sopa de verduras (f)   *vegetable soup*
sorpresa (f)   *surprise*
sos   *you are* (fam, Argentina)
su   *your* (pol), *his her*
suave   *mild*
sueldo (m)   *salary*
suerte (f)   *luck*

suéter (m)   *sweater*
sugerencia (f)   *suggestion*
sugerir   *to suggest*
sur (m)   *south*

tableta (f)   *tablet*
tal: ¿qué tal?   *how are you?* (fam), *how about it?*
talla (f)   *size* (clothes)
talón (m)   *receipt*
tamaño (m)   *size*
también   *also*
tampoco   *neither*
tan   *so*
tan amable   *so kind*
tantos/as   *so many*
tarde   *late*
tarde (f)   *afternoon, early evening*
tarjeta (f)   *card*
tarjeta de crédito (f)   *credit card*
tarjeta de embarque (f)   *boarding card*
te   *you, to you, yourself* (fam)
té (m)   *tea*
teléfono (m)   *telephone*
teléfono celular (m)   *cell phone*
templo (m)   *temple*
temporada (f)   *season*
temprano   *early*
tendencia (f)   *tendency*
tener   *to have*
tercero/a   *third*
terminar   *to finish*
terrestre   *land* (adj)
ti   *you* (fam)
tiempo (m)   *weather; time*
tiempo libre (m)   *spare time*
tienda (f)   *shop*
tienda de regalos (f)   *gift shop*
tinto   *red* (wine), *coffee* (Colombia)
típico/a   *typical*
todavía   *still, yet*
todo/a   *all, every*
tomar   *to drink, to have; to take, to catch* (bus, train, etc.)
tomar el desayuno   *to have breakfast*
tomar (el) sol   *to sunbathe*
tomate (m)   *tomato*
trabajar   *to work*
trabajo (m)   *work*

traer   *to bring*
tráfico (m)   *traffic*
tranquilo/a   *quiet*
traslado (m)   *transfer*
tratar de   *to try to*
tratarse de   *to have to do with, to be a question of*
tren (m)   *train*
tú   *you* (fam)
tu   *your* (fam)

último/a   *last*
universidad (f)   *university*
uno/a   *a, one*
usar   *to use*
usted   *you* (pol)
ustedes   *you* (pl)
utilizar   *to use*

vacaciones (m, pl)   *holidays*
valer   *to cost*
valija (f)   *suitcase* (Argentina)
variar   *to vary*
veces (f, pl)   *times*
vecino/a   *neighbour*
vender   *to sell*
venir   *to come*
ventana (f)   *window*
ver   *to see*

verano (m)   *summer*
verdad   *true*
verdadero/a   *true, real*
verde   *green*
verdura (f)   *vegetable*
vez (f)   *time*
de vez en cuando   *from time to time*
viajar   *to travel*
viaje (m)   *journey, trip*
vida (f)   *life*
viento (m)   *wind*
viernes (m)   *Friday*
vino (m)   *wine*
visitar   *to visit*
vivienda (f)   *housing, house*
vivir   *to live*
volver   *to come back*
vos   *you* (fam, Argentina)
vuelo (m)   *flight*

y   *and*
ya   *already, soon*
ya que   *since, as, for*
yo   *I*
yo mismo/a   *I myself*

zapatos (m)   *shoe*
zócalo (m)   *plaza* (Mexico)
zona (f)   *district, zone*

INDEX